P9-EMQ-158

Side by Side

The Autobiography of Helen Joseph

William Morrow and Company, Inc.
New York

This book was first published by Zed Books Ltd. in
London, England.

Library of Congress Cataloging-in-Publication Data

Joseph, Helen.
  Side by side.

  Originally published: London: Zed Books, 1986.
  Includes index.
  1. Joseph, Helen. 2. Civil rights workers—South
Africa—Biography. 3. South Africa—Race relations.
4. Apartheid—South Africa. I. Title.
DT779.95.J67A3   1986   323.4′092′4 [B]   86-23747
ISBN 0-688-07103-1

Printed in the United States of America

First U.S. Edition

1 2 3 4 5 6 7 8 9 10

The author will be sharing the royalties from this book
with the South African Council of Churches.

To Nelson and Winnie Mandela

"These Freedoms We Will Fight For, Side by Side,
Throughout Our Lives, Until We Have Won Our Liberty"
The ANC Freedom Charter

Contents

Acknowledgements

My thanks are due to all the friends who have helped me to produce this book – to one more than any other, but all gave me the confidence to undertake this work. In other circumstances I would have wished to acknowledge their help and assistance by name. They know who they are.

Billie and Helen Joseph in their garden. July 1939

Hyderabad, Deccan, India 1930

At a conference in the Trade Hall, Johannesburg. July 1953

A Lieutenant in the Women's Auxiliary Air Force,
Johannesburg 1945

On a country-wide tour in July 1956 with other leaders, organising for women's protest to the Union Buildings, Pretoria. L to R: H.J., Robert Resha, Norman Levy and Bertha Mashaba

Going from Marshall Square Police Station to the Johannesburg Magistrate's Court in December 1956 at the start of the Treason Trial

Executive members of the Federation of South African Women. R to L:
Philippa Levy (COD), Francis Baard, ANCWL (PE), Mrs Naidoo
(Transvaal Indian Congress), Unknown, Lilian Ngoyi (National President
of ANCWL and FSAW), Amina Kachalia (Transvaal Indian Congress),
Violet Weinberg (COD), Ruth Matserane (ANCWL), Esme Goldberg
(COD). H.J. was National Secretary but could not attend the National
Conference in August 1961 at Port Elizabeth because of banning orders.

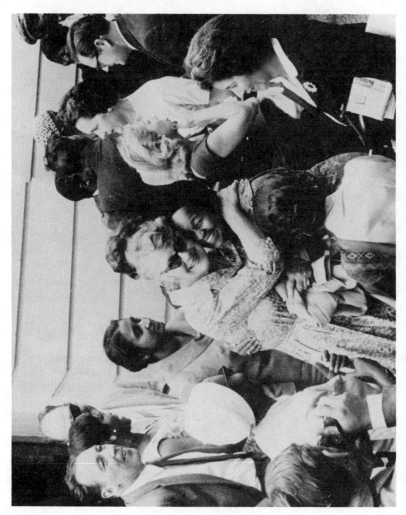

Acquitted of high treason after 4½ years. Centre: Helen Joseph and Martha Mathlaka.

Standing at the garden gate, beginning of house arrest. October 1962.

Photograph taken for jacket of *If This Be Treason*. 1962   *Eli Weinberg*

Arm-in-arm. Robert
Resha (L) and Oliver
Tambo (R) in Dar
Es Salaam, 1963.

Reunion with Lilian Ngoyi (former President of Federation of South African Women) after 10 years of separation through banning.

Photograph for jacket of *Tomorrow's Sun*. 1966.

Winnie Mandela interviewing Wits students on Helen Joseph's verandah.

Addressing Wits University students on campus during schools boycott
(last campus meeting before being banned).

Giving the Academic Freedom Lecture at the University of Cape Town.
August 1983

United Democratic Front Rally on February 10 1985 in Jabulani, Soweto, when Zinzi Mandela read her father's declaration rejecting the Prime Minister's offer of conditional release, to the 15,000 present. Picture shows HJ and Zinzi Mandela sitting together on the platform with Bishop Tutu's daughter on Zinzi's right. *Morris Zwi*

On the verandah with cat and dog, Abigail. *Morris Zwi*

Helen Joseph in her kitchen at 80. June 1985. *Morris Zwi*

At home in Norwood. May 1985. *Paul Weinberg*

Part One

Chapter I

Twenty thousand strong we marched

> We shall not rest until we have won for our children their fundamental right to freedom, justice and security.

I shall never forget what I saw on 9 August 1956 — thousands of women standing in silence for a full thirty minutes, arms raised high in the clenched fist of the Congress salute.

Twenty thousand women of all races, from all parts of South Africa, were massed together in the huge stone amphitheatre of the Union Buildings in Pretoria, the administrative seat of the Union goverment, high on a hill. The brilliant colours of African headscarves, the brightness of Indian saris and the emerald green of the blouses worn by Congress women merged into an unstructured design, woven together by the very darkness of those thousands of faces.

They had marched, that 20,000, pressed solidly together, not in formal ranks, from the lowest of the Union Buildings terraced gardens, climbing up those many steps, terrace by terrace, behind their leaders.

Lilian Ngoyi, Rahima Moosa, Sophie Williams and I, Helen Joseph, together with four women from more distant areas, had led the women up to the topmost terrace and into the amphitheatre. I turned my head once as we came up. I could see nothing but women following us, thousands of women marching, carrying letters of defiant protest against unjust laws, against the hated pass system, against passes for African women.

> We represent and we speak on behalf of thousands of women — women who could not be with us. But all over this country, at this moment, women are watching and thinking of us. Their hearts are with us.
>
> We are women from every part of South Africa. We are women of every race; we come from the cities and the towns, from the reserves and the villages — we come as women united in our purpose to save the African women from the degradation of passes.
>
> Raids, arrests, loss of pay, long hours at the pass office, weeks in the cells awaiting trial, forced farm labour — this is what the pass laws have brought to African men . . . punishment and misery, not for a crime, but for the lack of a pass. We African women know too well the effect of this law upon our homes, upon our children. We who are not African women know how our sisters suffer . . .
>
> *We shall not rest* until all pass laws and all forms of permits restricting our

1

freedom have been abolished.

We shall not rest until we have won for our children their fundamental right to freedom, justice and security.

We took those letters of protest into the Union Buildings, to the offices of the Prime Minister, Johannes Strijdom. He was not there. We flooded his office with them and returned to the thousands of women waiting for us, packed so tightly together, overflowing the amphitheatre. We stood on the little stone rostrum, looking down on the women again, and Lilian Ngoyi called on them to stand in silent protest for thirty minutes. As she raised her right arm in the Congress salute, 20,000 arms went up and stayed up for those endless minutes. We knew that all over South Africa, women in other cities and towns were also gathered in protest. We were not just 20,000 women, but many thousands more.

The clock struck three and then a quarter past; it was the only sound. I looked at those many faces until they became only one face, the face of the suffering black people of South Africa. I know that there were tears in my eyes and I think that there were many who wept with me.

At the end of that half hour, Lilian began to sing, softly at first, "Nkosi Sikelele" ("Lord, give strength to Africa!"). For blacks it has become their national anthem and the voices rose, joining Lilian, ever louder and stronger. Then I heard the new song, composed specially for the protest, by a woman from the Orange Free State, "Wathint' a bafazi, wa uthint' imbolodo uzo kufa" ("You have struck a rock, you have tampered with the women, you shall be destroyed!"). It was meant for Strijdom, the Prime Minister, the grim-faced, dedicated apostle of apartheid and white domination, implacable enemy of the struggle of the black people for freedom and justice. As it was always sung in the Sotho language, the implication of the last phrase usually passed unnoticed by whites.

The protest over, the women went away, down the terrace steps, with the same dignity and discipline with which they had come, but now singing, down to the public road and the lovely gardens stood empty again. Yet not really empty, for I think the indomitable spirit remained. Perhaps it is still there, unseen, unheard, unfelt, for the women that day had made the Union Buildings their own.

That was on 9 August 1956. Today, nearly thirty years later, it is celebrated as National Women's Day, both here in South Africa amongst those who carry on the struggle for freedom and in other lands where the liberation movement, led by the African National Congress, is known and honoured. How it came to pass that we made our protest that day at the Union Buildings — the most hallowed seat of white government — is a small part, but nevertheless a part of the history of our country, South Africa.

It is even more a part of the story of South Africa's liberation from fearsome racist oppression and domination. It is a story that continues even to this day. It is a story that will be told by others in the years to come, perhaps by some now in gaol. Some who have fled South Africa have already told parts of the story. It is a story that must be told and because I played a small part in this great struggle, I am proud to be one of those who help to tell it.

The Federation of South African Women came into being in the early 1950s, at the same time as the effect of the notorious Suppression of Communism Act was being felt. The Act had been passed in 1950, two years after the Nationalist Party had come to power. It was ostensibly to combat the threat of communism, but its real purpose was to harass and hamstring all opponents of the government. By this Act, the Minister of Justice could, through "banning" orders, restrict the freedom of association and movement of any person whom he "deemed" to be furthering the aims of communism.

It takes little imagination to realise the effects of a banning order. It is a subtle technique whereby your life is confused, disordered, where you live in limbo. In a strange way it may be almost worse than gaol, for in gaol at least you are clear what the situation is. In gaol you understand that in the minds of the authorities you form sufficient of a threat to be removed from society. With a banning order your freedoms are reduced to a degree that makes normal life impossible, but does not remove you from society.

By the end of 1953 a temporary halt occurred in the flood of repressive restriction orders issued under the Suppression of Communism Act. A banned man had appealed against the validity of his banning orders on the grounds that he had not been granted a hearing before they were served on him. He had taken his case to the highest court in the land and there his appeal had been upheld. Overnight, people had found that their banning orders were invalid.

Although this freedom was not to last for long (by the following May the Act had been amended to provide for the banning of people without a hearing), the loophole had allowed, in those few months of respite, two banned women to bring into being a new and unique multiracial women's organisation. They were also able themselves to attend and speak at its inaugural conference.

Ray Alexander and Hilda Bernstein were two feminist stalwarts amongst the leaders in the liberation struggle. Ray was a well-known and much loved trade union leader. Latvian born, with an accent she was never to lose completely, Ray won all hearts with her outgoing warmth and her "My dear . . ." and she meant it. In trade union circles she is a legend. Many tales are told of her early union organising days, going from town to town by train, from factory to factory on foot. A staunch Communist Party member, she was elected to Parliament by Africans when they still had three representatives, but was barred from taking her seat through the provisions of the Suppression of Communism Act.

Hilda Bernstein was in many ways like Ray — a warm-hearted communist, free from the chauvinism so often a feature of communism. She was elected by whites in 1943 to the Johannesburg City Council — the only communist ever to achieve this. During the Sharpeville Emergency of 1960 we were detained together in Pretoria Central gaol and her gay spirit helped all of us there. Hilda's intense love for her own children flowed outwards into deep concern for the

3

sufferings of all women and particularly for black women.

Undeterred by their previous banning orders, these two women set about realising a dream they shared of a mass women's organisation of all races that would take its stand on women's rights and play its part in the struggle for the liberation of both men and women. I am sure that they could not have foreseen the amazing progress of this new organisation, reaching its peak in that gathering of 20,000 women at the Union Buildings on 9 August.

I heard from Hilda about the plans for an inaugural conference to launch this new body of women, unique because of its multiracial character. Many women of all races would speak on issues close to them and to their daily lives. Additionally, Olive Schreiner's book *Women and Labour* had impressed me greatly. I was thus delighted to assist with the organising of this conference, with their sights set on their own rights as women. However, by far the most organising was done by Hilda and Ray through their widespread contacts with women, built up over many years. They had the eager help of the African National Congress Women's League and several trade unions.

The conference drew over 150 women from all over the country, some wearing brilliantly coloured national dress, all eager to participate in the proceedings. Interpreters were sometimes hard put to accommodate the variety of languages — English, Zulu, Xhosa, Sotho and Afrikaans.

An impressive Women's Charter was presented to the conference and adopted. It had considerable feminist emphasis but also reflected clearly the conditions of oppressed black people. The conference was highlighted by the speeches of the women from the floor during periods of discussion.

Lilian Ngoyi protested against Bantu education, the government plan for separate and inferior education for blacks. "Bantu education makes African women like fowls laying eggs for others to take away and do what they like with!" she declared. Then she spoke of the shanty towns where she herself had once lived: "where a man must dress with the blanket between his teeth because his family sleeps in the same room".

Lilian accused African husbands of holding back their wives from the conference. She was a widow but I doubt that any husband would have been able to hold her back. That was the first time I saw Lilian Ngoyi, later to become the greatest leader of women in the 1950s. Soon afterwards she came to see me in my office, a slender woman dressed simply but smartly in a black suit, wearing a little round black hat. I never saw her in anything but one of these little black hats. She did not wear the customary beret of so many African women of that time.

Lilian was beautiful then, beautiful and black; in her forties, but looking only thirty, head often tilted a little to one side on her slim neck, laughing eyes and a flashing smile to show an enchanting little gap in her front teeth. I could not of course know how closely our lives would be bound together as leaders in the Federation of South African Women, in and out of goal together, on trial together for over four years, banned and separated from each other over long periods — or that we should walk together leading 20,000 women in protest against passes. She became one of my closest and dearest friends — a joy and a delight to be with, even though this was not to be very often.

The conference allowed, for the first time, the voices of the women of South Africa to be heard. They listened with interest to the scheduled speakers on women of India, of China, on the need for a women's organisation, on the need for world peace. Their own emphasis was on the struggle of men and women together for freedom and justice, on the need to stand together in that struggle and the determination of women to fight for the rights of their children.

My own most worthwhile experience of that conference was in fact afterwards, when the other organisers had returned to their homes and children and I was left to entertain twenty black women from other areas until their departure later in the day. Entertaining black friends in South Africa is always a problem because of the lack of multiracial amenities, but we were soon off on a black bus for a picnic with boxes of minerals, fruit and buns. I think this was what I had been waiting for so long — complete acceptance as a person — and I had got it. Songs, laughter, dancing and then to the railway station and a joyous farewell, with anticipation of another conference.

That first conference of the Federation was a very deep experience for me and I was moved when I was elected to the national executive, for I had been quite happy to be a backroom person at the conference.

The conference had indeed been held just in time for Ray and Hilda to speak there, for it was only a few weeks before the new amendment to the Suppression of Communism Act was passed and both women were soon re-banned. They had used their respite heroically to bring this new organisation into being, for it was undoubtedly to become the most dynamic of women's organisations in the history of South Africa.

Lilian Ngoyi and I grew to know each other quite well and since she worked in a Johannesburg clothing factory, we would occasionally meet for a sandwich in a car during her short lunch break. I began to understand better the acute transport problems for African people, especially women; long bus queues stretching around two sides of a street block, unbelievably crowded trains, passengers clinging outside onto closed doors, and the dangerous walk home from the railway station or bus stop through dark, totally unlit streets. These difficulties made evening meetings for the Federation women impossible, so we had to rely on weekends which meant that again the women had to travel in from the townships. Nevertheless our first Transvaal provincial conference was successful.

Josie Palmer, veteran leader of African protest against location permits even in the 1930s was elected Transvaal President and I became Honorary Secretary. This time I was not a white woman doing things *for* black people but a member of a mixed committee headed by a black woman. It was different — and better than anything I had known before.

Towards the end of 1954, the Johannesburg Municipality announced a sharp increase in rentals for Soweto, the sprawling, spreading township housing the ill-paid workers and their families, the people who had no money for an increase in rent. The Federation took up the issue, calling another multiracial conference. Once again women spoke from the floor, describing their pitiful homes and their inability to meet any increase of rent.

5

I wished that the hall could have been filled with housewives from white suburbs to hear them. But it wasn't, nor was the Federation ever able to attract more than a handful of white women from the Black Sash or the Liberal Party to attend its conferences. Our identification with the African National Congress and the liberation movement saw to that. It was a small price to pay for the tremendous feeling of oneness with the national struggle for freedom.

From its early days the Federation had felt drawn to the Women's International Democratic Federation, formed in Europe at the end of the Second World War, to unite women in defence of their rights and to work for peace and social progress. It claimed to represent 140 million women from all parts of the world, through its affiliated organisations. Both Ray and Hilda were in close contact with this International Federation and cherished the idea of the South African Federation affiliating to it. We certainly maintained contact with it, but never got as far as even debating affiliation, certainly not in the Transvaal.

This International Federation had what was, for us, a most attractive policy of inviting women to attend their conference in Europe and then sending them on sponsored tours, mainly to the Soviet Union, Hungary, Romania, even as far as the People's Republic of China. I am sure the Federation would have gladly accepted invitations to conferences and sponsored tours to the West just as happily, but none came our way. The World Federation was to hold a World Congress of Mothers in Lausanne and the Federation was invited to send two delegates to the preparatory council meeting in Geneva in February as well as to the congress later in the year.

The Transvaal and Cape regions were the best established areas of the Federation so we were to send one delegate from each region. For us in the Transvaal there was one outstanding choice, Lilian Ngoyi. We knew that this great speaker and leader would not merely hold her own with women from other lands but would be our ambassador to bring the sufferings of black people and the struggle for liberation to the notice of women outside South Africa. Dora Tamana was chosen as the other delegate.

We began to prepare for the women to go. In those days it was not yet illegal to leave South Africa without a passport, although travel companies were reluctant to carry passportless passengers for fear of compromising themselves with the South African authorities. Passports for white political people were not impossible to obtain, though often difficult. For blacks there were almost insuperable difficulties. Radically political blacks just did not get passports, so means had to be found to get them transported without documents. There was no difficulty at the London end, merely separate queues for those with and those without passports.

I was going to Europe on leave for a few months, for the first time in nearly twenty years. I was therefore delighted when arrangements were made for me to fly from London to attend the Geneva Council meeting as an observer, in addition to our two special delegates. I still had a valid passport so would have no difficulties and I should hear from Hilda when and where to meet the two women on their arrival in London in January 1955.

6

I reached London just after the New Year and found letters from Hilda to tell me that the plans for sending Lilian and Dora by sea had misfired because they had been discovered, passportless, on board ship before it sailed from Cape Town. The captain had refused to transport them, despite their paid passages. They had come undaunted to Johannesburg, from where they would be sent somehow to London where I must meet them.

On the day they were expected, I waited for hours at the airport, fearful for them. Then I found a friendly porter to take a note through the customs and immigration barriers to say "I am here, waiting for you." They came at last, triumphant and excited, and we hugged each other, a little surprised that no one thought this in any way odd for a white and two blacks.

They told me of their adventures. On the ship they had hidden themselves in the lavatory waiting for the ship to sail before they dared to come out. They had been terrified when loud knocks and a command to come out had been heard. How they were found out none of us knows and we never shall. They could do nothing but open the door. The plan had failed somewhere along the way.

Once in Johannesburg, it had been easier to get onto an aeroplane, but they were very apprehensive until the plane actually took off. Racially-mixed air travel was still comparatively rare in South Africa and at first the two black women encountered hostile looks and whispered comments from the passengers. Then the captain announced that this was his plane and that there would be no apartheid on board. All his passengers were equal.

After hearing this, I was convinced that nothing could daunt Lilian and Dora. They would overcome all obstacles. We had a couple of weeks together in London and were preparing to go to Geneva when International Federation officials informed us that it had been decided that Lilian and Dora should not go to Switzerland at this stage for the council meetings as they might encounter difficulties there about passports and might even be sent back to South Africa. It would be simpler for them to fly direct to East Berlin from where they could set off on extensive travels, returning later for the Congress of Mothers in Lausanne. It would not matter so much if they were then sent back to South Africa because by that time they would already be on their way back.

I went alone to Geneva for the preparatory council meeting, now promoted to delegate, feeling very inadequate about representing South African women at this large gathering of women from all over the world. But I went, and there I met women from Burma, Indochina, the USA and Canada, the Argentine and near East countries and from every country in Europe.

I listened carefully to their speeches, in many cases accounts of suffering and disabilities comparable to the South Africa scene. From others I heard affirmation of their countries' achievements and a will to assist others still striving for basic human rights. I sat there, full of admiration for these dynamic, eloquent women leaders. I think I had not fully realised the implication of being a delegate and no longer an observer, for I was startled when I was asked on which day I would be ready to address the conference and report on South Africa.

I was still an inexperienced public speaker and no orator. I was white and had no real right to describe the unshared sufferings of others in my colour-ridden land, whereas these hundreds of delegates could and did speak from their own experience.

I drafted a speech for one of the organisers to consider, but she said it was too flat and I am sure it was. Then we talked about my life in South Africa and I told her, not only of our Federation, but also of the unjust conditions of life and particularly of the government plan forcibly to remove the African people of Sophiatown in the western areas of Johannesburg to another area and the growing protest against it. Since I left South Africa, news of the impending removal and the Congress Alliance protest plans had been sparse in the overseas press, but I had learnt enough to know that the government intended to go its own ruthless way. The forced move would be taking place in February and the African people would try by all peaceful means to resist that move.

My thoughts turned away from Geneva and back to Sophiatown and the protest. When I had finished, I was told "that's it! That is what you must tell the women tomorrow."

When I faced those women from all over the world, I wanted them to understand the agony of Sophiatown and the oppression of the people by their white overlords. I spoke for Lilian and Dora, I spoke for the women of our Federation and for the black women of our land, and I wanted to convey the strength of our hope for the future. When I came to the end I affirmed, "where you stand today, we shall stand tomorrow!"

Then the miracle happened. That gathering of women rose to their feet in a standing ovation, not to me as a speaker, but to the women of South Africa whose message I had brought. For me it was a tremendous moment of disbelief but also of joy and of complete unity with the women there.

I went back to London to find that Lilian and Dora had already left on their great adventure so I could not tell them about the conference. I had hoped, secretly, and vainly, that perhaps I too might have been invited to visit some other country, for there seemed to be many invitations floating around, though almost entirely to black women. However, it did not happen. I think my disabilities were that I was white and not ideologically committed.

Chapter II

Partners in protest

Soon after my return to South Africa in 1955, I had a brief personal link with the Black Sash, an activist organisation of women voters, which therefore excluded black women since they had no vote. It seemed a little ironic that the women were white but their sashes were black. This racial barrier, however, was later removed.

The Nationalist Party government was intent on removing all coloured voters from the common voters' roll. The common coloured vote was entrenched in the constitution of South Africa, but for the Nationalist government there must be only one parliamentary vote, the white vote. This move had aroused widespread indignation and protest, amongst whites as well as coloureds. White women had established the Defend the Constitution League and embarked on a national campaign of protest, mounting demonstrations outside the Houses of Parliament in Cape Town and at the Union Buildings in Pretoria. For these occasions the women wore black sashes in mourning for the constitution of South Africa, so soon to be violated, despite all protest.

These women, standing in silent protest wearing their black sashes, came to be known as the "Black Sash", adopting it as the name of their organisation. For nearly thirty years they have stubbornly continued to stand in silence, in smaller groups now, but still undeterred by the refusal of the government to heed their protest against racial discrimination and injustice.

In June 1955 the Black Sash called on women voters to join them at the foot of General Botha's statue in the grounds of the Union Buildings for a three-day vigil in protest against the removal of the coloured vote.

I joined them there on the second day and we spent two very cold June nights sleeping on mattresses on the grass, though almost smothered in blankets. I suppose there were about 100 women, not more, but the protest was significant because it was by white women protesting against unjust laws affecting coloured voters and not themselves.

I found these women determined and friendly but I knew that some of my friends and I were but cuckoos in this liberal nest, for we were totally identified with the liberation struggle and they were not. Nevertheless, we had to admit that this protest had reached the ranks of white women where we, with our radical multiracial emphasis in the Federation, had never been able to penetrate.

I wore a black sash for the occasion and on our return to Johannesburg even spoke briefly at a meeting on the City Hall steps where the protesters were welcomed back.

In August the Federation called a special conference, our own Congress of Mothers, in support of the World Congress of Mothers in Switzerland, where we knew our delegates, Lilian and Dora, would be speaking. I reported to our conference as a matter of interest that I had joined the Black Sash at the Union Buildings and described our nights of vigil there. I was not prepared, nor I think were any of us, for what followed.

Margaret Gazo, veteran of the ANC Women's League, spoke from the floor. "The white women did not invite us to join their protest," she said, "but we must go to the Union Buildings ourselves to protest against the laws which oppress us and we shall invite the white women to join us. We too shall sleep there, for we shall not leave the Union Buildings until our demands have been granted."

Her proposal was received with great enthusiasm but, as Secretary, I was torn between my joy at this defiant protest and my anxiety about just how it could be organised. How could we stay there indefinitely? My mind ran on babies and food — and "loos". I was thankful when finally a more realistic view prevailed and the protest was reduced to one day only. It was a momentous decision, for this would be the first time that black people would go to the Union Buildings in protest. After that every other conference discussion simply faded into the background.

We swung immediately into action, for 27 October, two months hence, had been decided on for our venture to Pretoria. We worked not only in the adjacent townships but went into the Transvaal at weekends, wherever it might be possible to organise women through African National Congress contacts to come to Pretoria.

Bertha Mashaba worked closely with me during all this intensive organising. She was a member of the executive of both the Federation and the ANC Women's League and worked in the offices of the African men's Clothing Workers' Union. At that time I was employed full time as Secretary of the Medical Aid Society which served the garment workers of the Transvaal. My office was conveniently just around the corner from Bertha's so we used to leave together after work, with large packets of fish and chips, to set off for the townships in whatever car I could borrow from my friends. Weekends, too, saw us campaigning together in the more distant areas.

There was little response from white women other than those who were affiliated members of the Federation. However, we had obeyed our mandate, we had invited them, and a few did come.

Organising with Bertha was fun. Tall, bespectacled, lively, she was not yet married so was free to accompany me. We knew all the back ways for me to slip illegally into black townships, though once I almost knocked down a black policeman in the dark, so close was my car. I had no permit to be where I was and I had a shock when I became aware of this dim figure beside my open window. "You nearly kissed him!" exclaimed Bertha and then proceeded to talk us out of this delicate situation with some explanation in Zulu which I couldn't follow.

Our protest was wide. There were many laws which oppressed black women, both as women and as mothers. We were not going to petition, we intended to demand the repeal of unjust laws. We would try to see the various Cabinet ministers and tell them so. Our first plan, indeed right up to a few days before 27 October, was to hold a large protest meeting on the public road, which runs between the Union Buildings and the terraced slopes below. From there we would send our delegates to the offices of the various ministers whom we intended to challenge.

Only three days before the protest, we were informed that the Pretoria City Council had refused permission for our meeting to be held. This was a heavy blow, for we knew by this time that many women would be converging on the Union Buildings. To stop them was unthinkable. We consulted a lawyer in Pretoria and came up with an ingenious scheme whereby each woman must sign her own letter of demand and bring it to the Union Buildings herself. It would not matter how many women came at the same time, as each would be there on her own business and there would be no common purpose.

Then the next blow fell. The Transportation Board refused to grant licences for the buses which the women had applied to hire to bring them from the townships to the Union Buildings. There was only one alternative — public transport involving two bus journeys and a train journey for almost every woman, more than doubling their travelling time.

Women in many areas had to be informed immediately that they must rearrange their journeys and raise the extra money they would need for the train fares. Telephone communication with women in the townships did not exist so it meant driving from area to area. Fortunately I had taken a week's leave from my office to cover the demonstration and I could spend the whole day contacting some of the women's groups, while Robert Resha, ANC Transvaal Secretary, who worked with us, went to the rest with the urgent message. "Your buses are cancelled. You must come by train."

The ANC branches rallied to the support of the women, calling public meetings the same night to raise the extra money in the traditional way of throwing coins onto a platform during the singing of freedom songs. In one black township, Brakpan, £400 was raised at one meeting and the men went themselves to the railway station to purchase the train tickets.

When I came home that night I drafted a letter of protest for each woman to sign when she reached the Union Buildings. There was no time for any committee discussions but I knew what the women would want to say. At the office of the Indian Youth Congress, ally of the ANC, the young men worked nearly all night to roneo 2,000 letters for the women to sign.

At daybreak on the morning of 27 October I drove into Orlando Township in Soweto to fetch Lilian Ngoyi. She and Dora Tamana had returned from their eight-month long international tour only a few weeks before. It was bitter for them to come back from the many lands where, for the first time in their lives, they had been treated as human beings and honoured leaders of their people. Now they had returned to the land of their humiliation, but it was the land of their birth. At the airport, Lilian had dropped to her knees on the tarmac and kissed the ground.

As I drove to Orlando I saw, high above me, on the railway embankment, a train packed with women, singing, their arms out of the windows in the Congress salute, telling the world they were on their way to Pretoria. Afterwards I learnt how the railway booking clerk had tried to stop the women, refusing to issue tickets to Pretoria. The women had then boarded the trains at the next station without tickets. They had made up their minds to go to Pretoria, and there they would go.

Our rather vague plan had been for the women to sign their protests at the gate below the terraces, where I had camped with the white Black Sash women only a few months before. Then they would walk up those many terraces and stone steps to hand in the protests to the organisers at the top and come down again. I visualised it as a colourful stream of women coming up and flowing down those gay flower-edged terraces. The women had their own ideas, and, as on future occasions, they made their own decisions. When I reached the top, I found them all there, sitting quietly in the amphitheatre, resting peacefully.

It had been a long and tiring morning for them. Babies were unstrapped from their mothers' backs and fed, umbrellas went up against the hot sun. Two thousand women were sitting where no black women had sat before. It was a triumph. Their signed protests had all been handed to their leaders and now they could rest. "We have not come here to beg or plead but to ask for what is our right as mothers, as women and as citizens of our country. . ."

We protested against the whole spectrum of unjust laws. We protested against ghetto housing and forced removals. We protested against passes, especially the passes so soon to be issued to African women, against Bantu education, black poverty, in fact everything which goes to make up the horror of the racial segregation which formed the background to our demands.

> We speak from our hearts as mothers, as women. Life cannot be stopped. We must love and marry and find a home. We must bear children in hope and in pain. We must love them as part of ourselves. We must help them to grow, we must endure all the longings and sufferings of motherhood. Because of this we are made strong to come here, to speak for our children, to strive for their future.
>
> We, the voters and the voteless, call upon you, the Ministers responsible for these Acts, and upon the government and the electorate of South Africa to hearken unto us.

Four women had been chosen as leaders for the day, Lilian Ngoyi, the African, Rahima Moosa, the Indian, Sophie Williams, the coloured and I, the white. We reflected the multiracial membership of the Federation of South African Women.

We took those piles of protests and left them outside the doors of the ministers' offices, when our knocking brought no response. I suppose we had really expected no less, in view of our unacknowledged letters announcing the forthcoming visit. It made no difference to us. We had recorded our protest for all time.

Back in the amphitheatre, Lilian could not make a speech. That would have turned that assembly of women into a meeting, forbidden by the Pretoria authorities. She announced curtly that we had delivered the protests but that the ministers had all run away. The women stood to sing "Nkosi Sikelele" and then it was over. The stream of women flowed down the terraces again to make their way back to the station, a long walk ahead for many of them. Taxis were few and costly and the regular buses neither near nor adequate.

The uniformed police had discreetly kept away from the demonstration or perhaps only out of sight. A few plain clothes detectives from the security branch took photographs but made no attempt to interfere with the women. Two or three ANC members, there out of curiosity, were the only other men to be seen. It was a women's affair.

In the townships, African men were waiting to welcome the women home. They gathered in crowds at the railway stations and the bus stops, even with their own local bands, in demonstration of their pride, in tribute to the courage of their women. That night I too went to a party. It was certainly not for me and I don't remember the occasion, but Nelson Mandela and Walter Sisulu, the ANC leaders, were there. From them I had an unforgettable welcome, and felt immensely rewarded for the weeks of organising.

The Nationalist Party press was incensed at our success in getting so many women to the Union Buildings, for that was really the essence of our triumph. We had not very confidently expected the ministers to be waiting to see us; we did not expect our demands to be met. But together we had presented them, and at the Union Buildings itself.

We were accused in the press of having succeeded only through trickery, presumably referring to each woman bringing her own signed protest, and there were some snide remarks about the "white master-mind" behind it all. (I suppose that referred to me!) Yet no action was taken against any of us, nor could any action be taken, because we had seen to it ourselves that we kept within the law. It was a protest, not an occasion for defiance. I felt, as I know other women did, that we had a tremendous moral obligation to see that all the women returned safely to their families.

In December of that year, I went to Bloemfontein in the Orange Free State, to the annual conference of the ANC. I was there when Lilian Ngoyi was elected to the national executive committee, a great and rare reward to this woman for her dedicated and courageous leadership of women over the past three years.

It was a moving experience and a great privilege for me to attend the conference of the ANC, to see these representative and responsible African men and women from all over South Africa. Dedicated to the cause of freedom and justice for their people, they were gathered together to plan for the coming years, ready to face years of hardship, even suffering and gaol, if need be, and to build on what had already been achieved.

The President of the Transvaal region of the Federation, Josie Palmer, became our first casualty in the Transvaal. She was banned in 1955, immediately after the October protest and ordered to resign from the Federation and other organisations. We wrote angrily to the Minister of Justice about the banning of our leader, assuring him that our work would go from strength to strength, regardless of such attacks upon our leaders.

Part of our Union Buildings protest had been against the threatened issuing of passes for African women and thus, when I was invited to write an article on "Women against passes" for a journal closely connected to the Congress movement, I gladly accepted it.

> Facing this new threat, [I had written] the African men and women have determined that the indignity of the pass system shall not be extended to African women. In every part of the country, in every town and village, the determination is clear. The question is not 'shall we carry passes or not?' but 'what shall we do when we are told to carry passes?' This question demands an answer from the liberation movement. The struggle against the pass laws is not a matter for African women alone. It is not a matter for the African people alone. It is part and parcel of the liberatory movement.

I had no idea that one day I should defend myself in court on a charge of high treason on this very extract from my article as a document "advocating extra-parliamentary, unconstitutional and illegal action, including the use of force and violence". I would never have thought that I had gone too far in this article, nor I am sure did anyone else in our organisation. I might even have thought that I had not gone far enough.

From January 1956 onwards, the government pass-issuing units began their work, at first confining themselves to very remote areas, to farms, even villages, where African women might still be unaware of the dangers of the passes.

The very word "pass" strikes horror into the hearts and minds of the African people, for the pass controls every aspect of their lives, houses, work, movement. The penalty for failure to produce a pass on demand is immediate arrest. By this means the white rulers, even before the Nationalist government, have exercised complete control over the black people. But under the Nationalist government the pass tyranny has been intensified.

The pass was, and is, the most powerful weapon of white domination over black. Officially it is now called a reference book, a more cosmetic name, but to Africans it remains the "dompas", the hated badge of slavery. For whites, Indians, coloureds, there is only the identity book, which does not have to be produced on demand, and which carries no gaol penalty for failure to do so.

In 1956 women in the towns and cities already knew how the pass system had brought harassment to their men. They had lived under the shadow of gaol, prison farm labour, the constant terror of arrest, a life of fear, of not knowing whether it would be this day or the next that the pass might prove to be irregular or even just left at home. Then it might be days, weeks, before a man could reach his family and his home again.

African women feared, with good reason, that if they, too, carried passes, they would be exposed to those dangers and the added agony of young children left alone, helpless. Their fears were well grounded. In 1980, twenty-five years later, in Johannesburg alone, 3,500 African women were arrested for pass offences.

In the rural areas there was little or no resistance by women to passes. They did not smell out the lies about the so-called benefits the passes would bring — easy identification on death was one of them! The passes were issued slowly to the women as the pass units went crawling from place to place. The small towns were next in line, but it was here that the resistance started.

When the women in Winberg, in the Free State, discovered how they had been deceived, they rebelled. Lilian Ngoyi and Robert Resha had been sent by the ANC to support the women's protest. Inspired by Lilian's dynamic leadership, the women collected their passes in bags and told the location superintendent to take back his rubbish. Then, according to Lilian, a bottle of paraffin appeared, somehow, from under someone's blanket — and the passes went up in flames. The Winberg women paid dearly for their defiance. They were arrested and charged with burning the passes, a criminal offence. Yet their example inspired many other women and led to epic resistance in several centres — Lichtenburg, Uitenhage, Zeerust, Standerton and many other towns. However, despite this, the passes were drawing nearer to the large cities.

The Cape region of the Federation had followed our Pretoria example with their own multiracial march through the city of Cape Town, while Durban had also held both multiracial and African protests against the passes for women.

Two thousand men and women attended the Federation mass meeting, "Transvaal Women's Day", held on 11 March 1956. Men and women alike were still excited about the Pretoria protest of the previous October and feeling was running high about the passes. Although most of the country-wide demonstrations and deputations to Bantu Commissioners' offices had come from the initiative of the ANC Women's League, the Federation had been very active in organising multiracial demonstrations in Johannesburg.

The news that women had been tricked into taking passes in the rural areas seemed to bring the anger of the African people right into the meeting on 11 March. I was not surprised nor even apprehensive this time when a proposal, indeed a demand, came that the women must go back to the Union Buildings, this time to Strijdom himself, the Prime Minister. Now it must be a national protest drawing women from all over South Africa. I knew that organising women on this scale would drain the resources of the Federation, but the defiant mood of the meeting was infectious and we left the hall talking of 20,000 women this time. Thursday 9 August was to be the great day. We always had to plan demonstrations for a Thursday, the traditional "Nanny's day off", so as to draw in domestic servants, though I doubt that we had much success in this area. Domestic servants at that time lived mostly in the backyard rooms of their

15

employers' homes, as they do even today, separated from normal home life and society. Those who lived in hostels could be contacted through township campaigning, but most African domestic workers came from rural areas, leading solitary backyard lives in the towns and cities. It was their very isolation that was to make the domestic servants such an easy prey, so amenable to pressure from their white madams that they must take the passes and not protest.

I drew up a very detailed campaign plan soon after the March meeting, but like any long-term plan, it tended to fall apart at times and I would have to re-draft it. It provided for a national tour and for weekend journeys to the northern and eastern Transvaal, and also for weekday visits to townships adjacent to Johannesburg. For these, at night, Robert Resha usually drove and I kept a good supply of scarves to tie over my head, keeping my coat collar turned up to hide my white neck and ears from the headlights of any following cars. I learned not to expose my white face by turning my head.

We implemented our campaign plans carefully, detailing duties to various committee members; I spent as much time as I could in Indian and coloured areas. I knew I would not have to organise the white women affiliated to the Federation. They were few in number, but they would go to Pretoria. We formally invited the women of the Black Sash and the Liberal Party and some other white women's organisations and a few did eventually join us on 9 August.

J.B. Marks, a dedicated veteran ANC leader, impressed by our week-by-week plans, called me the "General" dispersing my forces before the battle. I had other helpers too, not members of the Federation, individual white women who would assist with typing and other work, though they would not identify themselves openly with the protest nor with us. I exploited this help to the full because we needed it badly.

As always, the Federation campaigned on a shoestring budget. I borrowed cars and begged petrol until I could afford to buy my own small Ford, "Congress Connie". We begged gifts of paper and stencils for leaflets. Somehow we always managed to get what we wanted, day by day, despite the fact that the Federation, like the ANC, never had enough money.

I happily gave my own time and it was always more important for me to be using my resources for the liberation struggle than to spend it idly on entertainment or holidays. It was not sacrifice. I was doing what I wanted to do. The fact that I could contribute more in money than the black women was of no significance. We all gave according to what we had and I am sure we never stopped to think who gave what. This was true of all ANC organisers too, for they gave their time and lived on sparse budgets themselves.

I had no family ties, no husband and no children, so there were no other calls on my private life. This simply meant, as in the case of black single women, that I had more time to give. Yet to be totally without a family is not to be envied.

Once again, Robert Resha, Bertha and I went campaigning in the Transvaal and on the East Rand and the West Rand, in "Congress Connie" this time. She

16

was a gallant little car, bouncing noisily over rough roads, hailed loudly by township children with shouts of "Africa!" as we approached, often when we were trying to be inconspicuous! She carried me right around South Africa on a tour as 9 August drew nearer.

Bertha and I took leave from our jobs at the beginning of July and we became four when Norman Levy joined us. He, like me, was a member of the Congress of Democrats, a white organisation formed in the 1950s to work for change. The purpose of our tour was, of course, to find out what the response to the call to Pretoria on 9 August would be and to address as many women as possible in support of it.

To Bloemfontein, Kimberley, Cape Town, Port Elizabeth, East London, Ladysmith, Durban — a 4,000-mile journey. We found friendly hospitality for us all in the main centres, but sometimes had to sleep in "Congress Connie" on the longer journeys. When we neared the Hex River Valley, we stopped at the top of the mountain to wait for the dawn and so that Bertha could see that picturesque descent into the valley between the great mountains on either side. But Bertha, tired from the long journey, was asleep. Every time we tried to per-suade her to look at the glorious scenery she smiled sleepily, said "yes, it's lovely" and went back to sleep again, burying her head under a blanket. Eventually we gave up and left her to sleep the rest of the way.

It was a long and intensive tour. Between us we must have addressed some forty meetings, large and small, private and public, always calling on women of all races to come to the Pretoria protest. We were welcomed enthusiastically as the Federation stock was very high after the first protest to Pretoria and we found excitement and determination everywhere. Only once, in Cape Town, did we experience any hostility. It was when Norman and I, as whites, were not made welcome by a small but vocal dissident group of anti-white Africanists at a meeting. Robert, however, handled the situation superbly. While he was speaking, I watched the tense black faces gradually soften and then he began to sing, leading the whole audience in a freedom song. He then turned to me and said, "Now you can speak."

When we were campaigning we had an agreement with Robert that he was never to speak first at any meeting, because none of us could hope to make any impact on an audience after this gifted speaker had finished. There never seemed anything more to say. On this critical occasion, Robert had insisted on speaking first and we realised that it had been necessary.

Robert Resha was without doubt one of the finest public speakers in the ANC. Prominent in the Youth League, a member of the ANC national executive, he was nevertheless always ready to join us on our organising expeditions, a tireless friend. To hear Robert speak at a meeting was almost like watching an orchestra being conducted. He drew out the emotions of his audience until he had their full attention, then he ended quietly with a freedom song in which all could participate. He was a man of his people, a true African patriot — journalist, sportsman, musician, he was all these and also a proud Xhosa from the Eastern Cape. Short, powerfully built, his strength seemed inexhaustible as he drove thousands of miles with us around the countryside, so often easing our way or solving our problems. Yet beneath that friendliness and charm, lay a deep pool of passionate, sometimes aggressive anger at the injustice of the system under which he and his people lived.

Only once was there a dispute between us during those months of campaigning together and that was on this tour. Yet even then it wasn't really a serious matter. The ANC wanted Robert to remain in Cape Town a day or two longer, while Norman, Bertha and I went on without him to Port Elizabeth. He was needed, as an ANC executive member, to sort out some local difficulty. Despite our objections, he had to stay.

The rest of us must, I think, have been very tired by our long journey at this stage and, unreasonably, we took his absence badly, feeling that Robert ought to have continued with us. I suppose it was partly the need for him to share the driving of the 600 miles to Port Elizabeth and also because we felt we might need him on our arrival there to introduce us to the ANC leaders. Childishly we decided to punish him by not meeting him at the airport; the ANC could do that. I remember that he joined us again during an ANC meeting, obviously disappointed that we had not met him, but wearing the tie I had given him for Christmas. I don't know about the others, but I recall feeling very ashamed of my pettiness.

In Port Elizabeth we found women already organising for Pretoria. ANC officials complained laughingly that the women had taken over the Congress office and turned the men into clerks and typists. We really hardly needed to address any meetings there, preparations were so far advanced, but a packed hall awaited us and we all spoke, to a great welcome. We left, confident that there would be a great delegation of African and coloured leaders from the town, despite the crippling rail fares of £10 a head for a third-class ticket in an overcrowded compartment.

"Congress Connie" behaved magnificently; not one puncture in all those thousands of miles. Four adults, plus bags and food for long journeys, were squashed into this small car. We divided our duties, Norman and Robert handling all luggage for the boot and the roof carrier, while Bertha and I scientifically stowed away hand luggage and food containers inside the car so that there would still be room enough for our legs. One of us was always supposed to stay awake to talk to the driver so that there should be no falling asleep at the wheel, especially during the long night drives, which we made in order to get as much working time as possible during the day.

We were far better prepared for this August protest than we had been the year before. We could avoid the obstacles that had nearly prevented the women from ever getting to the Union Buildings. All transport plans were limited to routine public transport, so that we did not have to apply for licences for private buses. The bus company did, however, agree to increase the number of buses on the normal route from the railway station to the point nearest to the Union Buildings. Women from other areas were advised to arrive in Pretoria the night before the protest. Overnight accommodation would be found for them.

We conducted a tart correspondence with the Prime Minister, advising him of our coming and requesting him to receive our representatives, African, coloured, Indian and white. We had a curt reply saying that he would be prepared to meet African women only, not a multiracial deputation. This we rejected indignantly: the Federation was a multiracial organisation and this was a multiracial protest.

In the week before the protest, reports began to come in from all quarters showing a massive response by women. Even the media began to speak of 20,000 women from all over South Africa. The senior Congress leaders became apprehensive, doubting our ability to handle the situation. Lilian and I were summoned to a secret meeting of the Congress leadership, mostly banned people, and asked if we knew what we were doing. Had we realised the enormous responsibility of gathering thousands of women together in the face of possible police interference? What would we do if all the leaders were arrested?

Lilian replied that if that happened, other leaders would take our places. The women would know what to do and we had confidence in them. What we did not disclose was our ultimate plan that if the police marched on us, armed, to arrest the women, we would kneel and lead the women in prayer and song, for we knew that thousands of women would then kneel behind us. This was not cynically designed as a strategy. We knew that this would be a natural reaction for thousands of women whose religious faith was as much a part of them as their dedication to the struggle for freedom and justice.

On the eve of the protest day, Lilian and I went to Pretoria to be with the women there and to be sure of being there ourselves the next morning. Seventy women were coming from Port Elizabeth and there would be groups from many other centres. Most of the delegates slept on their blankets in a large township hall, although I think very few slept much as they sang for most of the night.

Once again, the Indian Youth Congress had roneoed thousands of protests until the supply of paper ran out. They had given us more than 14,000 copies and I thought it might be enough. Secretly, I doubted whether we could reach that stirring target of 20,000 people. I was wrong. As the women gathered together, now for the second time on the green grass below the terraced gardens of the Union Buildings, I could see only a solid packed mass facing us as we stood, the leaders for the day, at the top of the first stone steps.

We walked together down the centre pathway that the women had left free for us. We turned at the end of that pathway and the women fell in behind us, following us up the steps and across the terraces, their protests in their hands. There were thousands who had no protests, but that no longer mattered. I could see that we were many many more than I had ever thought possible. The 20,000 had become a reality. They stood together, women of all races, from all parts of South Africa, in that huge amphitheatre of the Union Buildings.

When it was over the women walked back to the bus terminus in twos and threes, singing now, never forming a procession, babies on their backs, baskets on their heads. They reached the buses as African men queued after work for their transport home, but when they saw the women coming, in their green blouses and skirts, they stood back. "Let the women go first," they said. It was a great tribute from weary men.

With so many women coming from all over South Africa to the protest, it was a golden opportunity to organise a Federation national conference in Johannesburg. The national executive committee members in Johannesburg undertook the arrangements for the conference, which was to be held the day after the protest.

There were over 400 delegates and altogether almost 1,000 people in the hall. All were eager to welcome the "Pretoria" women and to hear them plan their future path, for the battle of the passes was not yet over, despite that astounding protest. The conference was spectacular, the women in triumphant mood, yet ready for sober discussion of Federation matters.

Presenting the report of the Federation's work in the Transvaal, I could not help feeling proud of our achievements. In two years, we had grown to the point when we could stage, first a protest of 2,000 from the Transvaal, and then 20,000 from all over South Africa. We had won recognition from the other regions and from other quarters too, and established the position of women as a vital element in the liberation struggle. Our path had not been our deliberate choice, it had been taken always in response to the pressure of events. The Federation was indeed the child of its time.

The other regions, too, had campaigned against unjust laws, against passes. They had joined us in our campaigns and we knew that in every other centre there had been anti-pass demonstrations on 9 August, in support of the Pretoria protest. Like us, they would continue to grow.

The conference decided that the headquarters of the Federation should move from Cape Town to Johannesburg. Lilian Ngoyi was elected National President and I became National Secretary. I was then even prouder of our Transvaal region, for this was a recognition of what we had achieved, even though we realised that our future course would not be easy and there would be much to be done.

The conference adopted the draft constitution and laid to rest an early difference with the African National Congress over the membership of the Federation — whether it should be composed of affiliated bodies or of individual members. I think we were always too busy in the Transvaal to be greatly concerned over this. We seemed to be progressing very well as a federation, but the former national executive in the Cape thought otherwise and favoured individual membership. The ANC had objected to this and would affiliate its many thousands of women in the ANC Women's League only on the basis of affiliated organisations or groups. There was, however, no real support at the conference for individual membership and it was settled and written into the constitution that the Federation of South African Women would be composed of affiliated organisations or groups.

Years later historians and researchers, some with a feminist bias, resenting the dominance of the African National Congress, were to criticise this decision. My view was, and still is, that in the heavy and growing pressure of the times, the Federation could not have stood as a unitary women's organisation. It needed the strength of its affiliated organisations, particularly that of the Women's League of the African National Congress.

20

Chapter III

My very ordinary life

On that day in August 1956, I was already fifty-one. I often wonder just how it took me so long to find the road to what must surely be one of the highest peaks of my whole life. On that day I walked with seven other women at the head of a march of 20,000 women of all races to the Prime Minister of South Africa.

Nor were these ordinary women. They represented the oppressed people of South Africa, coming in defiant protest against the passes which would deprive them and their children even further of freedom, justice and security. Yet they had chosen me, Helen Joseph, to be amongst their leaders on that unforgettable day.

Looking back now at the age of eighty, it seems to me that perhaps for twenty years I travelled inevitably, if unknowingly, uncaringly, along the road towards that great day and what followed after it. As a white in South Africa, I belonged to an unjust society, protected, cosseted by the colour of my skin. I had left England when I was twenty-two. It was only when in my forties, during and after the Second World War, that I began to open my eyes to the real world around me.

I was born in Sussex, England, in 1905. I grew up in an ordinary middle-class family. My early years until the 1914-18 war were remarkable only by their total unremarkability. I remember little of those times. My father, Samuel Fennell, was called up at once because he belonged to the Sussex Yeomanry, then still a mounted unit, but soon to become dismounted. I remember him as a warrant officer, going first to Gallipoli, from where the British troops were evacuated; then to Egypt and to Palestine. He wrote vivid letters to his two children, enclosing pressed flowers for me from Jerusalem and Bethlehem.

In England, my brother and I were growing up in a small terrace house in a London suburb. There were blackouts and air raids — although blackouts were not as total as in the next war. Yet as a small girl when I went to post letters for my mother, I ran quickly from lamp post to lamp post at night because below each lamp was a very small circle of light and only darkness in between.

Air raids were at first Zeppelin raids. When the sirens were heard, our neighbours, wives also of men gone to the war, used to come to our kitchen for cocoa and cake and comfort from my mother. She had held herself rather socially aloof in peacetime, but on those dark nights of barrage and bombs, the barriers went down. From the window we watched the first Zeppelin go down in flames — a fiery falling blaze in the blackness of the night lit only by searchlights. In the mornings we would sometimes find pieces of shrapnel outside our front door. Soon there were daylight raids, with aircraft all over the sky and smoke bubbles around them from our guns.

The air raids were taken pretty much as a matter of course — not that we had to endure anything like the 1940 blitz — but it must have been a huge strain on the wives and mothers. My father came back from the Middle East in 1917 for a few weeks' leave, the first time he had been home for over three years. Then he was off again to France and Belgium until the end of the war.

By the time it was all over, I was a weekly boarder at a convent school and on Armistice Day the Reverend Mother allowed me to borrow a bicycle from a day scholar to go to my mother. I found her crying in the kitchen, just sitting crying quietly at the table. At thirteen I could not understand her tears.

After the war, we moved to Epping Town, on the edge of the forest, fifteen miles from the city. There were Christmasses with great blazing log fires in the open fireplaces of that lovely old Elizabethan house with its Georgian front, which my father had bought on his return from the war. There were lazy summer days in the old, old garden. My brother Frank and I, with only fifteen months separating us, became very close, sharing our train journeys to the city of London and the daily walks to and from the railway station.

We had been educated at private schools — middle-class snobbishness undoubtedly — Frank in a grammar school and I at convents. I remember the little chapel with the windows opening onto the garden and the lovely roses in the summer. I was a Protestant in this Roman Catholic fold, but the convent was really a place of love for me. I don't remember tensions and punishments, but even now I still remember the names and faces of the nuns I loved so much.

I felt spiritually drawn to Roman Catholicism. I wanted to become a Roman Catholic, wanted the colour and the ritual lacking in the only Anglican churches I had known. But after I left the convent, my mother arranged for me to be confirmed in the Anglican church, her church. My father acknowledged none. It was meaningful for me at that time, there is no doubt of that, but my faith was not rooted deeply enough to hold me once I had left school.

In 1923 I started at King's College, University of London. My father could only afford to send one of us to university and had wanted my brother to go. Frank chose a business career so I was able to go instead. Commuting daily from Epping involved a walk to the station, forty minutes in the train to Liverpool Street station and a bus or tube train to the Strand. It was strenuous and I envied the more fortunate hostel students — they had more time to enjoy themselves than I had with three hours daily travelling. Few students' families, and certainly not mine, owned cars in the 1920s and university students accepted daily travel as part of life.

For college dances, I put my dress and shoes into a briefcase and changed in the students' cloakroom, queuing up at the hand basin for a quick wash. At 10.30, when the dance ended, I put my coat over my evening clothes and made my way by bus to Liverpool Street station to meet my brother for the last train to Epping and the mile walk home.

My university honours course was in English, but I doubt that I had any great aptitude for it, and certainly not for philology, to which London University attached much importance. In 1926, the General Transport Workers went out on strike and the whole country was paralysed — immobilised. I went to live with an aunt in Clapham, from where I could walk the four miles to Kings' College. Many of the students drove trams and buses and trains — which I suppose illustrates the political level of Kings' College. I didn't think of them as scabs. I thought they were pretty noble.

After four years at the university, I obtained a not very distinguished second class honours degree, but I had no professional training. It seems I would have to become a teacher, and to seek a job abroad where a teacher's training certificate would not be required. After some time I obtained a post as English teacher in the Mahbubia Girls school in Hyderabad Deccan in India. The prospect of going abroad was exciting.

I was vague indeed about what would be required of me as a school teacher, but I went back to my convent school a few times to take practice classes in English. I was very excited about going to India and my interest was mostly engaged in acquiring new dresses for the great adventure. I certainly did not foresee — how could I? — that this journey was not just a journey to India, but a journey into a new life, a life that would bring me ultimately to confrontation and imprisonment, but also a joy and comradeship that would transcend all else.

My knowledge of India was limited to Kipling's *Plain Tales from the Hills* and the novels of one B.M. Croker, whose work I am sure has long since disappeared from library shelves. I did not, in my excitement, give any thought to reading about India or trying to know her as a country. I doubt if I even appreciated the difference between British India and the India of the Princes where I was going. That I learnt as I went along.

I went off, at twenty-two, alone, on a P & O liner. I was both tearful and terrified, but my father had been adamant that I could not change my mind at the last moment. The liner pulled away from the dock — that tearing moment of parting — and a strange young man at my side lent me a large handkerchief to dry my tears. I felt that life had not changed so much after all.

I learnt a little about India between Tilbury Docks and Bombay, making friends during those carefree weeks on board and feeling superior because I was not part of the "fishing fleet" — a derisory term used for the annual influx of marriageable girls to the India of clubs and picnics and innumerable unattached young men. Yet in a way I suppose I really was part of the fishing fleet, as I certainly hoped to get married in India. I was not cherishing any ideas about a vocation as a teacher.

I grew to love that Mahbubia School and the Indian girls and their families. Hyderabad was the largest and the richest and probably the most corrupt and oppressive of all the princely states. The Nizam of Hyderabad, supported by an enormously wealthy and powerful Moslem aristocracy, ruled tyrannically over millions of Hindus, mostly at the lowest level of subsistence. Notwithstanding all this, I absorbed very little of Indian politics in those years and became only marginally aware of the Indian National Congress and the non-violent struggle of the Indian people for independence. Nor was I aware of the stark poverty all around me. In the princely state of Hyderabad our lives were untouched by that struggle. We were encapsulated in our pleasant social life, but had I wanted to, I could then have learnt so much about the Indian fight for freedom and justice, so similar to the struggle which was to absorb me in South Africa later.

I was in India from 1928 to 1930, a critical period when Nehru was emerging as the dominant figure and the Indian Congress had taken its stand on complete independence from the British Empire. Gandhi's defiance of the salt tax inspired 100,000 men and women to passive resistance and imprisonment on an unparalleled scale. A quarter of a million workers went on strike in Bengal, 100,000 workers in Bombay, yet in Hyderabad we went our ways, untouched by the cataclysmic events in British India.

Early one morning towards the end of my three-year contract, I rode a horse too high-spirited for me to handle. The horse bolted and together we collided with a bullock cart on a narrow road. I fell on my head and lay for two days, unconscious in hospital. I survived, but was warned that I could only do very light work for some time to come. By this time I was senior teacher at the school, involving heavy duties and responsibilities, so I did not apply to extend my contract and instead looked around for something else. I found nothing in India and finally took myself off to South Africa to a university friend whose father was the principal of a small preparatory school for boys in Durban.

I sadly left India and the Indian people I had grown to love so much. Indian friends had warned me what to expect in South Africa — the colour bar, racial discrimination — but it was too late to change my mind. Just prior to leaving I had been staying in Bombay with Indian friends, a most natural thing for me, not fully comprehending that this would be forbidden in South Africa. Indeed I hoped that my stay in South Africa would not be long and that I should soon be returning to India.

Despite the warnings, South Africa came as a shock after India. I was resentful at first, even openly, that my Indian friends were not accepted in this land of apartheid. Initially, however, I didn't meet any Indian people so I wasn't constantly reminded of the differences. I had not known any Africans before arriving in South Africa except for the isolated black student at university, and then we had little contact. In Durban I seemed to be in contact only with black domestic workers.

Within a few months I met sophisticated, charming, Billie Joseph, seventeen years older than I. I was very lonely and unable to hold out against the gay life he offered me. My longing for India faded and so did my sense of outrage at the racist society I found here. I agreed to marry Billie and to remain in South Africa.

My father disapproved of my marriage and refused to have anything to do with me for some years. Billie was Jewish, he had been divorced and he was much older than I. Nevertheless, at twenty-six, I could make my own choice. We married and moved into Durban society. I rode, played tennis and learned to play bridge. We lived in an attractive Spanish house in Durban North, high on a slope looking down to the sea and across to Durban and the Bluff headland five miles away. I loved my garden, spending much time in it.

We had no children, by design. Billie had two children from his first marriage, not even ten years my junior. He was not eager to start with babies again and, for myself, I held back because I soon became aware that our marriage was not too stable. I, who had never even met divorced people until my arrival in South Africa, assumed that divorce was nothing unusual. Many of my new friends were already into their second marriages. We led a very social life as Billie was very popular. I was shy at first, perhaps because his friends were all much older than I. I did not work because Billie did not want me to and working wives did not fit into our way of life.

Our marriage gradually sank to a very low level and Billie and I more and more went each our own way. My attitude soon became that anything he could do I could do better. His physical attraction for other women was not fading and, being very much younger, it was easy for me to find some sort of cheap compensation with other men. I was looking in the wrong places for what I had not found in my marriage. We did not quarrel often or openly and we managed to preserve the facade of a friendly couple. Our married life had always been very social and gay, and outwardly it remained that way.

In September 1939 war with Germany was declared and I wept openly as we listened to the radio announcements. Billie and our friends were jubilant that Hitler was to be challenged, but I could only say, "People will be killed! People will be killed!"

The war did not make much difference to our lives at first; South Africa was far from the actual conflict, whether in Europe or North Africa. Durban had a blackout because it was on the coast and petrol was eventually rationed, but there was still plenty for normal use. For the Durban July Handicap, South Africa's greatest horse race, we still had our picnic at the side of the race course, although beer and sausage rolls replaced champagne and caviare.

My father volunteered as a Royal Air Force reservist some months before the outbreak of war. He was then sixty-five and was duly called up when war broke out. He wrote that he was now an "erk", an aircraftsman, the lowest rank in the Air Force. "Something less than a private," was how he described himself. My brother Frank had become an officer in the Royal Army Service Corps and very soon he went to France and was evacuated at the time of Dunkirk. After a couple of years Billie decided that he must join the South African Dental Corps and went off, leaving his dental practice to his partner.

I lacked the initiative or the determination to join up myself until one day I read a press announcement, calling for university and professional women to attend an intensive training course for welfare and information officers — the female counterpart of the male information officers in the South African Army Education Service. Any women selected at the end of the course would become full-time lieutenants in the Women's Auxiliary Air Force or the Women's Auxiliary Army Services. Others could remain in the forces as privates or simply go home again.

25

The welfare aspect appealed to me, although I had no clear idea about what might be expected of me. I went off to Pretoria, driving there in my car on black market petrol. I slept overnight at a hotel on the way so that I could reach the WAAF camp and the end of my 400-mile journey in the morning to report for the course. I found a few other women there who, like myself, had been attracted by this novel project, but I lost sight of them during that endless day of attestation when I learnt the first lesson of army service — to sit and wait.

I was held up almost at the last stage of the procedure because I found a question on the attestation form about my church. I wrote "none" because I felt that I could not honestly say that I belonged to any church. Far from it, I had attended church services only a few times in the past fifteen years and even then not of my own volition, but because I had been staying with church-going friends and had not wanted to embarrass them. Yet I was no atheist and could not really call myself an agnostic. I had never denied my God, I would not have dared to. I believed in God, but my faith was no longer strong enough to hold me in prayer and worship.

An officer instructed me brusquely to fill in my form properly and told me that I must belong to some church. When I insisted that I did not and that I could not make a false attestation, I found myself in great difficulty. I had not then realised — and no one explained to me — that all the air force was interested in was to know how to bury me. Finally the officer gave in and accepted my attestation form with no church stated. Probably she just filled it in herself afterwards since I never heard anything more about it. I suppose it was just stubbornness on my part, but I objected to being bullied into doing something which I thought was dishonest.

As the course progressed, I came to understand what it was all about. If we were accepted, our mandate would be to inculcate a "liberal, tolerant attitude of mind" in the women serving in the forces. Truly an astounding mission to the white women of the WAAF, born and bred in a society which denied human rights to others on grounds of colour and race. For our task, we must be (and in my case become) politically well-informed ourselves and able to inform others in our weekly lectures to them.

I was among those selected. A nightmare fortnight followed of practical induction into air force camp conditions and procedures, even parade ground drill. We trainee officers were separated from each other and allocated to large huts, where we were expected to make contact with the lower ranks of WAAFs.

My group were artisans, tough young women doing quite heavy mechanical work in the aircraft hangars. They were totally disinterested in the stranger in the corner of their hut whom they knew was about to become an officer. I tried to hide this fact by keeping my officer's barathea uniform in my car, in which I could change when I went out of camp. Otherwise I remained in the very unbecoming regulation khaki drill shirt and skirt issued to me on arrival. No one spoke to me, though sometimes I knew they were speaking of me in Afrikaans. Finally I achieved social contact by dispensing sweets and cigarettes, feeling no shame about my purchased popularity, only wishing that I had thought of it earlier.

The welfare and information officers were then sent about their various duties on different airstations. I set off apprehensively for Bloemfontein in the Orange Free State, wondering how it was all going to turn out. Billie had had enough of the Dental Corps and had managed to be boarded out on medical grounds, returning to his dental practice in Durban. So he was out and I was in.

It was a strange experience for I was in a totally new environment and I had to do a great deal of study for the background of the lectures. We had been given a schedule of the areas we were supposed to cover. These included local and central government, health and education services, women's problems and disabilities, socialism, communism, liberalism, trade unionism, "native" affairs and Indian and coloured affairs — and then a free hand for any other topics that might arise. It seemed a formidable assignment. I realised that I should set about educating myself before I could do anything about educating others.

A new world was opening up for me, a new vision and new knowledge. I began to view the South African scene with new and better-informed eyes. As I studied the conditions in which black children struggled for education and opportunity, and compared them to how most whites lived, I began to feel ashamed of my own position as a white. Talking about democracy brought home to me that the black people did not share it with me. I had a parliamentary vote and they did not. As I spelt it out to the WAAFs, so I spelt it out to myself, questioning my own values as never before. I did not turn immediately into a socialist, far from it, but I began to see people as human beings, regardless of colour, began to have some idea of how the other half of the South African world lived. To some extent I was still fumbling, the ties to my comfortable civilian way of life were still strong and I could not really see myself living any other way.

We also lectured on the war, of course, presenting it as the struggle for a better world, for democracy, for human rights. When I talked about the national income I saw the figures, so unevenly distributed amongst the different racial groups. When I talked about education, I saw how much was spent on white schoolchildren and how little on blacks. When I talked about agriculture and the land, I saw that only 13 per cent was available for black people, yet they formed over 85 per cent of the population. I wondered what sort of South Africa we were fighting for. There was no one for me to talk to about all this, so it lay fallow in my mind. But the seeds were there.

A few months before the war ended, I was undecided what I should do when it was over. Dancing one night in camp with an air force colonel, he asked me what I thought of doing when I was demobilised and when I said I was thinking about returning to England, he said, "Oh no, people like you will be needed in South Africa." Years later, when I had been tried for high treason, house-arrested and banned, I wondered if he ever remembered saying that.

Billie had returned to Durban four years earlier, and whereas in the first ten years of marriage, he had not been constant to any woman, let alone me, now there was one who seemed to be settled in his life.

27

When an exciting post as acting director of a community health centre in Johannesburg was offered to me, I accepted it. I told Billie I should not be returning and suggested divorce, but he refused to consider it and I was not particularly interested in it either. I was only relieved that I need not go back to the strain of a marriage in name only. Nor did I wish to resume the kind of life I had known before, seeking compensation wherever I could find it. I had no bitter feelings about Billie. He had been good to me and it was the fault of neither of us that we could not satisfy each other in marriage. It would be better for us to part while we could still be friendly towards each other.

Very soon after I had started work at the centre, I realised that the academic background I had was inadequate to direct the activities of this bustling community health centre, with its scientific analytic approach to health. I often wondered why I had been offered the job. When I learnt that there was a diploma course in sociology and social work at the Witwatersrand University, I was immediately interested, especially as it was intended for people like me who had obtained their university degrees before there were any faculties of social science. I enrolled gladly, with the help of a demobilisation bursary to cover my fees and books, and managed to fit in the lecture times without affecting my centre work.

I learnt a great deal in the social work and social legislation classes which brought home to me even more strongly the glaring disparities between white and black in every field. I loved my work at the centre, identifying with these white people at a low economic level, struggling against poverty and unemployment. I enjoyed watching the children's play groups and their lively concerts, rising far above their squalid surroundings.

My job was to co-ordinate the work that was going on, rather than to introduce new features, for the director, overseas for two years' study leave, had laid the foundations and I must build on them, not restructure the centre in any way. I was interested in the analysis and measurement of what we were doing and modelled my reports faithfully on the director's initial comprehensive survey. Most of all I enjoyed the adult education activities, especially the talks and debates. Here, for the first time, I met educated Africans, invited occasionally to take part in a symposium or debate. But beyond polite cups of tea, there was no inter-racial social contact and I suspect that, if it had been introduced, there would have been acute tension at the low socio-economic level of the white centre membership, who saw black people as a threat to themselves, their security, their employment and to the security of their children.

I was becoming aware that the need for help, for social service, was even greater amongst the coloured and African people than amongst the poorest of the whites. It was hard for me to accept all this because I loved the centre, its staff, its work and above all its members. My work there had become a way of life for me and I was making new friends amongst like-minded people. Nevertheless, when the National War Memorial Health Foundation advertised for a supervisor of community centres for the coloured people in the Western Cape, I applied for the post.

The Foundation came into being at the end of the war, when the soldiers "up north" had themselves decided that they did not wish for masses of stone and mortar as monuments to their dead comrades. They wanted living memorials to represent the freedoms for which they had fought, particularly freedom from want. Each soldier gave a day's pay and the funds were entrusted to the Foundation to inaugurate and maintain promotive health projects in the fields of nutrition, education, recreation and social services. All these were to be established in community health centres. I was engaged for this post and went to live in the Cape.

My work lay in the sandy barren Cape Flats in Elsie's River, where many coloured people lived. Once again my work made heavy inroads into my life. I discovered on arrival that the title "supervisor" was not strictly accurate. I should first have to create the community centres before I could supervise them.

For two happy years I worked closely with the coloured people. They accepted me and loved me in a way that I had not known before. We worked together. The Foundation provided the funds but we created the centres ourselves, starting from small beginnings that they grew with the needs and the goodwill of the neighbourhood. From one very small centre we grew to a larger one and then to a third, still larger, always repeating our pattern of promotive health activities, a crèche, children's groups, adult groups, co-operative vegetable clubs and grocery clubs, sewing groups. We brought health promotion right into the lives of these underprivileged people. I found them outgoing, warm, lovable and supportive as we laughed and stormed our way through all our troubles. I believed then, as I still do, that these living community health centres were the finest memorials to the dead, whose graves are scattered over the battlefields of North Africa and Italy. South Africa has kept faith with her dead sons.

It was my work in Elsie's River that finally brought me to the realisation that all our social services were only alleviating the existing evils, not eradicating them. Whatever and however much we achieved, the basic poverty, the injustice, the affront to human dignity, all these were still there. Our little islands of concern were not affecting the total situation. Yet I realised, too, that misery has to be alleviated. Obviously these new and deepening insights would not have taken me very far in any political activity, since the Foundation staff were not permitted any political involvement. So many of its projects depended on government subsidies. Then a friend telephoned me to say that the Medical Aid Society of the Transvaal Clothing Industry was looking for a new Secretary-Director. If I were interested I could fly up for an interview with Solly Sachs, famous General Secretary of the Garment Workers' Union. The clothing industry employed thousands of coloured and African workers, as well as whites and Indians, and since the militant and radical trade union was so political itself, there could be no obstacle to any political activity for me. I accepted the post.

I returned to Elsie's River, to tell everyone what I had done, feeling that I had betrayed them, but the centre staff and members accepted my decision with compassion and understanding, assuring me that they would bring up our child, the centre, even if they had to do it without me and I should still be proud of it. They did — and I was.

In a couple of months I was gone, back in Johannesburg by March 1951 with a sad heart and yet feeling that I could not have done otherwise. I had to move onwards and outwards.

Billie eventually asked for a divorce and I had agreed. The worst aspect of it for me was not the ending of the marriage but the trauma of the divorce court. Despite my oath to tell the truth, I had told a lie in court, when I had said that Billie had refused to make a home for me after the war. It was I who had refused to return to him. My lawyers had insisted that I must divorce Billie and not let him divorce me and he had agreed. The thought of that lie spoken on oath haunted me for a very long time and I believed that sooner or later God would punish me for it. In a bizarre way, this was the nearest I had come to God for many years.

Chapter IV

Becoming an activist

I remember well that first meeting with the redoubtable Solly Sachs, when I flew to Johannesburg for the interview. He didn't seem at all interested in what I had done already and only talked about the coloured people, impressing on me that the Medical Aid Society's function was to give the workers whatever benefits they were entitled to — "not a penny less, not a penny more!" I sensed his great concern for the clothing workers as people, and although I had not intended to come to any immediate decision at this first interview, when he asked me abruptly, "well, do you want the job?", I said "yes".

Solly used to say of himself, "I am a Jew. I have a rough voice and a Lithuanian accent, I am ugly and I had everything against me. . ." Yet he had captured and held the loyalty of thousands of Afrikaner women in the clothing industry.

As the first months of my new job passed, I found myself in a very close relationship with Solly. He was unlike anyone I had ever met before. He didn't belong to my middle-class life, which he contemptuously called "spit and polish". Nor did I fit into his life. He had come with his family from Lithuania and they had settled inevitably into the Eastern Jewish community in South Africa, which had clung to many of the traditional ways of life. These Solly himself had thrown off, but many of his friends, and to a great extent his family, still belonged to that tight Jewish community. Solly's mind and his total commitment to the cause of the garment workers went far beyond all this. Perhaps this is what drew me to him and led me to try and identify with him. It was never the other way round, for Solly never tried to identify with anyone. He could be tremendously arrogant, even abrasive, yet he was capable of great affection, even tenderness.

Solly had said of himself that he was ugly. In fact when I first met him I found him almost repellent. It was not his features, as they were good, strong and Slav, but his skin was acne-scarred and had been discoloured since his youth. When I became accustomed to it, I never thought him ugly again. Indeed his curling silver hair gave him almost an air of distinction and he carried himself well, despite a slight stoop when he was tired or deep in thought.

We were an oddly assorted pair but he taught me human values which I had not appreciated before — and much else too. His intense love for the workers, his determination to fight for them, to carry on the struggle in which he had won so many victories for them during the past twenty years, inspired me, and I am sure played a part in setting my feet on the road which I was to walk for the rest of my life. He scoffed at my lack of political erudition but I learnt more from listening to him than I ever learnt from the "masters" whom he was always urging me to read.

I had begun my work at the Medical Aid Society in March 1951. It took me a little while to learn about this new work, but personalities in the management committee soon emerged. There was Solly himself, and in the union I found Afrikaner women of outstanding personality and leadership. One and all they had come into Johannesburg during the depression years, driven off the land by poverty into clothing factories to work for 12/6 a week. One was Johanna Cornelius, later to become General Secretary of this militant union. It is said that she addressed public meetings in her old school blazer, quite unconscious of the strange impression she must have created. Her words as a young girl speaking at a large public meeting in Germiston still ring out strongly. "We are tired of slaving for a few pence," she declared, "our fathers rebelled for freedom and we are their daughters." The young Johanna knew gaol, police persecution, physical assault for the sake of her fellow workers in the factories. She became a dynamic trade union leader, greatly loved for her warmth and compassion.

There were others too. Anna Scheepers, President of the union for many years, was noted for her skill as negotiator in disputes with employers. Johanna's sister, Hester Cornelius, was the national organiser and there were many more like her. They were indeed the rebels' daughters who had built up the militant Garment Workers' Union, led and guided by Solly Sachs.

In May 1951, the Separate Representation of Voters Act was passed, removing the coloured voters from the common voters' roll. This proposal had aroused a storm of protest after the Act was passed and the Torch Commando took the lead, starting off as a war veterans' organisation. It soon widened its ranks and together with a few of my friends I marched in procession across Johannesburg by night carrying flaming torches.

This was really my first political activity, and very impersonal it was, for we marched in the dark, 4,000 of us, eight abreast. At its zenith, the Torch Commando numbered a quarter of a million followers, but the Nationalist government achieved its aim ultimately by increasing the Senate in order to get the required two-thirds majority needed to change the coloured vote. It had been a short but bitter battle, in which the Black Sash also played its part.

Later in the year came my first continuous period of political activity, when Solly, Johanna Cornelius and Anna Scheepers all stood in the municipal elections as Labour Party candidates. Solly had impressed on me that the Labour Party stood for all workers, but it seemed to me that it was really a white workers' party. However, there wasn't any other political option for me at that stage, so I joined the Labour Party and became engrossed in Solly's election campaign. He stood in Doornfontein, mainly a working-class area and mostly English-speaking, but with a fair sprinkling of Jewish immigrants from Europe.

I was suddenly busy every night for a couple of months, either helping at the election office or, less happily, canvassing. Solly decided that my English accent would either outrage the Doorfontein Afrikaners or be unintelligible to the Middle European immigrants. I was limited to canvassing the obviously English names on the voters' roll. I was not much good at this, partly because I was not sufficiently informed about the South African scene and partly because I was shy and not capable of thrusting myself through front doors as Solly and others could. I was grateful for the few cups of tea that I was offered, but I am very sure that I did not win any votes for Solly.

It was an exciting two months for me and out of it came a lasting friendship with Violet Weinberg, Solly's election agent. She was working with the Garment Workers' Union, in charge of the workers' Provident Fund. Neither Solly nor Anna nor Johanna won any seats in the election. Violet, from previous experience, said sadly, "wouldn't it be nice if we could win — even just once?"

I accepted that the Medical Aid Society work was to some extent constructive and not merely palliative, but it still did not help my growing feeling that it was the system itself, the colour bar, that had to be attacked.

At the Medical Aid Society office I came into contact with the Garment Workers' Union officials, black and white, and, for almost the first time, met black people as equals in status and responsibility. Yet even this was confined to a work association and I cannot say that I really knew any of them socially, black or white, except Solly and Violet.

Since the passing of the Suppression of Communism Act in 1950, several left-wing political leaders, both black and white, and some trade union leaders too, had been ordered to resign from their organisations, forbidden to attend meetings or leave the areas where they lived and worked. In May 1952, Solly Sachs, despite having been expelled from the Communist Party in 1932, was ordered to resign as General Secretary of the Garment Workers' Union, not to attend gatherings or leave the magisterial area of Johannesburg. I was soon caught up into the fury of thousands of garment workers that their leader, the man who had led them to their victories during the past twenty years, should be thus summarily removed from them.

Within a few days, a public protest meeting was held on the City Hall steps, the Hyde Park Corner of Johannesburg's political organisations. This was on the morning of 24 May 1952, a Saturday morning. Thousands of workers attended, black and white, and I marched in my first daylight procession from the Trades Hall to the City Hall. I felt very conspicuous, despite the size of the procession with Solly himself at the head of it. When we reached the City Hall, we saw the coloured workers arriving, marching eight abreast, in their thousands. Solly had publicly announced his intention of addressing the meeting. It was his defiant act of public protest. As he took the microphone and began to speak to the cheering crowds, the police burst out from the doors of the City Hall behind him and pulled him violently backwards with them until the doors closed again. The workers were incensed and there was a spontaneous surge forward. The City Hall doors flew open again. I was standing nearby and saw it all. The police burst out and charged the crowds with batons and even bits of broken chairs. The helpless people were literally beaten back, beaten to their knees as the police chased them, nearly all women, down the steps into the roadway.

It was a horrifying sight, women and a few old men, with bleeding heads, scrambling to their feet to get away. I had not known that police could act like this. I watched their faces as they rushed past me. They were young, but not too young to relish this brutality, legalised and official. It was later described as a riot, but that was no riot, for there was no violence among the workers. It came only from the police. About sixty people were treated at the hospital and many privately.

I went with some of the union leaders to the police station where Solly was held, to take food and books to him. He was brought out from the cells to us without his collar and tie. Somehow that really seemed to mark him, for me, as a prisoner. He insisted that he was perfectly all right and being well treated. He was released on bail that evening.

Meanwhile the union called for a one-day protest strike for the Monday when another mass meeting would be held on the City Hall steps. That Monday morning Solly first appeared in the magistrate's court and was charged with breaking his banning orders. His case was then remanded to a later date. A few hours later he came to the meeting, defying his banning orders for the second time.

Thousands of workers were gathered on the City Hall steps, just as they had been on the Saturday. I think there were even more of them this time. As Solly came towards the platform, he was arrested by the police. He told them there was no need for them to break any more heads, he would go quietly with them. He was once more led off to the police station. The union leaders continued the meeting and the police did not interfere again, but feelings were running very high among the workers. On this occasion, Solly was refused bail until the following morning. I suppose it was feared that he would go straight back to the meeting. And I think he would have done. He came to trial later on two counts of violating his bans and was sentenced to six month's gaol on each count but he remained on bail pending his appeal to the higher courts against the conviction.

Weeks of protests, meetings and demonstrations followed, all against Solly's bans, and I became part of them. I stood with a placard in Eloff Street, Johannesburg's main thoroughfare. I rode to Pretoria in a bus filled with garment workers, mostly Afrikaners, joining them in their folk songs. I found all this exciting, yet still felt that I was really on the outside looking in. I was not a union official, I was not a garment worker, I had never worked in a factory of any sort.

Solly's case came before the Appeal Court at the end of the year in Bloemfontein. He argued his case himself before the five judges. "The five old men of Bloemfontein," he used to call them. He had considerable ability and experience in the law and he had decided that neither he nor his union could afford legal representation at this high and costly level. The appeal judges complimented Solly on his able presentation of his case but refused to set aside his convictions. The magistrate's judgement was upheld and consequently the validity of his banning orders. His six-month gaol sentence was, however, suspended for three years, provided he did not commit a similar offence.

It was a bitter disappointment to Solly. He felt he had achieved nothing. He wanted only one thing, to have his bans set aside and to be free to return to his union, the organisation he had built and led for twenty-four years. All political work and trade union activity was now closed to him and he decided to leave South Africa. I thought he should stay, despite the restrictions. His influence in the trade union movement was still very strong and his presence in South Africa would continue to be valuable. I could not see that he would serve South Africa more by leaving, whatever he might achieve overseas. Of course, personally, I also wished that he would stay, but I don't believe that this had anything to do with my conviction that he could do more by remaining in South Africa.

It was now pretty clear that there was no permanent future for me with Solly. I had begun to doubt whether I could really fit into his intensely individualistic personal life. Perhaps my middle-class conventions were too strong, but I was not content to accept the second-class role which seemed to be all that Solly was prepared to allow me. In fact, I learnt long afterwards that he decided not to marry me because he was looking for some woman with "epic" qualities to share his life. I doubt that, for Solly, I ever graduated from the "wishy washy" liberal he used to call me.

Nevertheless I followed him to London, spending time in France with him before I went on to London and then to Geneva. After that I joined him briefly in Manchester, where he had obtained a research fellowship at the university. That visit finally convinced me that I could not adjust myself to his life. In any event, by now I felt committed to the struggle in South Africa in whatever way would be possible and Solly had decided that his future lay in England.

The main political event of the year 1952 was the Defiance Campaign, organised by the Congress movement. It had brought together the African National Congress, the South African Indian Congress and the Cape Coloured Franchise Action Council. They united in this great protest against injustice, and thus the struggle for the liberation of the black people. It was also the beginning of the Congress Alliance.

The particular unjust laws chosen for protest were those relating to the pass system, the culling of cattle (a long-standing grievance in African rural areas) and the Suppression of Communism Act, especially for its banning of black leaders. The Separate Representation of Voters Act was of course also included, for its arbitrary removal of coloured voters from the common voters' roll.

Passive, non-violent resistance in the tradition of the South African Indian Congress in 1908 and 1946 had been decided on. Volunteers must defy the laws, but only selected volunteers, who must be trained to defy, to undergo harsh gaol conditions and not break, must be trained not to retaliate whatever violence might be inflicted on them.

6 April 1952 was to be celebrated throughout South Africa as the 300th

anniversary of Van Riebeek's landing at the Cape. It was a joyous occasion, no doubt, for whites, but for the blacks it merely marked 300 years of wrong. The congresses decided to launch the Defiance Campaign on 6 April, with nationwide meetings calling for volunteers. Many thousands responded and actual defiance began on 26 June.

Nearly 200 were arrested on that day for defying curfew regulations or entering post offices or railway stations through "whites-only" entrances. Defiers intended in all cases to go to gaol without paying fines, but in some later cases they were turned out of gaol against their will. Money found on their persons was taken by the police to pay the fines.

The campaign continued and grew. At first the sentences passed on defiers were fairly light, a month or two in gaol, but they became increasingly severe as the campaign proceeded. In August, the peak month, over 2,000 were arrested. Everything was highly organised, even the names of the intended defiers and the time, date and place of the intended offence, were published by the congresses. There were some reports of ill-treatment in the gaols, but generally the groups of defiers established themselves effectively through their own discipline, their songs and their determination and unfailing cheerfulness. It became an honour to be a defier.

I was of course, aware of the Defiance Campaign which had attracted considerable press publicity. The idea of non-violent resistance to injustice appealed to me strongly. I believed, on the example of India, that if it grew to fully national proportions, the government would have to negotiate, even on its own repressive laws. Yet it did not really touch me personally. I was still moving in the trade union field, though not even as a significant part of that, and I was kept very busy at the Medical Aid Society office. As the months went by, however, this amazing campaign of self-discipline and self-sacrifice made me feel ever more ashamed that I was part of the unjust system and not part of the campaign against it. I think that this was true of many other white people. It was only at the end of the year that a handful of whites actually went to gaol. They were all very much more politically involved than I was, so I lived on with my sense of guilt, which I did not yet see clearly as white guilt. That came later.

Overseas publicity and sympathy for the Defiance Campaign was growing steadily. Some 8,000 men and women defied the unjust laws and went singing to gaol. No violence of any sort arose out of actual defiance episodes, but in the last two months of the year, ugly rioting was sparked off by police violence, when police fired into crowds. It soon became clear that the Congress could and did discipline effectively its own members, especially the volunteers, but they could not exercise control over masses inflamed by police violence.

Even before the end of 1952, government regulations had raised maximum penalties for defiers to three years' imprisonment or a fine of £300. When Parliament met at the beginning of 1953, drastic repressive laws were passed, specially designed to crush passive resistance and to make it impossible for it ever to be revived in this form. Whipping, up to twelve strokes, had been introduced as an additional penalty for defiers. Inciting others to commit an offence by way of protest became a new offence for which fines or imprisonment were up to £500 or five years in gaol. A second new crime also came into being: assisting materially in any way whatsoever any person campaiging against any law by way of an unlawful act — even members of the family.

These laws dealt the fatal blow to the Defiance Campaign and it had to be called off. Hitherto the gaol sentences for defiers had been one or two months, but the possibility of three years' imprisonment was a different matter. The defiers refused to pay fines because this would violate the principle of courting imprisonment as an act of defiance. Yet the Defiance Campaign had not failed, as it had strengthened the determination of the oppressed people to continue their struggle for freedom and justice. Their sacrifice had not been in vain, for it had highlighted the evil regime of the Nationalist government, heaping injustice upon injustice. As for me, I was still hoping for ways to become directly and personally involved. I had joined the Labour Party when Solly had told me to stop criticising it, get into it and do something about it. I still saw it as a party involved in the interests of white workers. I found I was regarded, and rightly so, as a newcomer amongst the experienced stalwarts of the labour movement, but much as I admired their dedication and leadership, I realised that I would not find here the political non-racial home which I sought.

It is of course quite possible that, had the Communist Party still been legal, I might have found my way into it and swallowed its doctrines for the sake of its multiracial membership. But the Communist Party, the only multiracial political organisation in the country, was banned, and there seemed nowhere for me to turn.

I had gone with Solly to Muizenberg in the Cape for his last holiday in South Africa. Understandably I was not very confident about my political future after he had gone. I walked on the beach with Violet Weinberg and I wondered how I should "fill my days" without all the various tasks which Solly had demanded of me and which I had carried out so gladly. Violet, too, spent much of her time assisting Solly in various ways, but she had a young family and was thus not as absorbed as I had allowed myself to become. I knew little of her political affiliation outside her support for the Garment Workers' Union, nor of her friends, but she did say that she thought there would be plenty for me to do and she offered to put me in touch with others in Johannesburg.

There had been an important meeting in Johannesburg at the end of 1952, attended by many whites, both radical and liberal, who were feeling much as I did, that the time had come for them to do something about their strong sense of outrage at the Nationalist government's oppressive regime and at the conditions of poverty, injustice and racial discrimination in which the black people lived. The United Party, the official opposition to the government, was conservative, still seeing the racial situation in terms of trusteeship, with the whites as guardians to wards, who were presumably never to come of age. Liberals could not find a political home there, nor in the relatively more radical but still narrow sphere of the Labour Party, which was, in any event, now little more than a shadow of its former militant self.

I do not know how I missed that meeting, other than that I simply did not know about it. The African National Congress and the South African Indian Congress had arranged the meeting to bring together this slowly growing number of whites sympathetic to their aims and to the Defiance Campaign. There were differing shades of political views at the meeting, mainly between those who wanted a loaded franchise for blacks and those who stood for universal adult franchise. One group took the lead afterwards in forming a white organisation to stand firmly alongside the congresses on universal adult franchise. This organisation was to become the South African Congress of Democrats.

To my surprise, I was invited to serve on the provisional committee for the formation of this new organisation. At the committee meetings I came into contact with Father Trevor Huddleston of the Anglican Church, and Father du Manoir of the Roman Catholic Church. Cecil Williams, Ruth First, Joe Slovo and 'Rusty' Bernstein were there too, all former members of the Communist Party and also of the Springbok Legion, a radical service organisation during the war. I served on this founding committee but don't think I contributed very much towards it, certainly not ideologically. I was still pretty ignorant, despite Solly's teaching. But it did not matter, for the really important thing was to get this new white organisation onto its feet to provide a political home for sympathetic whites within the orbit of the Congress alliance.

It was through this committee, however, that I became aware of the "black spots" issue. The government planned to separate white from black, to unscramble enormous residential areas where blacks and white lived adjacent to each other. Sophiatown, Newclare and Martindale, the oldest black settlements in Johannesburg, nestled comfortably side by side amidst several white suburbs of western Johannesburg. These were amongst the very few areas where blacks owned freehold property, made doubly precious because there a black man could own the very land on which his home stood.

Sophiatown was the largest of these three areas, well-established, though admittedly a slum in parts, but this was due to overcrowding under the pressure of the black housing shortage. It was not, and never had been, a prescribed area controlled by a white location superintendent, holding the power of residence in his hand, the power to decide who should be allowed to live there, or even enter the township. Sophiatown was free and friendly, almost the last bastion of black freehold land in Johannesburg. Despite poverty, squalor and violence, Sophiatown was exuberant, alive. Its people were strong. It was a living community, an organism grown up in its own environment. But Sophiatown was also a black spot to the white voters who had the power to have it removed, this black spot surrounded by white suburbs. For this reason alone it could not be allowed to remain.

No one, certainly no one in Sophiatown, was fooled by official statements about slum clearance. All the slum clearance that was needed was to provide proper housing and freehold rights elsewhere. The people of Sophiatown did not want to be removed against their will. They did not want to be herded into Johannesburg's controlled black townships to live under the "permit" system.

The government named its shameful plan the "Western Areas Removal Scheme". It stirred the consciences, at last, of some of the Johannesburg whites, and a Western Areas Protest Committee was formed, quickly followed by other protest committees. The congresses were represented on these committees and I soon became involved. We went on deputations to the City Council, sat at tables in white suburbs and in the centre of the city, collecting signatures for our protests. Most of white Johannesburg was too timid to give names and addresses, even the few who showed interest. We collected money for telegrams and postcards to MPs urging them to oppose the scheme. I felt some sympathy towards the frightened whites, for I too was very frightened when I started collecting signatures. I was convinced I would be arrested, although I was not sure for what offence, as I was too ashamed to discuss my fears with anybody. I was thankful when it rained and our tables had to be moved.

It was about the Western Areas Removal Scheme that I had addressed the council meeting in Geneva. While I was overseas, the first people had been removed from Sophiatown, despite all the protests, the Congress organisation, the weekly Sophiatown meetings and the Congress leaflets proclaiming "We Shall Not Move." It took, however, 2,000 armed police and army reinforcements to ensure that the people did move and 100 African families and their household goods were loaded onto government lorries. They were taken to a controlled location called Meadowlands and put into little matchbox houses, four times the distance from their work. The authorities had to bring the move forward by three days so as to forestall any resistance or response to the ANC call for a general stay-at-home from work on the day of the removals.

Some of the people from Sophiatown had moved voluntarily. What else could they do in the face of 2,000 armed police, there to remove 100 families? Yet such was the discipline of the ANC that despite the provocation of the very presence of the police, there was neither rioting nor bloodshed. Other removals followed later, though never as large, nor as heavily policed, as the first. After several years every black family had left Sophiatown. The long green grass grew in the streets where the houses had stood, marking it as the grave of the life, love and laughter that had once been Sophiatown.

Today a white suburb stands where once Sophiatown stood. Over "Freedom Square", where we held our meetings, a primary school has been built. White children now play in well-ordered playgrounds where once black children ran freely in the streets. The name of this suburb is "Triomf", which is the Afrikaans word for "triumph". What triumph? The triumph of the armed police who carted the families away? Or the triumph of the bulldozer that crushed their homes into the ground? Or the triumph of the Nationalist government, hell bent on separating black from white, on removing the "black spot" that had soiled white suburbs by its proximity?

Meanwhile, preparations were going ahead for the formation of the Congress of Democrats in Johannesburg. In October 1953, a national conference was held, attended by the Cape Town Democratic League, delegates from Port Elizabeth and Cape Town and, of course, our newly-formed Johannesburg Congress of Democrats.

The South African Congress of Democrats was formed and I was elected to the national executive committee. I was already secretary of a Johannesburg branch. At last I was a member of an organisation which identified itself with the struggle for freedom and justice, with the African National Congress and the South African Indian Congress and the newly-formed South African Coloured People's Organisation. Like them we stood unequivocally on the United Nations Declaration of Human Rights. I had found a political home, even if it was not itself multiracial in composition.

There had, in fact, been considerable division of opinion on whether the Congress of Democrats should have a multiracial membership or not, but the ANC had been adamant on this point. The Congress of Democrats must be white. As whites we could be equal partners in the Congress but we would not be welcome to compete with the other congresses for membership.

Our political task was to work amongst the white people, the voters like ourselves, to spread amongst them our rejection of all forms of racial discrimination, our demand for full equality of opportunity, for equal rights for all people, to persuade them that only in the acceptance of this lay any future peace for the people of South Africa. It would be no easy task but it was there for us to do.

Several people at the conference pressed for multiracial membership, but the ANC viewpoint finally prevailed. The South African Congress of Democrats, the COD, as it became known, was formed with a white membership, to be the white wing of the Congress Alliance.

Chapter V

South Africa belongs to all who live in it

The Congress Alliance, functioning with a closely co-ordinated leadership, was working on the preparations for the coming Congress of the People, the mass multiracial gathering to be held the following year, 1955. Other organisations, such as the Liberal Party, the Labour Party, even the United Party and the Nationalist Party, had been invited to become co-sponsors of the Congress of the People. In the event, however, the Congress Alliance, which had taken the lead, stood alone as the only sponsors of the imaginative and comprehensive plan to call the people of South Africa, black and white, to come together and adopt a people's Freedom Charter.

The Congress of the People activities brought me to an inspiring new level of personal activity, for as the campaign unfolded there were joint meetings of the national executives of the Congress Alliance organisations. These were exciting meetings, always held in great secrecy, for fear of police raids or other interference, and there were always some banned leaders amongst us. Sometimes we had narrow escapes.

On one occasion we met in a top-storey flat in Johannesburg where we had felt very secure. We finished our business and came down in the lifts, banned and unbanned together. As we came out of the building into the street, we saw four senior members of the security branch of the police coming across the road towards us. We stood and laughed and laughed. It might have been very serious for several of us who were banned, and we had no means of knowing how our plans had leaked, but the police had come just ten minutes too late! They could do nothing but turn around in the face of our mocking laughter and walk back to their car.

Another meeting that I remember especially was held in Evaton, an Indian suburb about twenty miles from Johannesburg. We drove there at night into the unlit streets until we came to a house, set a little way back from the road. One by one we filed quietly, almost surreptitiously, into the back yard and through the back door into a room lit only by one petrol lamp. I don't know what purpose that room usually served, but that night there was only a bare centre table, several chairs and a few wooden benches. Our friends were there from other cities, Cape Town, Port Elizabeth, Durban, having travelled many hundreds of miles.

It was the first time that I saw Chief Albert Luthuli, President General of the African National Congress. His dark face was softly etched in the lamplight, unforgettable, with the wise kind eyes and the ready smile that had already inspired thousands to follow him into gaol in the Defiance Campaign.

Albert Luthuli had come into the political field late in his life, when he was nearly fifty — like me. He had been a highly respected educationist and a lay preacher in the Methodist Church. He was chosen by his people in the Groutville Reserve in Natal to be their chief. When he was elected Natal President of the ANC, and because he supported and led the Defiance Campaign, he was dismissed by the government from his chieftainship. He was officially no longer a chief, but to the end of his life he remained "Chief Luthuli" to his people.

Of all the national leaders, Chief, as he was called by all of us, was the most beloved. He drew love and loyalty and he gave it. It was at that Evaton meeting that he said, "People ask me why I work with communists and my reply is that I have one enemy, the Nationalist government, and I will not fight on two fronts. I shall work with all who are prepared to stand with me in the struggle for the liberation of our country."

Chief had spelt it out very clearly on behalf of the African National Congress. It was his reply to persistent criticism of the Congress Alliance who would not reject those, black or white, who had made a great contribution as leaders when they had been free to do so, no matter whether or not they were communists.

Not surprisingly the two campaigns, for the Congress of the People and against the Western Areas Removal Scheme, aroused considerable interest on the part of the security police, eager as always to intimidate and suppress Congress activities. On 24 June 1954, a Western Areas protest conference was held in the Johannesburg Trades Hall, the historic venue of so many labour and trade union activities. It was invaded by armed policemen and security branch men who took the names and addresses of all the persons present.

I was not at this conference, but I was there a week later for the conference for the Congress of the People. This time the organisers were more than ready for such police action. I was standing next to the entrance when five security branch detectives, led by Colonel Att Spengler, the former rugby player, marched in, shoving aside anyone who tried to stop them, including me. The detectives sat down and began taking notes of the speeches, but two of the conference organisers left the meeting with an urgent petition to a judge, sitting "in chambers". Victory was ours when Judge Blackwell issued an interdict against the police. "South Africa is not yet a police state," he said, and the police could not enter a closed conference without a warrant. Colonel Spengler and his team were loudly booed out of the hall and as soon as the doors closed behind them, the conference came to its feet, singing "Nkosi Sikelele" in triumph.

1954 was a campaign year and my weekends, especially Sundays, were taken up with attending meetings, often in Sophiatown. I was, as yet, no public speaker, but I used to convey greetings and support on behalf of the Congress of Democrats, usually standing on the wagon which served as a platform for outdoor meetings. In July, a special anti-removal mass meeting was held on

Freedom Square there. Chief Luthuli was to speak, but on arrival in Johannesburg, he was met by police with a banning order forbidding him to attend any gatherings or be away from his home area in Natal.

A huge crowd of 10,000 people had attended this rally in order to hear Chief speak. My friend Violet's banned husband, Eli Weinberg, stood on an adjacent roof-top taking photographs, thinking that he would not be regarded as illegally attending a meeting. Subsequently he was arrested and charged with violating his banning orders, but acquitted.

The banning of leaders went on steadily. Bram Fischer, the first National President of the Congress of Democrats, was one of the early victims, soon followed by several of our executive members and officials too. The African National Congress paid the heaviest price with Nelson Mandela, their Transvaal President and President of the African National Congress Youth League, together with Walter Sisulu, Secretary General of the ANC, in addition to Chief Luthuli being banned. Altogether almost fifty of the Congress Alliance leaders and trade unionists had been banned. It could have been a crippling blow, yet somehow the congresses rallied and continued.

Loyalty to the banned leaders was affirmed over and over again. "All the banned leaders belong to you," declared Walter Sisulu, before he was himself banned. "They will remain your leaders because they still belong to our liberation struggle and they will still find a way to make their contribution. They have not been rejected by us, but forcibly thrown out by our enemies." As the first leading members were removed by banning orders, others came to take their places, until they themselves were banned.

After Chief was confined to Groutville, the joint Congress executives had to meet with him there secretly, in an isolated school building, deep in the sugarcane fields on the Natal north coast. We used to leave Johannesburg after work on Friday afternoon and drive 400 miles to Durban, arriving in the early hours of Saturday morning. After a few hours' sleep, we would leave for our rendezvous for the meeting, which would last all day. The Indians, coloureds and whites would then leave for Durban, while the African National Congress went straight into an all-night sitting of their own executive committee, lasting well into Sunday morning.

Strict security was observed for these joint executive meetings and this included all our arrangements for accommodation in Durban overnight. On one occasion, we arrived at about one o'clock on a Saturday morning, only to discover from a very sleepy host that we were not expected because the so very carefully worded telegram to warn him of our arrival had been so cryptic that it was unintelligible!

These meetings were especially valuable for me because there I met the leaders of the other congresses and from the other regions. It was a unique privilege. I was always with our National President and one or two others, so I did not have to do much talking myself. I was able just to listen and admire the stature of these national leaders. I was always learning.

The Federation of South African women had been asked to arrange overnight accommodation for the delegates to the coming Congress of the People. We had no idea how many people to expect, but we estimated it could run into 1,000 or more. We did not view this request as any sort of implied relegation of women to the domestic area. On the contrary, it gave us several weeks of intensive organising through small house meetings, mainly of women, at which we could discuss more important issues as well as beds.

The word "bed" was a little misleading, for in the cramped overcrowded little houses there were few beds and all we looked for was space for a mattress on the floor or a doubling up in someone's bed. It was not a case of "how many spare beds have you?" but "how many people do you have space for?" The answers came — one, two, three, even four people. I wondered how they could all fit in.

Bertha was my tireless comrade, always ready to go with me at night into the townships. Robert often came with us, to guide us in the areas which we did not know well. We would go from street to street, contacting women, talking about the Freedom Charter and the Congress of the People, calling for space for the delegates to sleep. In Soweto we could not work much later than nine o'clock, unless by pre-arrangement, as black working people needed to go to bed early in order to be ready for the five o'clock start the next morning.

Our lists of "spaces" grew to over 1,000: then we were satisfied, because we knew that many of the delegates would have relatives with whom they could stay in the township. When we had finished for the night, I used to drive Bertha to her home in the Germiston location on the other side of Johannesburg, slipping in quietly and illegally, and then quickly out again.

At the same time we had been organising women for a Federation Conference on 29 May, where we would consider, as women, what demands should be sent in for the Freedom Charter. Our regional committee drafted a comprehensive set of demands, covering almost every aspect of daily life, and it came out very much like the final form of the Freedom Charter. This was not really surprising for, as in the charter, the demands of the women reflected the hardships and struggles of their daily life.

At the Federation Conference we discussed the suggested demands very carefully and only two were dropped. One was the section calling for better conditions in the "reserves", the parts of South Africa set aside for occupation by Africans, the 13 per cent of the land for 85 per cent of the people. I was still ignorant of much that mattered to the African people and had not appreciated that the demand would be for a just redistribution of the land, not better reserves. I had accepted, as I accepted so much else, the factual existence of the reserves and demanded, therefore, amelioration of what ought not to be.

The other demand which was rejected was also my contribution — for better birth control clinics. This was my social work approach and drew lively protest from both men and women. (There were always a few men at our women's conferences, probably out of curiosity.) No one must tamper with the right to bear children, no matter what the social or health consequences. I know that especially in urban areas, health education has brought a somewhat different approach now to birth control, but at that time there were strong political overtones, a suspicion that the "system" sought to reduce the numbers of

African people, while encouraging an increase in the white birthrate.

Our demands reflected very clearly the direction of the thinking of the women of the Federation. The stress was on the struggle for liberation of men and women together. Separationist feminist liberation did not feature strongly beyond the call for the vote for women, election to state bodies, equal rights in marriage and guardianship and equal work for equal pay.

Rights denied to women must of course find a place in any charter of rights or any demands, but the intimate daily issues were at the heart of the thinking of these women. Demands for better living conditions in all spheres, for mothers, for children, for families, for houses and a better environment, for the removal of migrant labour — these were the issues which the Federation women had discussed in our committee meetings and which had formed the pattern of the demands which I had drafted and which the committee put to the conference.

It seems to me that here, as so often is the case in women's conferences, the women themselves shaped the course which the Federation would follow, for they were mothers demanding better conditions for their children. It was to be a pattern from which the Federation did not move away in the years to come.

Excitement and preparation grew as 25 June approached. It was clearly going to be a conference of the people, delegated by the people at every level, not by organisations on behalf of large numbers of people but by the people of the farms and villages, the streets, the suburbs and the mine compounds, direct to the Congress of the People.

Organising for the collection of demands for the Freedom Charter was in full swing and the demands were coming in in response to the call to the Congress of the People, widely circulated throughout the country.

> We call the people of South Africa, black and white
> Let us speak together of freedom
> Let us work together for the Freedom Charter
> Let us go forward together to Freedom!

It was to be a meeting of people of all races, elected from every town and village, every farm and factory, every mine and kraal, every street and suburb in the whole land who would write their demands into the Freedom Charter.

On the morning of 25 June I left my flat, a little apprehensively, as I had arranged for the care of my cat in case I did not return that night. Police harassment at all levels was mounting rapidly and we might not escape arrest on some pretext or other, despite the legality of what we were doing.

The congress was to be held on a football ground in Kliptown outside Johannesburg, adjacent to Soweto, as no hall would be large enough for this gathering. It had to be held in an area where all must be free to come, black and white. It was all rather primitive and very simple, but the people gave it dignity, the mass of people coming together to spell out their own freedom charter. There were too few seats and many of the delegates sat on the ground. The only structure was the speakers' platform, with the huge four-spokes wheel to represent the four organisations which made up the Congress Alliance. I was to be a speaker in the section dealing with houses, security and comfort. I felt greatly honoured.

I watched the groups coming into the enclosure bearing banners, "Let us speak of Freedom!", "Let us go forward to Freedom!" They came from far and near; some had travelled all night in trucks or Kombis (Volkswagen Microbuses). Not every group had reached Kliptown, for the police had been busy stopping vehicles, on every possible traffic pretext, from continuing their journey.

I could feel the strength and the indomitable purpose of these people as they marched in. They had sent their demands ahead of them. There had been 1,000 and more, sometimes only scraps of paper, sometimes formally set out. They had come to this congress to hear, to discuss and to adopt their own charter for the future, born of their heartaches and their hopes. It was a simple beginning for a charter which has proved indestructible, which refuses to die, despite sporadic bannings of sundry editions of it. A printed piece of paper can be banned but not the ideas expressed in it.

On the first day all went well. The wired-off enclosure for delegates holding some 3,000 people, was soon full, but there were easily another 2,000 spectators outside. Most of that day was taken up with greetings, the opening prayers and the Isitwalandwe presentations to three great men, Father Trevor Huddleston, Dr Yusuf Dadoo and Chief Luthuli. This award of the title of Isitwalandwe by the African National Congress was recognition of exceptional contribution and sacrifice by individuals.

Father Trevor Huddleston, Anglican priest of Sophiatown, was greatly loved by thousands for his many years of refusal to compromise in any way with the evils of apartheid. Yusuf Dadoo, President of the South African Indian Congress, was a famous leader of both the Indian Passive Resistance Campaign of the 1940s and the Defiance Campaign of 1952. He had taken the lead in establishing close co-operation between the Indian Congress and the African National Congress at leadership and campaign levels. Chief Luthuli was the beloved President General of the ANC. A distinguished and worthy trio indeed, but only one could be present. Chief Luthuli and Dr Dadoo could not attend because both were banned from gatherings and restricted to their residential areas. Chief Luthuli's daughter accepted the honour on behalf of her father and Dr Dadoo's mother, a little elderly lady, spoke on her son's behalf. "Freedom does not fall from heaven, the people have to struggle."

The congress had inevitably started late because of transport delays and the almost uninterrupted arrival of delegates who had travelled all night, many hundreds of miles, to get to Kliptown. The first day closed with the reading of the draft Freedom Charter. By this time it was almost dark, and the temporary lighting system had failed, which meant that the despatch of delegates to their accommodation had to be handled by the light of only one hurricane lantern. All the carefully prepared accommodation lists became meaningless in the dark and chaos that ensued. Groups of delegates, still clutching the bags and blankets they had held onto all day, were led away by volunteers into the darkness. I never knew whether they reached the correct houses, but they did all find places to stretch their weary bodies and the comfort of hot coffee and food.

The draft Freedom Charter had been read to the congress and the next day, Sunday, it was heard again.

... South Africa belongs to all who live in it, black and white!
... And we pledge ourselves to strive together, sparing neither strength nor courage, until the democratic changes here set out have been won.

THE PEOPLE SHALL GOVERN.
ALL NATIONAL GROUPS SHALL HAVE EQUAL RIGHTS.
THE PEOPLE SHALL SHARE IN THE COUNTRY'S WEALTH.
THE LAND SHALL BE SHARED AMONGST THOSE WHO WORK IT.
ALL SHALL BE EQUAL BEFORE THE LAW.
ALL SHALL ENJOY EQUAL HUMAN RIGHTS.
THERE SHALL BE WORK AND SECURITY.
THE DOORS OF LEARNING AND CULTURE SHALL BE OPENED.
THERE SHALL BE HOUSES, SECURITY AND COMFORT.
THERE SHALL BE PEACE AND FRIENDSHIP.

These freedoms we will fight for, side by side, throughout our lives, until we have won our liberty.

The affirmations came over loud and clear as the delegates spoke to them, adopted them, and the draft charter began to take on a reality, moving forward, section by section, until there were only two sections left for discussion and adoption.

I was on the platform, the four-spoked Congress wheel behind me, waiting to make my speech on houses, security and comfort. It was nearly four o'clock when I became aware of a stirring amongst the crowd. I saw that we were surrounded by armed police and a posse was moving towards the platform, a dozen or so detectives in plain clothes, escorted by police carrying sten guns.

The crowd seemed stunned, all eyes on the advancing police, who mounted the platform and presented the chairman with a warrant to investigate high treason. It seemed incredible, unreal; high treason at this gathering of peaceful people adopting a freedom charter. The chairman informed the delegates of the reason for this police invasion and asked if they wished to proceed with the congress. The crowd roared its assent and rose to its feet in a defiant "Nkosi Sikelele".

I gave my speech, surrounded as we all were on the platform, by the armed policemen. The microphone had been damaged in the confusion. There was barely standing room for us and the policemen on the platform, but someone held the microphone wobbling in front of me. I saw police already working their way up and down the rows of delegates, searching as they went, opening bags, looking for documents, not weapons. The police had the weapons, not the people in the crowd.

As I spoke, I looked at the people, 3,000 of them, seated in front of me, so many bright headscarves, so many people proudly displaying the black, green and yellow of the ANC colours. They were indifferent to the searching police, as if they had been tiresome insects. They were no longer watching them, their eyes were on their leaders and I realised, almost unbelieving, that they were in fact listening to what I was saying; my "social worker's speech", incongruously delivered in an atmosphere of armed police provocation. What I spoke of lay very close to the lives of these delegates, the right to homes and houses, the ending of hunger, the provision of medical care, the care of the aged, the sick, the young and the family.

Ironically, the next and last section of the charter was on peace and friendship. Peace and friendship, faced by guns, by armed police with searching hands, humiliating by their very presence. Yet the Congress of the People could not really be humiliated, could not be soiled. It rose triumphantly above this police action. Every section of the charter had been presented, discussed and adopted. It was no longer a draft but a reality; the programme of the people, their own programme for the future, their promise to their children of a land that should be free.

The police must have seized thousands of copies of the draft charter but nothing they could do could touch the charter itself. Its ideas and its message were now enshrined in the hearts and the minds of the delegates, who would carry it far and wide to the people of South Africa for them to make it their own.

"Nkosi Sikelele" was sung again. The Congress of the People was over and it had triumphed. But the delegates could not leave because the police were still searching, recording names and addresses, photographing people. My anger grew as the search proceeded — the deliberate humiliation of 3,000 people who had come together, not for violence, not for subversion, not for treason, but simply to speak of their lives and to look forward to their ultimate freedom from oppression. Yet stronger than my anger was my pride in the people.

It grew dark but the police were better prepared than we had been the night before, having brought a supply of lamps and torches. By nine o'clock it was all over, the last delegate had been searched and the police went away. Soon the site of the conference became a football field again, a deserted littered piece of land as after any football match.

To us it is still hallowed ground and will be so for as long as the Freedom Charter lives and that is immortal. Resha had declared at the end of the congress, defiantly, in the face of the police: "This ground on which we are standing here today is holy, friends. This shall be the monument of the people of South Africa."

Chapter VI

HEAR US!

The Congress of the People was over. We had come down from the mountain, down to our daily lives. The delegates from other areas had driven home through the night after a very late start, interminably delayed by the police searches. Those of us who lived in Johannesburg had gone back to our jobs. I know that I felt a little dazed by what had happened, curious about this treason-clouded future, but not yet apprehensive because it was all so unreal. I had seen the mass endurance of the delegates, their dignity unassailable, their commitment unshaken. "Throughout our lives, side by side!", we had pledged ourselves. This seemed to strengthen my position, for I was not alone. I was side by side with thousands, there could be no turning back for me. I was now where I belonged, with the oppressed people, moving into the next stage of the struggle for peace, justice and freedom.

The Freedom Charter had now to be ratified by each of the sponsoring congresses, and public support for it must also be canvassed. The Congress Alliance set its sights very high — a million endorsing signatures to be collected from the public, black and white, within a year. A national consultative committee was set up to co-ordinate the congress plans for this goal. I represented the Congress of Democrats on this committee, and was also there on behalf of the Federation of South African Women, though not as an official representative. That would indeed have been unnecessary, since our affiliated organisations were usually themselves offshoots of the congresses.

During 1955 there had been another ugly government measure to be challenged in addition to the Western Areas Removal and the rape of Sophiatown. The Bantu Education Act had already been passed and on 1 April, the Department of Native Affairs was to take over all African education, hitherto largely provided by church and mission schools, subsidised from government funds. This move was intended to give effect to Dr Verwoerd's infamous statement, "There is no room for the Bantu in the European community, above the level of certain forms of labour."

Henceforth African children were to be taught only as much as would fit them for the lowest forms of employment in the service of the white man. The education of their children lies very close to African hearts. Even today there is rankling resentment at the disparity of government expenditure, ten times as much being spent on white education as on black. The Bantu Education Act was suspect to the blacks because it would provide a special kind of education for their children, undeniably inferior to that provided for the white children. On this issue, African feeling had been running very high ever since the Act had been passed. In December 1954, the ANC had called for a total rejection of Bantu education. By the time I returned from Europe, the total rejection had developed into indefinite withdrawal of pupils from primary schools in protest.

A conference of 700 delegates from organisations opposed to Bantu education had been called by the ANC. Norman Levy and I were to represent the Congress of Democrats. We drove through the night to Port Elizabeth with Robert Resha and others from the ANC. This was my first experience of a large, mainly African, conference and I was impressed by the lively yet disciplined atmosphere.

Most of the delegates represented Congress branches, especially from the militant Eastern Cape area around Port Elizabeth. The Congress volunteers, from the former Defiance Campaign days, were out in full force in khaki shirts and black berets to welcome and usher in visiting delegates and to maintain order. Many African women were already wearing the newly adopted black skirt and green blouse of the ANC Women's League, with the green stripe and the additional yellow stripe which distinguished it from the uniform of the Women's Federation.

Freedom songs are an integral part of any Congress meeting. With delight, I heard hundreds of voices singing the songs I was beginning to know so well but could not sing. I used to "la-la" happily except for the occasional phrases I did know. The occasion was serious indeed, but the conference had life and laughter in it.

The ANC national executive met during the weekend and decided to embark upon the immediate withdrawal of children from African primary schools. Obviously the provision of alternative education of some sort ranked high in the discussions, but no blueprint for it was adopted other than general agreement that the children must be provided with some educative occupation. It was from this conference that the African Education Movement, an informal educational council, was formed, centred in Johannesburg.

On the long drive back we talked a lot about the proposals for the informal clubs for the boycotting children. The conference had finally accepted this structure to provide some sort of education. Obviously the clubs would be manned by teachers whose classes were out on boycott, yet the Act was strict about the requirement that any form of teaching be registered as a school with the Department of Education. We could hardly suppose that any of our clubs intending to assist boycotting children and parents would be registered. Norman was a teacher and I had been one, so we were eager to help as much as possible with what were soon to be known as cultural clubs, a good cover title.

In the car, Robert nobly tried to teach me some of the African freedom songs, but, alas, my ignorance of the African language, combined with my unfortunate lack of a musical ear, proved too strong and we gave up in despair and laughter. I was destined to continue my "la-la-ing".

We needed petrol urgently after closing hours and had to persuade a sleepy, white, petrol pump-owner to fill our tank. We decided that we ought not to put him off with our odd mixture of races, all crowded together into the car. I was put into the driver's seat, Norman was squashed into the back with instructions not to show his white face, while Robert got out and knocked up the white petrol pump-owner from his bed, appealing to him to help us out because his "Missus" had to get back to Johannesburg. He confided that she was very cross because he had not filled up properly with petrol on leaving.

Back in Johannesburg, there were meetings of the African Education Movement. We all strongly supported the idea of organising training conferences to assist the cultural club leaders who were trying to educate and occupy large numbers of children, of all ages, in playgrounds, in any open space, with no school equipment of any sort, not even schoolbooks or slates, since any teaching would soon label the club as an illegal, unregistered school.

These club leaders' conferences were to occupy a great deal of my time for the next twelve months. Norman and I, with other helpers, planned the conferences. We prepared masses of roneod material, including action arithmetic games and counting songs, geography lessons, where we could "chat" about the continents, for lack of atlases. We produced history stories, for which we rewrote the history of South Africa in our own version, oddly unlike the orthodox school history books. Everything had to be some sort of game or informal group activity.

At first, we confined our conferences to one-day affairs, Saturday or Sunday. Beginning them in July 1955, we held them every two weeks, in any black area where Norman and I, and any other whites, could legally be. These were mostly coloured areas or in Alexandra Township, which was not under municipal control.

The conferences were friendly, informal and gay. The club leaders enthusiastically welcomed our material for varying their own programmes. They were finding it difficult to adapt their usual formal teaching habits, trying at the same time to keep large groups of children, out of doors, both entertained and instructed, as far as possible.

James Hadebe from the ANC, singer, musician, teacher, composed his own musical multiplication tables in Zulu and Sotho. The children sang them joyously. Permeating everything, of course, was the sense of defiant protest, triumph in the rejection of Bantu education. The clubs themselves were symbols of protest. There was considerable harassment by police, clubs were raided, leaders prosecuted, the children, too. Club leaders were banned, even deported, but the spirit of defiance was high and the clubs survived.

We became more ambitious in January 1956, attempting a five-day conference in Alexandra Township. Father Trevor Huddleston opened the conference on the first day. Security branch detectives sat outside for the whole five days, for we insisted that this was a private affair and we would not let them in without a warrant to enter, which they did not have. They did, however, do a great deal of looking through the windows and listening outside the doors.

The Transvaal and the Eastern Cape were the main centres for the withdrawal of children from the primary schools. Over 7,000 children were withdrawn by their parents from government schools during that year. The anger of the parents was directed against Bantu education not only because it was separate, but because it was both inferior and racist, inadequate to the needs of any children. To take their children away from school was indeed a costly decision, for education is very highly prized, but the parents saw it as lower than the cost of exposing their children to the poison of Bantu education.

From Port Elizabeth in the Eastern Cape came urgent messages that we must come there too, so off we went during the Easter holidays, but there we almost came to grief. Norman and I had gone with Robert and James Hadebe, with a carload of training material, even the home-made instruments for a percussion band, which an enthusiastic nursery school teacher had pressed upon us for demonstration in our conference. We had assumed that, as in the Transvaal, whites could be in coloured municipal areas. So, on arrival we had secured the use of a coloured church hall.

There was a Congress meeting on the night of our arrival, and our conference was formally approved. Congress volunteers were sent in all directions to outlying areas to instruct the club leaders to be at the hall next morning. I was amazed at this tremendous discipline, in which volunteers accepted instructions, quietly leaving the meeting immediately to carry them out. The volunteer spirit of the Eastern Cape ANC, which had led 5,000 men and women into passive resistance and gaol, was still strong.

Thirty club leaders reported by eight o'clock the next morning at the hall and we began the conference. On the second day, we were interrupted by the security police. Norman and I were carted off ignominiously to the location Superintendent's office, there to be shown regulations which required whites to have permits to be in a coloured area. With the security branch breathing down our necks, we did not go through the farce of applying for permits. They took our names and Johannesburg addresses but we refused to answer any questions about what we were doing there, and they did not insist. It would have gone differently with us today for that refusal.

We were taken back to the hall to collect our belongings. We informed Robert and the club leaders of what had happened, but we knew that the conference could not continue without us, the trainers. Robert told us to wait outside the location gates. We stood there disconsolately for a little while until we saw the club leaders, headed by Robert and James, approaching in a single-file procession, carrying all our conference gear. Norman and I joined in, the percussion band struck up and we marched singing in an unrecognised protest to the centre of the town. There we broke up and Norman, Robert and I drove off, the security branch hard on our tail. I asked myself, could it really be only three years since I had so timidly marched with the garment workers to Solly's protest meeting or sat in fear at signature tables?

Robert told us that the club leaders were determined to finish their training conference; we must be ready early next morning and he would fetch us. Before dawn, we were collected in a truck with our goods and driven to a house about twenty miles away in the low hill area between Port Elizabeth and Uitenhage, from where we had been routed the previous day. There we found our club leaders, a few dozing, but many still singing.

We went off silently, in single file, carrying food for the day and our conference material. We were led in the half darkness up into the hills to a lonely clearing which was to be our clubhouse for the day. There under the sun and the blue sky, we taught and laughed and sang, even jumping around to keep ourselves awake, for some of the club leaders had had no sleep at all. In this area of the Eastern Cape, a meeting of more than ten Africans was illegal, but we had volunteer guards posted in the bushes all around us.

We telescoped our teaching programme to put as much as possible into one day, a long day, for the club leaders wanted as much as we could press into the few hours we had together. When the sun went down, we, too, went down the hill again to say goodbye to our friends, promising to return.

In 1956, while we were touring the country, organising for the protest to Pretoria, we managed to fit in an afternoon with the club leaders in Port Elizabeth. It wasn't a training conference, there wasn't time for that, but we spent the afternoon discussing problems, sharing them and exchanging experiences. It was good to be together with committed people again, still determined to carry on despite the increasing police harassment. The children were still out of school, and remained out for many more months.

Then the pressure of events began to tell. The children were showing signs of a desperate need for formal education, parents were worrying about the future of their children without school certificates, and the boycott gradually fell away. It had not failed, it had not been defeated, it had made its mark. A generation later, in 1976, the black children of South Africa came out again in protest, walking in their thousands away from Bantu education.

It was in 1955 that the Congress of the People had been raided "to investigate treason". Somehow we had become conditioned to the word, for it subsequently appeared frequently on police warrants for the increasing number of police raids on offices and homes. We had become used to these raids, too, and tended to shrug them off. The first raid on my flat had appalled me. The very thought of hostile hands fingering my private papers, of hostile eyes reading my private letters, was utterly repulsive. Yet, since I had chosen the road of public political action, I could not hope to escape such police attention.

We had been warned by the Minister of Justice in a public statement that he intended to arrest some 200 people on a charge of high treason. The figure of 200 made it seem unreal. We could at any time have singled out twenty or even thirty leaders whom he might want to attack, but 200! And for treason? It belonged to the absurd. It could have nothing to do with *our* struggle — it must be a bluff, a ploy to placate the reactionary whites. I certainly never thought seriously that the Congress of the People, the Freedom Charter, the Women's Federation or the protests to Pretoria could ever be associated with high treason.

On 2 December 1956, the Federation held its Transvaal provincial conference, electing its officers for the coming year. Lilian Ngoyi was re-elected

Transvaal President and I again became Transvaal Secretary. I don't think that it seemed odd to anyone at the conference that we were also National President and Secretary. We were unanimously elected; the women wanted us. The conference adopted a programme of anti-pass demonstrations, collection of anti-pass pledges, and signatures for the Freedom Charter, also opposition to the Group Areas Act.

It was just three days later that the police struck. Like many others, I was raided before dawn and arrested. Like any expectant mother, I had packed a suitcase with a few clothes, thinking that if there were to be 200 arrests I might be one of them and I ought to be prepared. Additionally, friends had warned me that rumours were floating around that arrests of some sort were imminent, involving a few days in gaol until bail could be arranged. I lived alone, there would be no one to collect things for me, so I got ready. Of course when the police arrived I didn't want to admit it, but I finally pulled that suitcase out from under my bed.

After my flat had been searched I was driven to a police station to be fingerprinted for the first time in my life. I was subjected to it on many occasions later, but that first time was a horrible experience. I had my hand seized and my thumb was roughly pressed down onto an inked pad. Then all my fingers in turn and then the other hand. It made me feel as though I had been convicted already, but I scarcely knew of what, for treason still meant nothing. Naturally I was scared and apprehensive, but trying not to show it. I simply did not know what might be in store. It certainly meant going to gaol that very day, that could be in no doubt. Yet my mind did not really grasp that the operative word was treason. That could mean hanging!

I was driven to my office for that too to be searched. There I was at least given a few moments, though still under police escort, to make emergency staff arrangements for an absence of how long I did not know. It was my first personal communication with anyone, because I had not been allowed to make any telephone calls from my flat. I knew that even in South African law, an accused is presumed innocent until found guilty, but I didn't feel that this was the case at all! What with fingerprinting and a police escort, I felt like what I was: a prisoner.

From my office I was taken to the main police station. I found some of my friends there too, though we were separated, white from black, men from women. None of us had any idea of the nationwide extent of the arrests. I caught a glimpse of Robert at the police station. He looked arrogant, defiant, almost triumphant. I gathered that Lilian and Bertha were also amongst those arrested.

During the afternoon we were taken to the magistrate's court where we were kept in dingy underground cells until we were moved upstairs to a court in batches of about twelve to be charged with high treason. I still seemed to be the only white woman arrested, though I heard whispered rumours that Yetta Barenblatt, the National Secretary of the Congress of Democrats, was still being held at the office during a police search. Just as we were herded into our separate black and white police vans, the door was flung open and Yetta was hustled in to join the five white men and me. Although sorry that she too had been arrested, I was thankful that I would no longer be alone in the women's gaol.

We were driven off to the Fort, Johannesburg's forbidding gaol, high on a hill, where we said goodbye to the men and Yetta and I were marched down the road to the women's section, rather forlornly clutching our suitcases. When we were finally admitted and taken to our cell, we were astounded to find three others there, two of our friends from Durban and one from Cape Town. From their accounts of being flown with others in large military aircraft, we realised that these arrests were really nationwide and becoming more and more sinister. Were we really all so dangerous?

We had sixteen days in the Fort before we were brought back to court, by now 156 alleged traitors in all. In the women's gaol we settled down fairly comfortably in a large cell. We became six when Ruth First joined us some days later. On one of the days we prowled around outside the cell, for once not under the eye of a wardress, and we came upon our black sisters. They were sitting on the stone floor in dark iron sheds. The doors were open and we saw that they had only mats to sleep on and no other furniture. We had time only to exchange loving greetings before we scurried back to our quarters, but we had seen enough to realise with shame how much better off we were in our large light cell with beds and a couple of chairs, even a cupboard. It was a bitter memory, despite the joy of actually seeing them.

Gaol food was not really a problem. As prisoners awaiting trial, we were allowed to have food sent in to us. Friends and lawyers visited us frequently and we learnt that we might soon be bailed out, perhaps before Christmas. After two weeks in gaol, we became a little anxious about it, when Christmas was only a week away. I had grown tired of flat life and had recently acquired a cottage. I was due to move into it on 1 January. I wanted a garden again, but most of all I wanted to have my black friends visit me without prying neighbours or inquisitive flat superintendents. It was not actually illegal to have black visitors, but it certainly aroused hostility and suspicion and led to fairly overt police surveillance.

In gaol, we chatted at first fairly light-heartedly, about being charged with high treason. We knew we could be on a capital charge, but I don't remember ever verbalising that aspect of it, although it must have been in our thoughts constantly. It seemed totally unreal that our activities, our non-violent policy, could have come into the orbit of high treason, even now that we were in gaol. Our legal advisers were, however, taking it more seriously.

We soon began to feel the weight of being confined, cut off from family and friends, except for the frustrating visits through bars during visiting hours. We resented being locked up in a cell, unlocked again at specific times and lights turned out by eight o'clock.

I think it was far easier for me to adjust to all this than for the others, because I had had those years in the air force camps. Much of my present condition reminded me of the first weeks there, even the tin plates. In fact I positively bloomed in gaol because I was having the regular meals and early nights which I had not had for so long during those years of intensive political activity. Nor had I any husband or children to worry about. We swept and polished the floor of our cell, giggling at the sight of each other on our knees. There was no other work for us to do, so we lived from one visiting day to the next, waiting to be released on bail.

Contact with any of the other prisoners held in the Fort before trial, or serving sentences there, was forbidden but we gathered that they awarded us a very high social status in prisoner society, even though they didn't understand what treason implied. We ourselves felt no shame at being in gaol on a political charge. Far from it, we were proud of it.

Sonia Bunting from Cape Town, Jackie Arenstein and Dorothy Shanley from Durban, Ruth, Yetta and I from Johannesburg, spent more than two weeks in that cell, except for the times when we were allowed into the yard, which amazed me with its green grass and flowers in bloom. For the past three years, I had been trying to suppress my fear of gaol, yet knowing that I might one day have to spend time there. Once there, it did not seem so bad.

I soon realised that I was in the company of high-powered, well-informed, primarily ideologically committed leftists, involved in the liberation struggle, whereas I was involved simply and solely in the liberation struggle and everything else came afterwards. I think Ruth and Jackie were ahead of the rest of us in political thinking, though Sonia and Dorothy and Yetta were also old Communist Party members. I really didn't belong in this political circle, yet we all got on very well together. I did not lose my nervous awe of the crisply intellectual Ruth, but I admired her chic foresight in coming to gaol in elegant black underwear, whereas the rest of us had just packed our oldest clothes.

We were brought to court again on 19 December. There was much pressing of our clothes, even in gaol, for this public appearance. Hustled into the front section of an enormous police van, we were taken to the men's gaol to collect our friends there. They were put into a different section behind us. Small barred windows prevented us from seeing much in the streets, but as we neared the court we could see huge massed crowds on the pavements, even in the street. They were pressing close to our van, even rocking it as it slowly forced its way into the yard. The great crowd, singing and waving, was shut out behind iron gates.

The first part of our trial was to be held in the Johannesburg Drill Hall, simply because there was no law court which could accommodate the 156 accused. The army, ever the eager supporter of the police, had made their large drill hall available and there it was, turned into a law court, with rows of seats for the accused, tables and chairs for the lawyers, a platform for the magistrate and very little space left for the public.

There were ugly scenes that day with the police opening fire on the huge crowds of people pressing to get into the Drill Hall where their leaders and their relations were on trial. We sat immobilised, helpless, unable to be with our people outside. We heard the shots, not knowing how many were wounded —

or killed. Later we learned that over twenty had been injured but none killed on this occasion. It was another example of lack of proper police control. White policemen in South Africa carry guns on all occasions and their flashpoint is soon reached.

The trial proceedings were unbelievably chaotic. Prisoners were eagerly greeting friends and families, hugging wives and children, until we were marshalled into the rows of seats only to find that we could not hear anything that was going on. It had apparently not dawned on the authorities that an adequate public address system would be required for 156 accused to be able to follow the case against them, or, since it was an open trial, that the public would also want to hear the proceedings.

We had arrived in chaos and we left in chaos. The application for bail had not been settled, so we all went back to the Fort that afternoon. The waiting crowds, bearing banners saying "Stand by our leaders!" sang again for us as the vans inched their way out into the street.

On arrival at the Drill Hall next day, we were confronted by an enormous wire cage, like something from the zoo. We were to sit in this so that we could have no contact with the public. We laughed, but our legal team was incensed, outraged by this insult to their clients and to themselves, too, as they were now unable to consult with us — the caged wild beasts. All the lawyers, attorneys and counsel, threatened to walk out unless the cage was removed, agreeing to remain only on the undertaking that the cage would be dismantled before we came to court again. Our supporters in the public gallery raged and then laughed with us as we put up notices on the cage, like "Don't feed the wild animals!", "Dangerous!" and "No monkey nuts!"

We listened to the prosecutor's opening address. He was Oswald Pirow, a former Minister of Justice, an implacable enemy of Solly Sachs in the past, and now our enemy, a formidable Nationalist Party leader. He thundered away, accusing us of incitement and preparation to overthrow the state by revolutionary methods, including violence. Like much else, it sounded unreal and irrelevant, like the warrants to investigate high treason. What had treason to do with us?

At last bail was allowed at a reduced figure after strong argument by our counsel. It stood finally at £250 for whites, £100 for Indians and coloureds and £50 for Africans. It seemed that treason also knew racial distinctions; compared with the astronomical amounts demanded for others in later trials, it appeared we were not considered very dangerous traitors after all. Or did it reflect an unwilling acceptance that we should stand trial, every one of us?

The issue of the bail bonds, necessary before we could be free, was a tedious proceeding. We were taken to the magistrate's court for this, still in custody. From five that afternoon until nine that night a team of magistrates sat, releasing us one by one until they came at last to me.

I almost failed to get out of gaol that night, not because I was a particularly dangerous criminal, but because I could not immediately produce my passport. I knew it was in the office safe, but only the General Secretary of the Industrial Council had the keys. Since it was 21 December, office Christmas parties abounded and he could not be found. Eventually, when I was being escorted to the police station for the night, too late even for gaol, my passport arrived. At last I too was free and home for Christmas.

Chapter VII

Democracy?

In January 1957 we were back again in the Drill Hall. The cage had been removed and our seats were now numbered. I found to my dismay that I was number thirteen, but there was nothing that I could do about it. The 156 persons occupied the greater part of the Drill Hall, but there was some space at the back which, to our anger, was separated into black and white. Yet the accused were not. Our division was only into regions. Johannesburg came first with by far the largest number, 77, almost half of all the accused.

We had been numbered in alphabetical order and I sat between Jack Hodgson of the Congress of Democrats and Paul Joseph of the Indian Congress. A white woman and a black man having the same surname caused some confusion from time to time, but not as great as that created by the identical twins, Norman and Leon Levy. They created havoc during identification by police witnesses.

The prosecutor completed his opening address and Vernon Berrangé of our defence team replied in an historic address. Pirow had included the Freedom Charter in his accusation of treason, but Vernon asserted:

> The defence will contend that the ideas and beliefs which are expressed in this Charter, although repugnant to the policy of the present government, are such as are shared by the overwhelming majority of mankind of all races and all colours, and also by the overwhelming majority of the citizens of this country . . .
>
> We will endeavour to show, in other words, that what are on trial here are not just 155 [sic] individuals, but the ideas which they and thousands of others in our country have openly espoused and expressed . . .
>
> They will assert and in due course ask the Court to hold that they are the victims of political kite flying on the part of those responsible for these prosecutions. We are going to endeavour to show that the prosecutions and the manner of their presentation are for the purpose only of testing the political breezes, in order to ascertain how far the originators thereof can go in their endeavours to stifle free speech, criticism of the policies of the government and everything, in fact, that the accused believe is implicit in the definition of the oft misused word "Democracy".
>
> They come of all races, but they hold one thing in common . . . they believe in the brotherhood of man and the desire to work for his betterment and towards his ultimate freedom . . .

59

We believe that, in the result, this trial will be answered in the right way by history.

Vernon Berrangé had spoken for us all and set the tone for the conduct of our case. We were determined to affirm, not merely to defend, our convictions and our activities.

Our bail conditions prohibited us from addressing meetings and also required us to report to a police station once a week. That was when my regular reporting to the police really began, but it was onerous, and we were all doing it and constantly reminding each other.

Just as our trial began in January, the great Alexandra Township bus boycott also began. Alexandra Township (popularly known as "Alex") was then a crowded black freehold township, some ten miles from the city. This boycott was not the first of its kind: that had been in 1943, when 15,000 Alex people walked ten miles to work and back again because they could not and would not accept an extra penny on the fares. I was then stationed as a WAAF officer at the Union Grounds in Johannesburg, right on the road from Alex into the city. I saw the boycotters, washerwomen with their huge bundles of washing on their heads, the factory workers who worked a fifty-hour week, and old men and children too. Alex walked for nine days, through the sun and the wind and the rain — and the Alexandra people won. The busfares remained at four pence a journey, already more than ill-paid workers could afford.

A year later, Alex walked again. I saw it again, the determination that could conquer exhaustion, a people who could walk twenty miles a day for seven weeks. I marvelled at it, the passive resistance of a people who were denied any say about the conditions of life in which they worked and travelled. They lived in poverty, they worked for exploitative wages, they lived ten miles away from their jobs, because the whites would tolerate them no nearer. They travelled in grossly overcrowded buses, for which they stood for hours in queues and which already cost them eight pence a day. It was the extra two pence that brought them out in defiance. They would not pay it because their wages were too low to stand the extra shilling a week.

The boycotters won again and the busfares remained at four pence a journey until 1957. Then Alex walked once more, refusing to pay an extra penny on the fares. "Asikwelwa!" they cried, "we will not ride!" Again I was on their road, this time sitting day after day in the Drill Hall, past which the people walked, in the wind and the rain and the mud. It was in the summer months, and the storms broke in the afternoons. While we sat in the Drill Hall, with transport to hand, the boycotters walked, sometimes soaking wet, and the next day they wore the same clothes to work, still wet.

Whites tried to help, as they had before, with car lifts, but this was hampered by traffic policemen pulling surplus passengers out of cars, threatening and sometimes carrying out prosecutions. The passengers were harassed for passes, taken off to police stations and even cyclists giving lifts had the valves of their tyres removed by the police. My "Congress Connie" was a little small for this job, but she could just squeeze in three portly ladies and I insisted that she was for women only — for the "aunties". I realised more fully now that the bus boycott had a significance deeper than the refusal to pay the extra penny a ride. It was the only weapon available to the people of Alex, the weapon of sacrifice and determination, of undiminished fortitude, against which neither the bus company nor their allies, the police, could prevail.

The treason trial continued in 1957, taking up most of the working time of all the accused but, as best we could, we continued defiantly with our political activities and made the most of the Congress leadership being together. Fourteen of our leading Federation women were amongst the accused. Five of us were from Johannesburg. We could and did continue with our Federation programme for the Transvaal, organising women's conferences against passes for women, in Pretoria and on the East and the West Rand, and collecting pledges of opposition against the Group Areas Act. We were also busy promoting and popularising the Freedom Charter, despite the attacks on it in the trial.

We had a full programme and it meant a lot of weekend organising for Bertha and me. Sometimes Lilian or other ANC Women's League organisers used to come with us. I could now go only rarely at night, because I was working at my offices during the evenings to make up for time spent at the trial. None of us, not Bertha, Lilian or I, could attend the conferences we organised because our bail conditions prevented us from attending political gatherings, nor could we address gatherings of any sort. Although we missed the actual conferences, we received very encouraging reports from these gatherings of African, Indian and coloured women, even a few whites. The spirit of the Federation was as strong as ever, despite the threat of the treason trial hovering over the leaders.

On 23 April, I was met on arrival at court by two special security branch detectives who handed me two banning orders, one prohibiting me from attending any gatherings, except purely social ones, and the other preventing me from leaving the magisterial areas of Johannesburg — and all this for five years.

I don't think I paid much attention that day to what was going on in our trial. Shocked and angry, I looked at those banning orders and tried to figure out just what they were going to mean to me, to my life. I wasn't banned from any organisations, but the prohibition on gatherings was more stringent than the bail terms. It seemed that holding me for months on end on a charge of high treason was not enough for the Minister of Justice, Charles Robbertse Swart, who eventually became the State President of South Africa. He did not know, of course, and nor did I, that in the end the trial would take up four years of the period of the ban.

Confinement to Johannesburg was frustrating, for I could no longer go to Pretoria, to the East and West Rand, or even to the further Transvaal areas. It meant the end of the precious organising expeditions with Bertha and Robert and the contact with the women.

I looked at the orders several times before I realised that the confinement to Johannesburg would take effect only after seven days. In the trial interval that morning, Robert and Bertha and I planned a hectic week of farewell visits, though we knew of course that I would meet the women again after five years. We went to the various areas every night that week. I decided that my office working hours could be made up afterwards. This last week was too precious to lose. So, night after night, while I still could, we went off to small gatherings of women in little houses in many different places. We drank tea and ate cakes to make these meetings into social gatherings. On the last night, after we had dropped Bertha in Germiston, Robert and I drove back rather silently and I thought dismally of the five years ahead.

I did not think then of how fortunate I was in that I had already had a few years of intense political activity, nor of the fortunate fact that I was in the treason trial where I could daily meet so many friends and colleagues in court. But I knew that others had been banned before me and others would be banned after me. I was only one amongst many.

We all drew close to each other in the first year of the treason trial, the preparatory examination in which we played no personal part. The prosecution would lead their evidence and then it would be for the magistrate to decide whether, on that evidence, he should commit us for trial in a higher court — or let us go.

The passing weeks brought sunshine and shadow. We began to realise that this part of the trial would go on for a long time. The prosecution was putting in masses of documents, found in police raids, literally hundreds of longhand reports of our speeches, taken down by semi-literate security branch detectives. These were astounding, incomprehensible, yet claiming to be verbatim reports. Vernon Berrangé exposed them for what they were — gibberish. Bertha raged one day, almost audibly, "that is NOT the way Helen speaks!" But it went on and on and the court record grew longer and longer.

The accused read, slept and even knitted if they were not in the front row. I was, but I still brought some of my Medical Aid Society work to court and signed hundreds of sick pay cheques, which our messenger brought each morning. The court orderly then brought them to me. I suppose it was actually contempt of court, but the magistrate sensibly turned a blind eye, for how could we retain an alert interest for hours, days and weeks on end, especially when we could hardly hear what most of the witnesses were saying?

I think, too, that the magistrate was, understandably, somewhat apprehensive about how he would handle so many of us if we became difficult. It almost happened once, when one of us, Joe Slovo, an advocate himself, clashed with the magistrate who then committed him for contempt of court. The magistrate had to face 155 furious persons, who had risen in a body and were advancing towards his rostrum. He certainly blanched and seemed uncertain of what to do, but it was Chief Luthuli who rushed to the front and called upon us to resume our seats. All except a few did so and the few were committed for contempt of court as well, but there were no serious consequences.

We laughed a lot too, at the comic placards, "soup with meat", "soup without meat", seized by police at the Congress of the People as they overturned the pots of food in their search. Now these placards appeared in court as evidence — of what? Treason? Or treason soup? We laughed at the motorcycle and sidecar solemnly rolled into court with a detective seated on it to write down what Vernon Berrangé read to him slowly and clearly, with an interpreter, in order to show that his six-line report of a thirty-minute speech, taken down while on his motorbike was rubbish. We laughed at the figure he cut when Vernon read to the magistrate the garbled nonsense which was all that this detective-turned-reporter had been able to write down of what Vernon read out.

We did not laugh at the financial ruin of so many of the accused, especially those who came from other areas, leaving jobs, professions, to face weeks and months of unemployment. Even for those who lived in and around Johannesburg, there was no possibility of work; the court proceedings filled our days and not more than a dozen of us had managed to hold onto our jobs by working at night.

On 26 June 1957, the second anniversary of the Congress of the People, we stood in silent prayer during the morning break. More than half the industrial workers in Johannesburg stayed at home that day, answering the Congress call. In the Eastern Cape and elsewhere there were mass meetings and torchlight processions. It was one of the Congress's finest demonstrations.

On the day that twenty-two African men were hanged for the killing of five policemen in a dagga (cannabis) raid in Bergville, we came to the court in mourning. I sat through the trial that day thinking of twenty-two living men executed on one morning.

We led a life within a life and became ever more firmly bound to our organisations and to our common struggle. The effort to turn us from our path had resulted only in a stronger determination to follow it, as almost the whole of the Congress leadership, from all over South Africa, sat together, discussed together, planned together for the future.

On 31 December 1956 I had moved into my little cottage with the tall trees, delighted to have a home of my own, pushing aside any intrusive doubts of how long I might be able to live in it. Many friends urged me not to go on with the purchase arrangements when I was arrested, but I would not listen. It was in some way a demonstration of my own faith in the future.

The year moved slowly on, with endless relays of detectives giving evidence, handing in our documents, until we came to Professor Andrew Murray, from Cape Town University, an expert on communism. He fared badly at Vernon's skilful hands, exposing himself in so many ways to our barely suppressed laughter and ridicule. We could not see his evidence as formidable.

At the end of September, the court adjourned until the beginning of 1958. The prosecution had at last come to the end of its case, and the magistrate needed time to arrive at his finding on the mass of evidence before him. I often wondered how much of it he actually managed to read. The accused from the other areas went back to their homes; the few of us still in our jobs welcomed the break, and many others, dependent on help from the Treason Trial Defence Fund, sought, but mostly did not find, temporary jobs. Yet it was a relief to all of us to be out of that Drill Hall, not to have to sit on those hard chairs for so many hours every day, not to have to listen to those relays of witnesses and all those documents being read into the record.

The Federation of South African Women had been active throughout most of the year, despite the immobilisation of fourteen of its leaders at this preparatory examination and my banning orders. Our special anniversary, 9 August, had been celebrated with anti-pass demonstrations and we had printed and sold thousands of "Women's Day" badges — a black mother with her child upon her back.

Passes for African women were, however, being issued in many areas in spite of the efforts of the ANC Women's League and the Federation in campaigns and protests. Then African nurses were called upon to supply identity numbers for registration with the Nursing Council. This aroused indignation amongst nurses, because an identity number could only be obtained by taking the reference book — the hated pass. Groups of black nurses in the Transvaal were holding angry protest meetings and nurses declared, "Our mothers were washerwomen and they educated us. We will go back to the washtubs but we will not carry passes."

These were brave words and the Federation took its stand alongside the nurses. We organised a demonstration of women, the mothers of the African nurses, to demand an interview with the matron of the huge black hospital in Johannesburg, the Baragwanath hospital, to protest against the requirement of identity numbers which would compel their daughters to take passes.

I think it was because of our famous protests to Pretoria that we drew such publicity, even before the demonstration. Baragwanath seemed to have panicked over this demonstration of women, although it was widely known that the purpose of the mothers was simply to bring their protest to the matron of this great hospital, requesting support for their stand.

It was to be on a Saturday morning and I drove out to watch. I could not get close because of my banning order, but even to get near I had to skirt a couple of police road blocks. All traffic which passed the hospital was being diverted to other roads. We learned afterwards that all walking patients had been sent home for the weekend and all except absolutely essential medical personnel had been told to stay at home that Saturday morning.

As I drew near, I saw the hospital surrounded by police, armed as usual. Facing them, on the other side of the road, were a few hundred African women, obviously the mothers of nurses and there to protest on behalf of their daughters. It was a hot morning and the umbrellas were up against the sun. Perhaps the police thought the umbrellas concealed secret weapons. It looked a little comic from where I stood as there seemed to be more policemen than protesters. Then I saw four Federation women in their green blouses, one of each race as usual, walk across the road to the hospital gates. I held my breath for a moment — would the police interfere with them? However, they were let in and they explained that they wished to see the matron. They were ushered into her office, where they were courteously received. They held a long discussion with the matron who agreed to forward their request to the Nursing Council that identity numbers should not be required for the registration of nurses.

It was all very peaceful and polite and it made the hordes of policemen look silly and superfluous. We heard later that there had been tear-gas canisters hidden behind the hospital hedges. For whom? A few hundred mothers who had walked a mile across the rough grass from Soweto? The press and the public laughed. Yet the women had been very serious and very dignified and they had succeeded. Soon afterwards the Nursing Council rather hastily withdrew their demand for identity numbers.

We had always known that at the end of the preparatory examination, a sort of pre-trial run, we might or might not be committed for trial in a higher court, but even that seemed far off. Early in 1958, we learned that the charges against sixty-five of us were withdrawn. This number included even the President General of the ANC, Chief Luthuli. I was amongst those who remained on trial.

The rest of us were committed for trial on a charge of high treason because we had "conspired with hostile intention against Her Majesty's government by committing hostile acts or inciting others to do so". Had it really taken more than a year to get to this point? I think that most of the time the actual idea of treason had faded from our minds as any sort of reality. I know it had from mine. But now it was real and we went through the ritual of the renewal of bail bonds, now for the Supreme Court, before we scattered again, now only ninety-one accused.

We waited for a new date for the proceedings to continue and for a new venue. No longer would we come daily to the Drill Hall, which had become so familiar to us that we felt the apprehension of the unknown in contemplating a trial in a more formal setting — where? For more than a year we had been on trial while the prosecution scraped the barrel, desperately trying to find evidence of treason. The Defiance Campaign, the Congress of the People, even the women's protests to Pretoria had all been dragged in. Yet these had all been peaceful, non-violent campaigns of protest — how could they be treason? Was it treason to ask for higher wages, for houses, for bread? Or to protest against passes, against banning without trial? Could the Freedom Charter be treason? A hostile act against Her Majesty's goverment?

I thought bitterly how right Vernon had been when he said that the trial was simply to see how far the government could go with its stifling of free speech, of democracy itself. I felt that we were trapped in some unbelievable situation. Did the future hold nothing but gaol for me? Yet in the midst of all this, I knew that I was totally and unalterably committed to the struggle for the liberation of the people of South Africa. I belonged now to the highest company in the land and wherever their road would take them, I must go too. There could be no turning back.

Chapter VIII

Treason – South African style (1)

Six months later, in August 1958, we came to trial. The government wanted us out of Johannesburg this time, to avoid huge crowds of Africans thronging the court precincts, as there had been at the beginning of the preparatory examination. The trial was to be moved to Pretoria, where the African population was much smaller and the Congress organisation not as strong as in Johannesburg.

Pretoria is thirty-five miles from Johannesburg city and almost fifty miles from Soweto where almost all the African accused lived; even those from other areas were accommodated there. Not one of us lived in Pretoria. The government provided a leviathan-type bus which picked up its treason passengers from Soweto for a long and exhausting journey of nearly 100 miles every day.

When we had been 156 accused, we had started off in the Johannesburg Drill Hall, in a military setting, the only place big enough for us all. Although the number had fallen to ninety-one the problem still remained because in the Pretoria Supreme Court there was no dock large enough to accommodate so many people. However, there was the "Old Synagogue", a large rather ornate structure, long since given up by the Jewish community. It was now standing empty, it was central, spacious, it had a gallery — it would do for us! It was still unmistakably a synagogue, but officially it became a "Special Criminal Court" for the Department of Justice. We went incongruously from army drill hall to synagogue and all in the name of justice.

This extra travelling would obviously make my already 'flexi' office-hours more difficult, as it would Stanley Lollan's of the South African Coloured People's Organisation also one of the remaining accused. He worked in the same office as I did and somehow we had to make up thirty-seven hours a week regularly. If there were any court adjournments we could revert temporarily to normal office hours. I reorganised my own office hours and Stanley shared them for we both had to hold on to our jobs.

We got ourselves to the office by 6.30 in the morning and worked there until 8.00. Robert Resha was holding down a reporter's job in the same way, so he would meet us as we left the office. Nelson Mandela drove in from Soweto to his law office at the other end of town for a couple of hours' early morning work and would meet us along the Pretoria road, leaving his car on the roadside for his return. We travelled the rest of the way together, often with an extra passenger. The treason bus was slow and ponderous and we needed speed so as to spend as little time on the road as possible.

"Congress Connie" would have been too small and too slow for this swift dash to Pretoria and back, so I bought, and nearly bankrupted myself in the buying, a fast French car. We named her "Treason Trixie". The court rose at four o'clock and we could be back in our offices before five. At 9 p.m. Stanley and I would lock up those huge empty offices, in which there had been only the two of us since five o'clock. There would be a quick break for a meat pie and coffee at seven so that we did not have to cook when we got home after that fifteen-hour day.

I don't know where we got the strength and perseverance to do all this, but somehow we managed it and saved our jobs. I arranged with my secretary to work flexi-time too, so that she could have some time with me before I left in the morning. She was loyal, devoted and efficient, even though she did not share all my political views. Her loyalty was deeply personal and I valued it greatly. Court adjournments were helpful to us and Stanley and I secretly welcomed each one, although our fellow accused resented them as delaying a long trial still longer.

It was those daily journeys which brought me closer to Nelson Mandela. I knew him already as a leader, but I got to know him as a person, sitting beside him as I drove, for Nelson's height and long legs could only be accommodated with comfort in the front seat of my car.

On trial he was Nelson Mandela, the ANC leader, standing tall, proud and dignified. He was exceptionally handsome with a magnificent physique, dark piercing eyes, sometimes narrowing above his high cheekbones until he looked almost oriental, sometimes opening wide in serious moments. But his infectious laughter and radiant smile often broke through his dignified reserve. He had the unique quality of being near to you and far away at the same time. Charismatic to a degree seldom seen, it is no wonder that even after more than twenty years on Robben Island, South Africa's dreaded maximum security gaol, he remains head and shoulders above everyone else. Mandela is recognised as the leader in the South African liberation struggle, respected and revered, not only by his fellow prisoners and by the African National Congress, but by thousands of people, black and white, the world over.

In our car he was Nelson, just one of us, as we shared our jokes and the peaches we bought and ate along the road — the "peach club" we called it. We shared so much else too, long political discussions, comment on the trial, which by now we accepted as a way of life. I don't recall any grumbling about it. We joked about our future sometimes and I would complain, "It's all right for you chaps, you will be together in gaol, but I'll get the husband poisoners because they are the only white women who get long sentences!" Sometimes Nelson would tell us of his childhood in the Transkei, the traditions and even the initiation rituals.

These journeys were friendly and fun-filled. We picked houses along the road for ourselves for the day when we should have freedom. Nelson's house was unpretentious and on the small side. We told him he wouldn't even be able to swing his lawyer's briefcase in it. Robert's house was odd, reminiscent of a series of dwindling dog kennels, but he stuck stubbornly to his choice. He could never explain it to us, even though we teased him that when we got freedom we wouldn't need to be reminded of chains, dog chains or any other sort. My choice was disapproved by Nelson as too bourgeois, with its well-planned garden and green lawns. I defended it on the grounds that it was painted green, black and yellow, the Congress colours. We chose a home for "Kathy", Ahmed Kathrada, the young Indian bachelor, so gay, who often travelled with us. We sat next to each other at the trial. His was a handsome villa with a large wing on either side "for all his Moslem wives!" Today few cars travel that old Pretoria road, but sometimes I take it just to look at our houses. I prefer it to the swift highway which has no memories for me. Our houses are still there, but Nelson and Kathy are serving life sentences in a maximum security prison and Robert is dead.

I know that Nelson sometimes thinks of those drives together for in one of his letters from Robben Island he wrote that one day he would like to drive me to a synagogue! I knew what he meant.

Beneath our laughter was concern for the future of our colleagues, our organisations, our struggle. The trial had begun with the highest in the legal profession in a titanic battle and we were in the middle. What did the future hold for us? It was an unspoken question but there would have to be an answer at some time.

For me those years of journeys to and from Pretoria were unique, privileged. It was then that Congress history opened up for me as never before. I was learning much too, from the many historic documents being read into the court record — as treason evidence.

Although the trial had opened in August, we remained locked for three more months in legal argument and technicalities, our defence counsel arguing for the quashing of the indictment altogether and the prosecution offering amendments. It was far above most of our heads, of course, except for a few legally qualified accused, such as Nelson Mandela, Joe Slovo and Duma Nokwe.

At the end of October, the state's indictment was actually withdrawn but only pending the framing of another, so we were not free. We were still out of gaol because we were pending trial and on bail, yet we had not been formally charged because there had been no satisfactory indictment. It was an odd position for ninety-one traitors, but it was to become even odder when it appeared that we were now divided into three groups. Thirty of us must stand trial in January 1959 and the remaining two groups on 24 April. On what criteria the division was made we did not know, nor did we ever know, but it brought us a two-month adjournment.

Nelson, Walter Sisulu, Robert, Lilian, Stanley and I were all among the thirty "first-liners" as we have been called. It seemed that the decision to try the remaining sixty-one would depend on whether *we* were acquitted or convicted. The prosecution apparently genuinely anticipated that our trial would last only four months, as it was not to begin until after Christmas. It proved to be an unreal calculation.

While we remained on trial, the units for issuing passes to African women were coming much closer to Johannesburg. Announcements were no longer made in advance as to when and where the units would operate. They just appeared without warning and the word went around. It was clear that Johannesburg had been left alone only for the time being, while the outlying areas were brought into line.

Just as in the Defiance Campaign, legislation was passed to hamper resistance to passes, and meetings of Africans outside the townships became illegal. This affected the Federation badly because it meant that while non-African women could not attend meetings inside the townships without permits, African women could not now attend them outside.

The first move by the authorities against Johannesburg was to request white housewives to send their domestic servants for "registration" — a deceptive term used to cover the intention to issue passes. While it may have deceived the white madams, it did not always deceive their domestics, but they were almost as powerless as their counterparts in the country. Nor did it deceive the ANC Women's League or the Federation. Pamphlets were swiftly distributed in white suburbs to point out the truth, that passes for women were not yet compulsory.

The anger of African women was aroused and within days hundreds of women marched in protest to the pass offices. They knew that they would be in illegal processions and holding illegal meetings, but this was spontaneous defiance of an unjust law. The first marchers came from Sophiatown and were taken into custody by the police before they reached the pass office. Then they were joined by crowds of women at the police station demanding to be arrested with them. Soon women were coming from Soweto and Alexandra Township, gathering outside the pass office.

I was not tied up with the trial on this day because this was during the long adjournment and I heard the news while I was working in my office. I did not propose to defy my banning order by joining the African women's protest, because it was theirs and theirs alone. But I thought I should be around to show solidarity and be seen to be near them on behalf of the Federation, but mostly for myself. I slipped down to the pass office during my lunch hour. There a fairly senior security branch detective was heard to comment, "Here comes that red bitch, Helen!"

I watched the laughing courage of the women as they were herded into huge police vans, helping each other in. They were driven off, singing and waving the Congress salute from the open backs of the police lorries. To see this was in itself a triumph. They knew that what they were doing was illegal, but this was their way of showing their contempt for the passes.

Soon there were almost 2,000 women in the Fort prison, where we had been in 1956 at the beginning of our trial. Many women had babies on their backs or at their breasts; some were pregnant. They were factory workers, domestic servants, housewives.

When they came to trial, they were still defiant, then returning, still singing, to the gaol to serve their sentences. "No bail, no fines!" they declared. It was the Women's League protest, and the Federation supported it to the full, doing whatever could be done to help the women still in the police cells awaiting trial. The police were, in fact, unable to cope with this load of women; their food resources were inadequate, as was the sanitation.

I was allowed into one of the big police cells, taking milk for the babies and food for the women. It was a moving, shocking sight seeing women sitting huddled together over every inch of the cell on a stone floor. Some mealie meal porridge, their only food, had been brought to them on an upturned dustbin lid. Babies were crying fretfully, hungry, but the mothers were still proud, defiant, smiling when they saw me with the milk for their children.

The pass protests and defiance lasted three full days. On the first day, 584 women were arrested in Johannesburg, 934 on the second day and 900 on the third. No wonder the police cells and the gaols were full.

The determination of the women did not weaken. Their decision had been taken to serve their full sentences in gaol, but their husbands were pressing for their wives to come out because of the care of the children and the care of the home. The ANC did not believe that the women could sustain a period in gaol because they had not been trained for it, but the Women's League and the Federation had confidence in the women, despite the spontaneous nature of the protests.

It was in fact the culmination of three years of growing anger against the issuing of passes to African women and there had been continuous propaganda and preparation by way of pamphlets, protests and meetings. However, the African National Congress asserted its authority at a special meeting with Lilian and me and we had to obey. We were disappointed and a little angry at first, but we were also disciplined and we were a part of the whole liberation struggle. There was no room for any rebellious spirit on our part and there was none. Bail and fines were paid and the women returned to their homes.

The Federation had also been active as far as it could be in this phase of the women's anti-pass campaign. We planned a mass rally of women of all races on the steps of City Hall, the time-honoured venue of protest meetings. The city council had cunningly planted shrubs and flower beds over most of the steps, obviously to prevent meetings of the former size, as in Solly's day. Very beautiful they were too, carefully guarded by stone borders, so that it was only possible to have some kind of gathering around the flower beds. But even those gatherings are gone now because every year outdoor meetings are banned in Johannesburg.

The Black Sash had been refused permission to hold a meeting there and it was absurd to suppose that we should succeed where the Black Sash had failed. We changed our plans and worked on a mini-Union Buildings plan for our protest, calling women of the East Rand and the West Rand, as well as Johannesburg itself, to come to the City Hall. There they would sign protests to hand to their leaders standing just outside the City Hall doors, flanked by other women holding placards. The protests were addressed to the Mayor of Johannesburg, calling upon him not to co-operate in any way in the issuing of passes to African women by demanding reference book numbers for township housing or lodgers' permits. He must make representations immediately for the suspension of the issuing of passes.

Several weeks of intensive organisation went into this protest and between 3,000 and 4,000 women came to the City Hall steps. They walked in twos and threes, as they had done in Pretoria, past policemen on every corner, careful not to block the pavements opposite the City Hall, not to linger as they handed over their protests. As many as could then made their way to a great welcome gathering in Sophiatown. I had been standing very near the City Hall, proud of this disciplined demonstration. I joined them in Sophiatown, but it had to be in an adjacent house, not at the actual welcome party, although I could hear their triumphant singing.

At the December conference of the ANC that year the women received their accolade. "We proudly salute the women freedom volunteers from Winberg, Lichtenberg, Zeerust, Sekhukhuniland, Uitenhage, Durban, Standerton, Pietermaritzburg — and two thousand Johannesburg women." I was proud too, that the Federation had played its part in some of this epic resistance.

We had gone back to Pretoria in January 1959, thirty of us, sitting again in that incongruous building converted into a Special Criminal Court. Our defence counsel had applied for the trial to be returned to Johannesburg, to avoid the long hours of travel for the accused and for themselves, arguing that otherwise adequate consultation with their clients would be almost impossible. There was no redress, however, and we sat on in the building designed for the worship of the Hebrew god. The Star of David hung high above the rostrum where those three red-robed judges were to preside for more than another two years over a treason court. Judge Rumpff, Judge Bekker, Judge Kennedy, they all became persons to us, even though we never exchanged words or even greetings with them.

Two of the judges became ill sometimes and the court would have to adjourn for a day or two. Judge Rumpff never missed a day, retaining his impressive calm demeanour throughout, but with occasional flashes of dry humour. Perhaps his most human trait was his impatience with the prosecution's inability to summarise documents or present their case in a disciplined manner acceptable to his high standards.

We thought our trial would be starting in earnest that January, but it did not. Argument began again on the indictment and went on beyond April, when the trial of the second batch of accused was supposed to begin. It had become an epic battle, with our defence counsel constantly on the attack, determined to expose and quash this inept indictment. The prosecution frequently retired to its corner to amend, to remedy the defects, coming back again and again with modified indictments but still intent on treason. It might have been amusing to watch the defence constantly on the attack and the prosecution always on the defensive, had we not been tied to the trial for more than two years already, immobilised, frustrated, many financially ruined.

I had thought I could not really add any other commitment to my life, divided between trial, travel, office and Federation tasks, but there was still a totally unpredicted call to come which had rather bizarre roots. Even in the preparatory examination I had developed double vision, so that I sometimes saw two magistrates and two court orderlies walking one behind the other to hand in documents. Yet I knew there was only one of each. An ophthalmologist advised me to read, knit, write, close my eyes frequently and do anything to stop myself from staring ahead. As I sat in the front row, knitting and closing my eyes were not possible, but I did write and do some of my medical aid work.

In Pretoria I was again in the front row, now as Accused No 2, and in this more formal atmosphere I could hardly walk in with an armful of office files. I certainly could not knit and there was a limit to the number of letters I could write. Reading made me sleepy. I then brought notebooks and scribbled random notes on the happenings of the trial, anything to keep my eyes away from three judges who became six if I looked at them for more than a minute or so — and where else could I look? Three judges were enough, six became unbearable.

During the preparatory examination and the first part of the trial, Lionel Forman, one of the accused, an advocate himself and a brilliant journalist, had been writing weekly summaries of the trial proceedings for widespread circulation by the Treason Trial Defence and Aid Fund. But Lionel was no longer in court with us, he was not one of the thirty.

My pointless and perpetual scribblings had not gone unnoticed and I was asked to take over the weekly summaries. I found it a difficult task because I had to concentrate all the time, but it kept my eyes off the judges and compelled me to take a more detailed interest in the proceedings. At the weekend I would type out my scribbled notes, they were then checked by a lawyer and edited by a journalist before they were roneod and circulated. I soon began to value court adjournments more than ever because the weekend typing removed me from what little was left of any social life.

For several months, the newspaper *New Age* had published shocking reports of inhuman conditions of African prison labour on potato farms. Some of these men had already been convicted for pass offences, others had been arrested and had "chosen" to work on a potato farm in preference to a trial and possible gaol. But clearly there was no real choice about it — it had more of a press gang dimension. The press reports revealed unbelievable conditions of life and work, for mere token wages. Men were locked up at night in crowded huts with no ventilation, no protection against the bitter cold of the winter nights. By day they wore potato sacks and worked under whiplash supervision. Beatings and brutal whippings were common.

In May 1959 the ANC called for a boycott of potatoes in protest against this inhuman treatment of prison labour on the farms. The boycott achieved astounding success almost everywhere. Potatoes became taboo. It was not a hardship for the few liberal white boycotters, as there were many palatable substitutes; however, the substitutes were more expensive, and this put them beyond the reach of African families. Yet the response to the boycott call was overwhelming from even the poorest people. It was aimed at the pockets of the very farmers who had so brutally treated the men, young and old, who had been sent away to work on potato farms. The potato farmers had needed cheap labour, starvation labour, and the police cells and the gaols had provided a convenient reservoir.

Within a few weeks the potato boycott skyrocketed to such an extent that sacks of potatoes piled up in markets and warehouses, even on railway sidings. They were still flowing in but the blacks would not buy and the sales to white consumers could not shift the mounting backlog. This boycott was one in which we could really participate, even at court, provided we refused to supplement the potatoes with substitutes. I do not suppose that this minimal self-restraint made any difference to the actual boycott. But it was important to us.

Perhaps the greatest sacrifice was made by black industrial workers, whose standard lunch was fish and chips. It was a real hardship to buy fish and bread instead, or only bread where the money could not stretch to fish. Chips were greatly missed. Yet the boycott was sustained for three months. The people gloated over reports of bags of potatoes rotting in the markets and farmers were in doubt as to whether to plant another crop of potatoes.

The boycott achieved its end. The government set up a commission of enquiry into prison farm labour. Not that any of us believed this was designed to probe and expose the whole vicious system. We knew it was intended only to save face in this horrifying exposure of the potato farm labour conditions. But at least the supply of prison labour to farms was suspended and the lorry loads of hopeless black men, despair on their faces, were no longer seen being driven off to face hunger, exhaustion and even whipping on these farms. Boycott had gained another victory.

Thankfully we went back to our usual treason lunches, so generously supplied by Pretoria friends. They were indeed nourishing, but not always my favourite diet. I enjoyed "Indian" week, with its savoury curries, but faltered sometimes over "African" week, with its meat and mealie meal. To bring my own packet of eggs, tomato and cheese was unthinkable, so I ate and then fought a losing battle at the weekends with encroaching poundage. Very occasionally friends from my pre-political days would take me out for dinner and I would indulge in gourmet food. The next day I would look a little sourly at my lunch plate, while my friends laughed, telling me I was back where I belonged.

At the end of May, Chief Luthuli, President General of the ANC, was served with banning orders for the third time and now for five years, not two. The conditions were similar to mine and those of so many of our leaders; no gatherings and he was confined to his home district in Natal. Chief, like me, had a period of grace, if you could call it that, of seven days before the confinement ban took effect. He came post-haste to Johannesburg to spend his last week of freedom at the headquarters of the ANC. His train journey was a triumphal tour as his people crowded onto the platforms of the railway stations to say goodbye to the Chief for the next five years. Yet Chief, even during this confinement, attracted many visitors from near and far, at national and international levels, despite very close and continuous police surveillance. The government's hoped-for isolation of this great man was only partially successful.

Less than a month after the ban on Chief Luthuli, Oliver Tambo, Acting President General; Duma Nokwe, Acting Secretary General; and the indefatigable and fiery Transvaal Volunteer-in-Chief, Robert Resha, all fell victims to similar bans, together with provincial Congress leaders.

It was a mighty swoop and inflicted considerable damage on ANC plans and preparations. I was now already through two years of my own ban and could appreciate the drastic effect of such restrictions on these recognised leaders, especially on Robert, accustomed to moving far and fast in his organisational work. He was such an eloquent speaker and now he was to be confined and silenced for the next five years.

By this time, in fact, most of the thirty accused had been banned. Kathrada, the Indian Youth Congress leader, said that if he didn't get banned soon, people would begin to suspect him!

Chapter IX

Treason – South African style (2)

The months of legal argument on the indictment were over at last and thirty "high traitors" pleaded not guilty to the charge of treason, two and a half years after they had been arrested. Each of us pleaded our innocence in our own language. I tried to make my plea loud and clear but I think I must have sounded very haughty as I said, "I plead not guilty to the charges as preferred against me." Nelson insisted afterwards that generations of British imperialism rang through the court as I spoke.

We listened to Advocate Pirow's opening address for the prosecution and I thought of what Vernon Berrangé had said in the preparatory examination. These political kites had been blown a long way since then.

Like all of us, I was angry, deeply angry, about the whole trial and what it had done to our lives. I was, all the same, immensely proud to be included in the front-line thirty, even though I did not know why I had been selected for this honour. I was proud to be sitting with them, close to them in so many ways, sharing their ordeal with them.

We were facing a capital charge, could there be anything more serious? We knew that for the Crown to prove treason, it had to prove that the ANC advocated a policy of violence and we could not believe that this would be possible. We had no need to fear the truth, yet we were human beings, with human fears as well as human hopes. Despite our confidence in our defence counsel, our organisations, ourselves and in each other, the unspoken question lay always close to the surface, "Would truth prevail against the hostility of the Nationalist government?"

For ten weeks we listened to our documents being read into the court record. We had heard them before in the preparatory examination. After a few weeks of this, we complained to the court that we could not hear what the prosecuting counsel was reading — the evidence against us. Judge Rumpff instructed the counsel to read louder, suggesting caustically that possibly a professional reader with a loud voice might have to be engaged. There was not much improvement, for the synagogue had been built for rabbis and readers with trained voices, not for the efforts of lawyers and detectives. We used to say sometimes:

We're here for what we didn't do,
We're here for what we didn't say,
And we'll be hanged for what we can't hear!

We could always hear what the judges said and usually what our own counsel said. When the prosecution spoke of "historical fact" we heard Advocate Maisels mutter, "Hysterical fact!" We heard him comment that if this were a cloak and dagger conspiracy, then it was all dagger and no cloak, since our documents had not been hidden away in secret places.

I listened, absorbed now, scribbling all the time, to our Congress history being unfolded, a unique record of a non-violent liberation struggle for nearly fifty years. Pirow's opening address had quoted extracts on which the prosecution would rely in its efforts to prove violence, communism, treason. Now we heard these gobbets being put back into context again.

The judges' pleas for summaries bore no fruit, for the Crown counsel continued to display an inability to summarise and drew much judicial contempt for their failure. The trial seemed to stretch out endlessly before us. "Freedom in our lifetime!" had been one of our much used slogans; Judge Kennedy was heard once to express the hope that the trial would end in *his* lifetime.

Yet it was not to end in Pirow's. On 12 October we came to court to hear that he had died suddenly the night before. The court was crowded with advocates to pay tribute to him. We had been divided amongst ourselves as to whether we should stand with the rest of the court in respect to his memory, but the text of his opening address was still fresh in our minds. He represented our enemy, the Nationalist government; he had formerly been a member of it. Not one of us stood for Pirow, we sat stony-faced, with folded arms, while the court stood.

Leaving the documents, the prosecution produced its showpiece, none other than Professor Andrew Murray, its expert on communism. He was the very witness who had taken such a battering from Vernon Berrangé two years before, in the preparatory examination. To our amazement here he was, back again, with seemingly renewed confidence.

At first we listened carefully, remembering his previous sorry exhibition, but the sheer length of his evidence now proved soporific. We were being submerged in communist doctrine, according to Professor Murray, and I noticed that several of my colleagues were sleeping through it. The opening of his evidence was inauspicious for the prosecution. Their star witness had furnished himself with notes from which he had hoped to read, but he was soon stopped by defence counsel's objections. Judge Rumpff commented curtly, "If he's an expert, then he's an expert." So why should he need to refresh his recollection?

After days of expounding communist doctrine, punctuated by damaging defence objections, the witness came at last to the Freedom Charter. Now we all listened, for we knew that the Freedom Charter was crucial to the trial. For us it was a declaration of faith, the affirmation of what we strove for, the statement of the hard facts of the life of the black people. We had adopted it four years before and it belonged to us.

The prosecution presented the Charter in its own way, trying to show, clause by clause, that it could be related to communist doctrine, that there was no clause that could not be. To me it sounded totally unreal. I knew the origin of the charter, that it told of the hopes of the people for a world in which their present sufferings would be no more, those sufferings which were reflected in every line of it. Why should a nation need a communist doctrine to tell them what they suffered, to spell out for them their hopes for the future? Had not the people done this for themselves.

Then we moved back again to documents, 400 documents, and books too, to be presented to the expert on communism for his verdict. They had all been once in our possession, or the co-conspirators', that shadowy body of our fellows in this huge conspiracy against the state. Presumably the state dared not bring a charge of treason against them for lack of evidence, but it had felt it could sally forth against *us* by throwing in everything it could scrape together in the hope that something might come forth eventually from this inchoate mass.

Our books, according to this expert, were communist classics, or contained communist material or propaganda. I remembered, ruefully, the ones I had once purchased, feeling that perhaps I ought to be a little better informed on communist ideology. But of course they were not the only political books I possessed, and I did not have them long. They were all removed by the police in a raid the morning after I had acquired them. It seemed that, for the prosecution, we could be damned for treason just for possessing such books, whether we had read them or not.

It was almost a comic proceeding. Counsel read an extract, the book was handed by the court orderly to the witness, putting it into his outstretched hand, and then the verdict would be announced. It was usually "straight from the shoulder communism", an odd phrase, but obviously dear to the witness. The volume would then be added to the evergrowing pile of books beside him.

It took only one day of this procedure to draw a protest from the judges and then only the title was read aloud. The extract was to be read into the record at some other time, outside court hours. Nevertheless it remained an agonisingly slow process, and a sort of stupor spread over the court, broken only by the rhythmic movements of the court orderly walking backwards and forwards.

At last this part was over. Professor Murray had had twelve days already in the witness box. He looked a little weary, but his real ordeal was still to come. Now we were all alert again when Advocate Maisels rose to his feet, tall and commanding, to cross-examine this witness.

We entered into a world of semantics, of the meaning of words and terms, as used by Professor Murray, as used by us. Confronted with his own articles written twenty years before, with his own evidence given only a few days before, Professor Murray started on a course of retreat before Maisels' attacks, attempting to defend his own use of words. He drew a devastating comment from Maisels of 'fascism'. "We hope to establish at the end of this cross-examination that you are about the only person who uses the word in this special fashion" and "I am going to suggest that this reply is due to tiredness on your part." To which Murray replied haughtily, "On the contrary, it is due to experience and knowledge."

Advocate Pirow had alleged in his opening address that we were inspired by communist fanaticism and racial hatred. Maisels declared that he would, by the presentation of objective facts, put forward another interpretation, the right of the human person to be treated as one.

The facts of South African life were then presented in their stark reality, as Advocate Maisels led the witness through the many statutes, based on deprivation and differentiation, rooted in race and colour. Statistics reinforced Maisels' searching questions, until Judge Rumpff asked, "where will it stop?", to which Maisels replied: "where did the Crown stop?", adding that the real inspiration of the accused was the miserable conditions prevailing for the black people in South Africa. He then proceeded with his exposition, putting his question on objective facts to which the witness could only answer "Yes". We heard those monosyllabic replies, "yes . . . yes . . . yes . . . !" like the sound of a paintbrush slapping paint on the devastating picture of black life in South Africa.

In reply to the suggestion that generally the tone of the speeches at the Congress of the People was moving, touching and humanitarian, the witness at last conceded that the charter itself was liberatory and humanitarian.

Eventually Professor Murray left the witness box. We thought that he had been routed, but I doubt that his self-esteem had really been punctured. He was merely a weary man, a little drawn and grey-faced, when he stepped down. Our esteem for Maisels and his defence team had risen very high indeed. Many of us thought that our case was already more than half won and we were jubilant. The court was exhausted, I think, because the trial was then adjourned until the following January, a break of almost two months.

October had brought sadness to us with the death of Lionel Forman, an accused with us until the separation into two trials. Aged only thirty-two, he had suffered from a heart condition all his young life and died during an operation. I thought how keenly he would have appreciated Maisels' handling of Murray and wished he could have been there to hear it — though not as an accused, for I did not wish that on anyone.

We reached the third part of the treason saga in January 1960, the reports of our "treason" or "violent" or "communist" speeches. We knew what to expect, for we had listened to it before. Now we should have to sit for more dreary hours listening to these incredibly distorted versions of our speeches. Yet they were not distorted by malice or deliberate untruth, but by the sheer inability of many of the detectives to get down on paper what we had actually said.

"We're here for what we didn't say . . ."

What it all added up to, except for a small proportion of reasonably accurate shorthand reports, was what these longhand reporters thought we said, or thought we might have said. The entire two-month performance would have been ludicrous, had it not been that we had been sitting on trial now for over three years. Was this a time to play yet another act in this bitter farce?

Our anger was not directed against the black witnesses as individuals. They were victims of a system which had pushed them into this humiliating exhibition of their own inadequacy, exposed them to the searing contempt of cross-examining lawyers. How could men, only half educated through no fault of their own, ever have been expected to make verbatim reports of speeches, not even in their own language. Perhaps they were literate in their own tongues. I don't know. They were certainly not in English.

Occasionally defence counsel would produce a time and motion study. There had been twelve meetings which had spread over a total of thirty-nine hours, but the longhand notes, when typed, had covered only one page for every three hours of speeches. "I always write the best way I can get along," one witness said, "It was the speech . . . in so far as I could get it down," said a white sergeant, at the same time insisting that this was the speech that had been made.

Yusuf Cachalia, one of the South African Indian Congress's best speakers, was reported to have said, "I one day read an article in an Afrikaans newspaper after the judge's decision. This article read thus: 'One who loves first, loves more.' Yes, of course they were correct to say so, because the Minister of Justice may after three months impose bans upon us."

Then followed this exchange in court:

Witness:	"I wrote what he said."
Defence Counsel:	"Nonsense, isn't it?"
Witness:	"If it is nonsense then he speaks nonsense."
Defence Counsel:	"You agree it's nonsense?"
Witness:	"HE said it. I wrote it down."
Defence Counsel:	"Do you agree it's nonsense?"
Mr Justice Rumpff (wearily):	"Does it matter, Mr Berrangé?"

I don't know how the judges had the patience to listen to weeks of this befuddled nonsense. I suppose they had no alternative because the Crown was presenting it all as evidence of complicity in a treasonable conspiracy, in some cases even as proof of our very acts of treason. Yet it was almost at the level of Alice in Wonderland: "Twas brillig and the slithy toves did gyre and gimble in the wabe."

Three and a quarter years after we had been arrested, the Crown closed its case. Now at last, in March 1960, it would be our turn. Our witnesses would be called, Chief Luthuli, Nelson Mandela, Professor Z.K. Matthews and others. Our leaders would speak for us and for the whole Congress Alliance. Dr Zami Conco from Natal was our first witness, the Deputy President General of the ANC. His evidence ended on 21 March, the day of the Sharpeville massacre, when sixty-seven unarmed Africans were shot dead by the police.

The ANC view on Africanism had always been clear. It had been set out again recently by the National Executive Committee at the ANC Annual Conference in 1958. The ANC accepted South Africa as a multiracial country in which all racial groups have the right to live in dignity and prosperity. ANC nationalism was neither exclusive nor racialistic, but broad and all-embracing. It had always been accepted by the ANC that freedom is indivisible and that the ANC must work with all forces prepared to struggle for the same ideals.

There was, however, an extremist Africanist view within the ANC membership that the SA liberation struggle must be conducted on the basis of narrow African nationalism alone, because Africans were indigenous to the soil and constituted the majority of the people. This was in direct opposition to the long-standing ANC policy of racial co-operation and to the ideal expressed in the Freedom Charter and adopted by the ANC "that South Africa belongs to all who live in it, black and white . . ."

In 1959, the Pan Africanist Congress had established itself, the result of an Africanist breakaway from the ANC. It seemed a strange time to be breaking away from the mother body with so many leaders still on trial. The ANC was itself fighting for survival against the tremendous onslaught of banning orders imposed on the leadership at all levels, and against the treason trial which threatened its very existence.

Despite the Africanist breakaway to form the Pan Africanist Congress, to be known thereafter as the PAC, the ANC remained consistent in its policy of uniting with other racial groups in the Congress Alliance, whilst preserving its own national identity.

At the 1959 ANC national conference, 31 March 1960 had been proclaimed as "Anti-Pass Day" when demonstrations against passes would be held throughout the country. The PAC, meeting just one week later in their conference, decided to launch their own "final and positive action against the pass laws". Their campaign was to have tragic consequences at Sharpeville. The situation seemed to have taken on a competitive dimension in the PAC's anxiety to achieve a following for their organisation.

Chief Luthuli emphasised the need for popular training in non-violent action and the danger of "reckless haste and impatience which might be suicidal and be playing into the hands of the goverment". I remembered the women's gaol protest in 1958 and how the Congress leaders had insisted that the women were not prepared and would not be able to sustain a long stay in gaol. I had come to see the wisdom of this but I did not foresee the terrible consequences of the ill-prepared PAC defiance.

Halfway through March, the PAC proclaimed their starting date as 21 March, ten days before 31 March, the date fixed by the ANC. The competitive inference was inescapable. The PAC call to its members was that they should congregate at municipal offices, leaving their passes at home and offering themselves for arrest for being unable to produce them. They would not pay fines nor accept bail nor legal defence. After serving their sentences in gaol, the protesters would again offer themselves for arrest. This was to be a campaign of "decisive and positive action" which the PAC leaders believed would mobilise hundreds of thousands of Africans in mass protest against the pass laws.

The ANC Secretary General informed Mr Robert Sobukwe, the PAC President, that the ANC could not support this campaign. "We realise that it is treacherous to the liberation movement to embark upon a campaign which has not been properly prepared for and which has no reasonable chance of success." These were strong and wise words, prophetic words, so soon to be proved true.

Even before we left court on the fateful 21 March, reports were filtering through, reports of demonstration and arrest, which grew into horrifying reports of police shooting and many dead in Sharpeville Location. Thousands of people had marched peacefully to the municipal office and formed a growing yet peaceful crowd there, joined by thousands more. Police reinforcements were rushed to the offices and then, just as outside the Johannesburg Drill Hall at the beginning of our trial, the police panicked and fired, claiming afterwards that it was in self-defence. No order to shoot was given but the crowd, after it turned to flee, was raked with gunfire and sixty-seven people lay dead, 180 wounded.

By the next morning, we knew of all the dead and wounded, we heard of mass demonstrations and shooting in the Cape and we knew the shame of sitting helpless, immobilised, in the treason court. President Luthuli called for a National Day of Mourning on the day when all the Sharpeville victims were to be buried. It was to be observed by people staying home from work. This time the ANC and the PAC worked together and the stay-at-home was almost totally observed in many large centres.

We were mourning the dead, but we were also watching the last rites of the African National Congress as a legal organisation. On 28 March, the Unlawful Organisations Bill was introduced in Parliament to outlaw the ANC, after fifty years of existence — and with it, the newly-formed PAC.

We knew that nothing could stop this Bill. It was a bizarre situation. We were in court to defend the ANC, its wisdom, its refusal to approve violent action. In the midst of all this, with the President General now in the witness box testifying to its non-violent policy, the organisation had been outlawed. If ever there was contempt of court, surely this Bill was it. It was on that day that Duma Nokwe said bitterly, "this trial is out of date". And so it was, but the sorry farce still had to be played out. The tragedy was that Sharpeville should never have happened. The rash action of the PAC had cost us — and them — very dearly and brought tragedy to many homes. There was, however, more to come. The government reacted by putting the whole of South Africa under a State of Emergency, taking into custody nearly 2,000 people of all races, in all centres.

I heard the knock at my door at three o'clock in the morning. I became hazily aware of car lights and sounds of people and there they were, the mixture as before. First a search, then a suitcase to be packed, this time with a warning to take plenty of clothes. "It might be for a long time." Then off to Marshall Square police station again, there to find three friends in the large cell of the treason days, also with their suitcases.

We sat around in the cell, not hungry, for food had been brought to us, but isolated, cut off from home and friends and children. Later in the day, we were allowed to sit in a small built-in yard, from which we could see only the sun and the sky above us. Then we heard the voices of our friends, "Helen, we are missing you!" called Bertha. "The world at 1 p.m." shouted Kathy and he gave us news of many others held like us. It was a "loo" communication service, possible only by standing on tip-toe on lavatory pans to shout through high-up gratings.

In the evening we all met in the charge office, some of the treason accused and many others. We learnt from our lawyers that hundreds had been arrested all over South Africa, under the State of Emergency regulations, but the police had jumped the gun before the regulations had actually been gazetted and the arrests were illegal. We should have to be released, but the presence of armed police all around us left no hope that we should be allowed to leave the police station. Sure enough, we were first released and then re-arrested, one by one, with a tap on the shoulder, a ludicrous performance for this was no knighthood, but a sentence to indefinite detention in gaol. The regulations had by this time been gazetted and were now law.

Many of our friends were pressing at the doors and windows, heavily guarded by the police with sten guns and revolvers, but they could not guard the fanlights. A flood of gifts came pouring through, sweets, biscuits, nuts, cigarettes, even playing cards, tumbling down amongst us. We were not forgotten.

We heard the freedom songs of our people as they marched around the police station and then we were herded back to our cells, but we could still hear the songs. We slept well that night, despite the horror of our detention, for we had not slept much, if at all, the night before. I remembered, uneasily, the warning when I was arrested, "It might be a long time," but it was no use worrying about the future. That would have to take care of itself as we could do nothing about it.

The next morning, I was taken away from my friends in the cell and bundled into a prison van, where I found Leon Levy, the only other white on the trial now, and learnt that we were being taken to Pretoria for the trial. It seemed a bit peculiar in the midst of all these arrests, but I was glad to know that I should be with the accused again. Freedom songs started up in the back of the van, for Leon and I were separated from our friends by our colour. We joined in enthusiastically; peering through the small windows, we could see people gazing curiously at this travelling choir.

Chapter X

Trial by detention

In Pretoria things had changed at court. Our van drove through the gates of the old synagogue. We heard shouts of greeting as we were driven in and knew that friends were gathered outside. We were offloaded in a yard sealed off from the public, because we were now detainees held completely incommunicado.

Here we found Nelson, Robert and others who had been held at Newlands police station in Johannesburg. At Marshall Square station, where we had been held, it seemed there were only whites, coloureds, Indians and African women. African men had been held in the Newlands police cells. We also found at court ten innocents among the accused who had brought themselves to court the previous day, surprised to find the rest of us missing. They had come free, but they left in police custody, all except one, Wilton Mkwayi, who had actually been pushed aside by the police and told to get out. He did — right out of South Africa — for a time. But he did return and now serves his life sentence in a maximum security prison with the Rivonia accused.

We heard with amusement of the court scene the previous day, with only ten of the accused present and no witness. The judges had not been informed and the court officials and prosecution knew nothing. It must have been an hilarious scene. The court dignity was affronted and the judges felt insulted, demanding information and the presence of all the accused and the witness, Chief Luthuli. A placatory prosecution team apologised and undertook to remedy the matter. The defence counsel and the judges, too, remained unmoved and the court had to be adjourned — for lack of accused. We laughed at this, but we did not laugh at Nelson's account of the treatment in the Newlands police station. To think of naked power, of man's brutality to man, is always horrifying. To hear of its exercise against your friends, is worse; to know that you yourself have been saved from it by your white skin, is the worst of all.

In the Newlands cells, fifty detainees had been locked up for the rest of the night, after their arrest at one o'clock in the morning, in a yard open to the sky and lit by one electric bulb. It was so small they could only stand and were given neither food nor blankets. In the morning they were taken to a cell, about eighteen feet square, with sanitation only from a drainage hole in the floor, flushed at the whim of the policeman in charge. Food, even drinking water, came only at three o'clock in the afternoon, twelve hours after the men had been brought to the cells. It was soft, thin, sour mealie porridge — to be eaten with hands that had not been washed all day. But to the hungry men it was food and it was eaten. At 6 p.m. it came again with some dirty blankets, considered good enough for any arrested black man.

At 8 p.m. they, like us, went through the farce of release and re-arrest, one by one, and then back to the filth and stench of the cell. They came to court next morning, still unwashed, packed like sardines in a police truck, to their trial in a formal court of law.

The court battle was still going on. The judges ruled that the trial should be adjourned until 19 April, nearly three weeks ahead. We climbed back into the prison van and were driven to the Pretoria local gaol, where Leon and all the black men got out. Lilian and I were taken a little further to a large stone building, which we learnt was the Pretoria Central gaol.

We felt terribly alone, the two of us, rattling around in that huge van; we knew we should be separated, white from black, but apart from that we did not know what our conditions would be for the next nineteen days. As we climbed out, Lilian burst out bitterly, "You are better off with your pink skin!" It was true. Her words have remained with me and there was nothing I could say or do.

Yet we were not entirely separated after all. Our cells were on the same row, high up under the roof but open to the rafters, except for wire netting stretched across the top of each cell. There were some other black prisoners in these punishment cells and we quickly learnt how sometimes to shout to each other across the tops of our cell walls.

It was as Lilian had said: my pink skin brought me a bed, sheets, blankets. The mattress was revolting, urine stained, but Lilian slept on a mat on the floor with only blankets. My food was better. I had a sanitary bucket with a lid. She had an open bucket covered with a cloth. I learnt to hate my pink skin but I could not change it nor expiate it.

The nineteen days dragged past. The highlights were the occasional books from the prison library, the escorted walk down the stairs to the ablution block for a tepid bath, watched by a wardress, and an occasional half hour in the exercise yard, round and round a huge palm tree which reminded me of the one in my Norwood garden. Sometimes this helped, sometimes it didn't.

Evenings brought the singing of the other women in these punishment cells. I heard their voices during the day as they called to each other, but they were nameless, disembodied. Sometimes I thought I heard Lilian as she called to them in her own language. The songs they sang at night were not freedom songs, only once did I hear them sing "Nkosi Sikelele". They mostly sang hymns, very beautifully in harmony, and when their voices died away, all would become very quiet.

After about ten days they left these cells and Lilian was moved away too. I did not know where she was. I was alone then, up in the rafters, except for the wardress bringing my food, putting it on the floor and then kicking it into the cell. Only one of them did that, however; the others were fairly kind, but uncomprehending.

I learnt that there was another white detainee there. It was Hannah Stanton, a Christian missionary. It was difficult to imagine what she could have done to bring about her detention without trial, but she had important British connections which brought relief to me as well. After two weeks we were actually allowed to exercise together, even to talk to one another! Daily we asked to share a cell, but at this time, with no success.

The treason accused returned to court on 19 April, excited to meet again and exchange our prison experiences. As whites, Leon and I had of course by far the best treatment, except that we were isolated and the others shared cells. Robert's account of the Africans' gaol conditions was as horrifying as Nelson's had been of the police cells, and it had gone on much longer.

The detainees had been put five in a cell, no larger than mine in the women's gaol. Their only sanitation was the same as Lilian's, a cloth-covered bucket, but for five people, not one, and standing next to the bucket of drinking water. As in Newlands, they had no toilet paper and only dirty blankets. Their food was the standard black prisoners' food, mealie pap and only occasionally some gristly meat and beans on top. For the first ten days they had no exercise at all and were not even let out for showers. Only in the last few days, after prolonged battles with their gaolers, was there any improvement.

Exchanging scraps of news amongst us, we learnt that nearly 2,000 people were now detained, including a good number of whites, but we did not know where they all were. Some appeared to be held in the Johannesburg Fort. We went into court for argument about whether the trial should continue during the Emergency.

The prosecution had offered to approach the Minister of Justice for assurances that any witnesses whom we might wish to call would not be victimised under the Emergency regulations, but our counsel had replied that he did not think we should accept such assurances as we obviously could not accept the minister's bona fides.

We learnt with sadness that on 8 April the ANC and the PAC had finally been declared illegal. It was also my birthday and Hannah, even before we were allowed to talk to each other, had sent a little mug of marigolds for my cell. I had not known then that it was the day of the banning of the ANC and with it the ANC Women's League. This was going to create a serious problem for the Federation, for the Women's League provided the greater portion of our affiliated membership.

Lilian told me that she was now with another black detainee, though no longer in my row of cells under the roof. Conditions were still very bad for her. We were now supposed to have visits from relatives, but her daughter Edith had come all the way from Soweto on two or three occasions, yet only once had they been allowed to see each other.

I had no family, but had had a visit from a friend, who undertook to let my Norwood cottage for me. It would be better than leaving it empty and there was no telling when I would get back to it again.

The trial adjourned for another week. To my surprise I found that even the forbidding gaol gate had lost its horror for me, as had the lonely cell, for I should see Hannah every day. During the week that followed we were at last allowed to share a cell and I moved in with my few possesions — a couple of library books, a pair of pyjamas, my toilet things and a tin of biscuits.

Even in those earlier weeks of isolation I had not thought of spiritual comfort nor reached out for it. I had listened to the African women singing their hymns at night, but I could not understand the words. I envied them a little because they seemed to find comfort in their singing, but I did not think very much about it. In Hannah I found a dedicated Christian who had involved herself in the suffering of others and was now paying a heavy price for it. I could see for myself how much her faith meant to her. She accepted me as I was, devoid of all meaningful Christian faith, but night and morning she knelt in prayer, drawing my respect, even my envy. Hannah had so much that I did not have, for she was very close to the God I had not dared to deny but had rejected for over thirty years. I knew it was more than neglect, it was rejection of a faith which I had discarded — for what? I could find no answer except my own superficial life values. Yet I could not talk to Hannah about it, for this faintly disturbed feeling was not yet at any level of articulate words. It was barely at thought level. I watched her twice a day, watched and wondered.

Only once did we speak of my lack of faith and I do not recall how it arose except that it related to what I saw as the church's failure to involve itself in the struggle for liberation. I remember speaking bitterly. I think I said that there would be no room for me in a church that could not stand up to be counted. That was all, and I suppose it was really nothing but a rationalisation of my own deeper guilt feeling that made me blame the church.

On 26 April, we came to court again to learn that some sort of indemnity for witnesses had been authorised, but neither we, nor our counsel, had been impressed. Advocate Maisels informed the court that his clients felt they could not properly present their case in the Emergency but that if the Court ordered the trial to continue, they must do so.

The court did order the trial to continue and then Duma Nokwe, one of the accused and himself an advocate, addressed the court on our behalf. He first presented our doubts and concerns and then stated bluntly that we had instructed our counsel to withdraw from the case because it would be "profitless to continue spending public money in conducting and defending this case".

We had discussed this in the court interval and had agreed unanimously on this step. We knew what it would entail but we felt that we had to make this stand, no matter what the outcome would be for us personally. It was a bold decision, boldly announced. Maisels followed with: "We have no further mandate and will consequently not trouble your lordships any further." He led his defence team out of the court and out of our lives for the next few months.

I know that I, for one, felt desperately alone, vulnerable, for a few moments. Then I looked at their lordships, for the court had been deeply affronted. I do not know whether they had expected this move, but they betrayed nothing of their feelings. Judge Rumpff sat, as though carved in stone, watching our counsel leave the court. Then the trial continued as though nothing had happened, except for the empty defence counsel table.

Chief Luthuli was brought to the witness box. This was the first time we had seen him since the detentions and we looked anxiously at him as we had heard that he, our chief, had actually been assaulted by the police when he was arrested. He had apparently been hit across the face and on the head. It was hard to believe that this had been done to this dignified, elderly man, the President General of the ANC, but it was true. His evidence in chief had been completed just before the arrests and he was now to be cross-examined by Advocate Trengove for the prosecution.

In our last discussions with our defence counsel, a strategy had been planned for the period of the Emergency, until we felt that we could call our counsel back. When Chief's cross-examination was finished, some of us were to follow him into the witness box. We must first give our evidence and then our fellow accused would have the right to cross-examine us before the prosecution took over.

It was decided that I should follow Chief and that Farid Adams, of the Indian Congress, should lead me in my evidence in chief. My task would be to set out our policy and to deny the allegations in the Crown's opening address, as Farid took me through the points, one by one. It would take time, but in the present circumstances, time did not matter. It was an enormous responsibility for me, but I saw it as a very great honour.

Nelson took over the battle of gaol conditions, demanding proper consultation facilities, which now ought to include Leon, Lilian and me, and should no longer be held in a dingy cell with no toilet facilities available. The court was requested to see that proper arrangements were made for us for the preparation of our defence.

We went back to gaol that day, uplifted by our defiance and the impact we had made, not only on the court, but on the authorities and on South Africa, yet also sobered by the implications of what we had taken on. I carried a copy of the Crown's opening address under my arm when I returned to the women's gaol and through the routine search of my person. Then I joined Hannah in our cell where she was waiting for me to tell her the events of the day. Even though I went only to court, I was Hannah's link with the outside world.

Our trial limped on again as Advocate Trengove returned to his cross-examination of Chief Luthuli. On the way back to the gaol, and coming down in the mornings, we sat together in the cab of the prison van. Because I was a white woman, I was not allowed to sit with the black accused, although we all sat together in court. We had insisted that Chief must also ride in front and not in the bumpy back of the van. His health was still precarious after his long illness and history of heart disease.

At first I was shy of talking to him, especially in the presence of the police driver, but gradually we were able to relax. Those brief moments became for me precious moments and then cherished memories, even though we could not talk of the things that were important to us.

We heard that the other white detainees still held in the Johannesburg gaol might soon be coming to join us in Pretoria. Hannah and I became aware of much bustling and gaol preparation. Two very large interleading dormitories were being prepared for all the women, one for sleeping, with twenty-two beds, and the other for communal living, with a stove, a sink, tables and chairs, even table tennis for our entertainment. There was also a triple-seated loo with only half doors.

Hannah and I were taken to view the new accommodation. Even the mattresses, bedding and pillows were new. We had become accustomed to our shabby existence in the death cell (for that was what we had discovered it to be), with Horace, the black gaol cat, lent to us every night to protect us from rat visitations. We wondered how we should fit in with so many other women. I was sure they would love Hannah — who could help it? — but I wasn't so sure about myself. However, the grapevine assured me that I should find some friends amongst the newcomers.

They came, these women detainees, excited, high-powered, triumphant over their defiant stand against being moved from Johannesburg. Almost all of them had to leave young children when they were arrested and in Pretoria they would be further from their families. They had physically refused to move and had been carried or dragged to the waiting prison transport. I don't think they were handled very gently, but surprisingly they were not charged with failure to obey prison orders. Hannah and I felt apologetic that we had never thought of defiance.

I had a warm and loving reunion with several friends. We sorted ourselves out and chose our beds, Hannah and I in a corner; she because she wanted a quiet spot for her prayers and I because I wanted to be near her.

Our privileged position as whites, even in gaol, was brought home to me more than ever by these amazing arrangements for our living quarters during detention. I knew that nothing like this would be provided for black detainees. It had to be accepted because there was no way to reject it. It was yet another example of the unjust racial disparity which was to haunt me throughout my life, especially when it touched me as personally as it did then. I had to go to court every day to meet my friends, my fellow accused, knowing that my conditions in gaol were so much better than theirs. Lilian had indeed spelt it out — I was better off with my pink skin.

It became a strange life for me because I was away from the gaol every day at court, then again in the evenings for consultation and briefing with the other accused in preparation for my rapidly approaching entry into the witness box. Chief's cross-examination ordeal would not go on much longer. It had been a very harsh experience for him even though he was now limited to two hours a day on medical grounds. I sat with him only on the morning journey, but I could see that he was physically exhausted, conserving what was left of his strength for the strain of Trengove's relentless cross-examination. I was becoming more and more nervous at what I might have to face; I tried desperately to give enough time to preparing my evidence, which was going to cover so much Congress history.

Our briefing sessions were extraordinary, totally against normal prison routine and regulations. After the four o'clock lock-up time, a gaol is completely locked up and there is no coming or going of any sort. The section keys are locked away for the night and I doubted whether even fire would bring them out again before morning. Yet here was I, being taken right out of the women's gaol at half past five and driven down to the men's gaol, accompanied by a security branch detective of course. I was escorted into what would normally have been the visitors' side of the prison visiting room. There, on the other side of the bars and the wire grill, would be Farid Adams with his typewriter, and Nelson, and Walter Sisulu, possibly Duma Nokwe as well, with Leon on my side. They would go through my evidence as I had prepared it the night before, sentence by sentence. They helped me clarify things and although they often suggested variations in the emphasis, they always left the final decision to me for it had to be my own statement. It was a unique, bizarre way to learn political history, but who ever had such illustrious tutors? They were the very Congress leaders themselves. They knew that the value of my evidence would lie largely in its sincerity.

Farid was to lead me in my evidence and his questions, too, were carefully prepared so as to draw out from me the substance of our liberation struggle. The struggle must speak for itself and I must be ready to deal with all the smears and allegations in Pirow's opening address and also with whatever was going to arise in cross-examination. It must all be from my own knowledge, because I would not be allowed to consult my notes.

Much of Congress history had already been presented to the court in our documents and through our speeches — on the rare occasions when they were intelligently reported. During these weeks of preparation I lived with the trial record and the opening address, working until late at night, even after I returned from the briefing sessions with the men.

In view of all this it was not surprising that I did not really become a part of the community of women detainees in which I was living. I had little time with them and was absorbed in studying for my evidence. Hannah, however, was totally accepted and loved, as I had been sure she would be. She was a gracious, pretty woman, somehow preserving her simple elegance, even in gaol. Tall, slender, short, curling silver hair above a smiling face too young for that silver, Hannah was then only in her early forties. She lived her faith and had no need to impose it on anyone else. She knelt in prayer at her bedside night and morning, while these dynamic women prisoners, atheists and communists all, gave her peace and quiet, accepting her completely. She had not only won their love but also their respect for her as a Christian.

While they were still in Johannesburg gaol, the women and the white men too, with whom they had established some sort of clandestine contact, decided that their detention was intolerable and they must protest. They must demand their release and the return to their children. In gaol there is only one way to protest and that is by a hunger strike. When they arrived in Pretoria the plan was already well under way, but they wanted the approval and co-operation of the other detainees, especially the black detainees.

Because I had contact with Lilian and the men on the trial, it was my task to carry messages, report on the discussions and the opinions of the congresses. I also had to ascertain whether the ANC and the Indian Congress would bring the other detainees out on hunger strike at the same time, as well as the treason accused.

The women were confident of support but the ANC was not sympathetic to the idea, maintaining that a hunger strike in these incommunicado conditions would achieve nothing as there would be no publicity. Moreover, this form of protest was alien to African tradition and culture and would be difficult to sustain, especially as the poor gaol food had already weakened the African detainees physically.

Nevertheless, for the sake of unity, since the white men and women in gaol were determined to carry out their hunger strike protest, the ANC and the Indian Congress agreed to go along with them for three days in a token hunger strike. I brought back the unpopular reply and it isolated me from my fellow prisoners. I conveyed the decision as best I could and the women then took a vote on the issue. Obedient to Congress discipline, I voted against the proposal for an indefinite hunger strike. Everyone else voted in favour of it.

The women's hunger strike was heroic and impressive. It was broken in the end after eight full days, by the sudden decision of the prison authorities to separate the women and send half of them to another gaol some distance away. The women then wisely decided that it would be too great a strain on their shockingly weakened physical condition to continue their hunger strike unless they could all be together.

Hannah and I had only joined the hunger strike for a couple of days. We knew that she was to be deported back to England at any moment and we wanted her to be fit enough to make forceful public statements about Sharpeville, the Emergency and detentions. I had been limited by the ANC because I would be going into the witness box soon.

My fellow detainees were all in favour of my drawing attention to the hunger strike by fainting in the witness box, but my fellow accused would have none of this and limited me to two days. I did not have hunger pains — I hadn't continued long enough for that, but my mind did feel cloudy and I was certainly very sick after the first cup of tea, for which I had longed so much. The worst aspect of it all for Hannah and me was that we crept into corners to eat because we couldn't bear the other women to see us when they were so hungry. We tried to expiate our guilt by carrying cups of water to the strikers, watching them grow weaker and weaker.

Just as the strike ended, Hannah was deported and left for England. We realised just what she had meant to all of us and missed her enormously.

I went into the witness box at last, in a state of absolute fright. I remember sitting during the lunch break, miserably reading the notes which I could not use. Then Nelson came over to me, took them out of my hand and ordered me into the yard to play scrabble. I relaxed then and became conscious of the warm support and affection of my fellow accused. I knew that I belonged with them, they trusted me and I must speak for them. I must not fail them.

Chapter XI

Witness for freedom

When I began to give evidence, my knees were actually trembling for the first time in my life. Somehow I managed to make my opening statement: I did not accept any of the Minister of Justice's assurances that I should not suffer any disabilities, such as further detention, from giving evidence during the Emergency. I added that I had no confidence whatsoever in his bona fides. It seemed to be a pretty bold statement but I wanted to make it.

I explained how I had become politically involved and also my functions in the Congress of Democrats and the Federation of South African Women. I said that I had no faith in a spontaneous voluntary change of heart by the white electorate. I believed that pressure, economic and moral, from outside and within South Africa, could bring about a change of mind. I added that this would obviously involve non-violent extra-parliamentary pressure in the form of strikes, boycotts and civil disobedience from the voteless four-fifths of the population. I denied any suggestion that the congresses were "bent upon a violent and forcible revolution" — a quotation from the Crown's opening address. Our aim was to establish a multiracial democracy through universal franchise. I denied that we wished to substitute a communist state for the present state. Our aim was to work for a state on the lines of the Freedom Charter but that the people must be free to choose for themselves the nature of the state they wanted.

I testified to Congress activity at length, especially the Western Areas Removal and the Bantu education protests and the campaign against passes for African women. Judge Rumpff and Judge Bekker asked me many questions. This was a great strain and I dreaded their interventions, sometimes confusing myself in my desperate attempt to make them understand what it was all about. I hated the distance between the witness box and the dock where my friends sat. They were so far away and the judges so close.

When Judge Rumpff asked me in what way I used the word "socialist", I replied that I used it in the sense of a greater sharing amongst the people which would require the nationalisation of some of the resources but I did not use it to the total exclusion of private enterprise.

I also had to answer searching questions on Robert Resha's speech to the volunteers in which he had said, "when you are disciplined and you are told by the organisation not to be violent, you must not be violent. If you are a true volunteer and you are called upon to be violent, then you must murder, murder!" For the prosecution this was the most important piece of evidence against us. To me it was so clear. Perhaps it was because I knew Robert so well. I knew of his passion for discipline and obedience and his whole speech seemed to me to be set in that context, not in the context of violence. The image was indeed a violent one, but it was an extreme example and nothing more. I realised that I did not convince the judges of this.

As the days went by — and they seemed to go very slowly — I became more relaxed. I replied to Farid's questions, so carefully prepared beforehand, to bring out our policies, our ideals, to destroy the terrible smears contained in the prosecution's opening address. I was proud to be part of the Congress Alliance. We had nothing to hide and here was the opportunity to affirm what we stood for, what we were fighting to achieve, a truly democratic state on the lines of the Freedom Charter.

It had taken five days of giving evidence to cover all that we wanted to put before the court and it seemed that their lordships became mighty tired of it. Occasionally Judge Rumpff would try to head Farid off, but he clung on doggedly, leading me through every section of the Freedom Charter.

We covered almost every aspect of the Congress activities and then went on to the council meeting of the Women's International Democratic Federation in Geneva and my speech there and also to my article "Women against Passes". According to the indictment, part of my speech and part of the article were both overt acts of treason.

Whenever the judges intervened with their questions, I wondered where they were leading me to and I became defensive. Always at the back of my mind was the knowledge that my answers could affect not only my own trial, but the fate of twenty-nine others. It was a heavy responsibility.

On the sixth day, Farid ended his questions and I became a witness under cross-examination by my fellow accused. Then everything changed. I had not known that I should be separated from the other accused. In later political trials this was not allowed, but we did not know we could challenge it. It meant being brought separately to court, sitting apart from my friends in the recesses, even eating my food sitting apart. It felt like a bad dream to be so cut off.

The accused cross-examined me for two days. Their questions were simple and direct. They wanted to tell the court, through me, of the conditions in which they lived, the injustices they suffered, so that the groundwork of all our activities should become clear; it was the desire for their human rights to be achieved peacefully, and not by violence.

They questioned me on farm labour, on the Western Areas Removals, on trade unions, on passes. It seemed to me that they were painting a picture, each one adding some strokes of the paintbrush. It was so different from the picture of South Africa which Murray had tried to paint. I wondered, not for the first time, whether their lordships could remain unmoved, could not see that it was South Africa that was on trial, not us, and that *we* were presenting the true indictment.

After this, Advocate Liebenberg began my cross-examination for the prosecution. I was thankful that it was not Advocate Trengove, the prosecutor who had cross-examined Chief Luthuli so aggressively, and felt that I ought to be able to handle this counsel's questions fairly well. My strength lay in the knowledge that I was telling the truth, simply trying to make everything clear and showing the falseness of the allegations of violence, of hostile intent to overthrow the present state by force.

Most of the cross-examination was directed towards the Congress of Democrats, attempting to show it as a communist-led organisation or a communist front. Often it became a debate of semantics. I was hammered on the meaning of words, of democracy and people's democracy, capitalism, imperialism, colonialism — and what I understood by them. What did my organisation mean by them? I sometimes felt that I could stand it no longer and had to resist an urge to walk right out of the witness box and out of the court! I knew, of course, that I should not get very far!

I fought my own battle against the quotations torn from our speeches, always demanding to see the whole document so as to put the quotation into context.

Sometimes Liebenberg accused me of dishonesty. "You are not telling us all you know . . . you seem to be abysmally ignorant of the policies of your organisation." Once I had to face forty-five minutes of uninterrupted questions from the judges. I almost broke down, but I only openly became tearful after reaching gaol.

As I anticipated, I had to face extensive questioning on my two "overt" acts; the quotation from my Geneva speech with reference to the Sophiatown removals being "the spark that might set off a mighty conflagration," and the quotation I had put into the women's mouths in my article, "what shall we do when we are told to carry passes?" Had I not clearly invited violence in the first quotation? Had I not encouraged illegal activity by suggesting that the women should refuse passes in the second?

I knew clearly what I had meant, but under the insidious heavy pressure of questions from the prosecuting advocate and the judges, I became somewhat confused and my answers less clear. It went on so long. I wished the clock would move faster. It was exhausting and each recess was a respite but I could never relax completely. As the days went by I felt my responsibility to my friends heavily and feared I might in some way be letting them down. The courtroom became that complex of attack and defence I had read about, but I had never expected to be a participant, fighting for ideals which most people in the civilised world took for granted.

Judge Rumpff also questioned me searchingly on my views on armed struggle — which would be of prime importance, the achievement of liberation or the method of achievement? I replied that I would not support violence to achieve liberation. I said that even if an oppressed people had arms and could shorten the struggle, I still would not support an armed conflict, even if the non-violent struggle took longer. I said that the aim would be less important than the fact that human life could be lost and suffering imposed. I would both regret and condemn any movement by the people to start an armed conflict, no matter for what purpose. I meant every word of it then, for the possibility that the ANC and its allies would eventually be compelled to involve themselves in armed struggle had not yet even been considered. I did not foresee the escalation of both institutional and actual violence by the government and the police which followed Sharpeville. I did not foresee the spiral of violence which was to come so soon.

On the fourteenth day my sojourn in the witness box was over and I could be with the other accused again. They gave me a great welcome, almost mobbing me. "Undented and undaunted!" cried Duma Nokwe, high praise indeed. I could hardly believe it. I had not failed them. There was much joy in our gaol, too, that my ordeal was over. From the gaol canteen we ordered supplementary food in addition to our rations and a celebration supper was cooked for me.

When we had been three months in detention, rumours of release began to circulate, yet the Emergency still showed no signs of ending. We had made a life of our own in gaol, as well as in court, sharing our chores and our cooking, playing bridge and scrabble, and endlessly knitting. I was given fewer chores and excused from cooking because of my long hours away at court. "Cooking" is perhaps not a good description, because all we could do was to improve the prison rations with what we bought from the canteen. Nevertheless, some surprisingly tasty dishes were concocted.

Then great news came: 1,200 detainees were to be released; on 1 July the prison matron told us, "everyone is going home except Joseph." It was a bad moment, but in the event I was not left alone at first because Yetta was held for another three weeks. It seemed to be only the treason trialists who were not to be released. When Yetta had gone, torn between her joy at going home and her grief at leaving me, I was truly alone, except for the time spent at the trial. Lilian was alone too. We had no contact with each other once inside the gaol gates.

At court things had changed. When so many detainees were released, it appeared that the end of the Emergency might possibly be very near. We called our legal counsel back and they studied the record of our evidence. Their immediate reaction was strong disapproval of Judge Rumpff's extensive questioning of our witnesses, especially Chief and me.

This led to an application for Judge Rumpff to recuse himself from the trial on the grounds that his questioning had given rise to a reasonable fear in our minds that we were not obtaining a fair trial. We believed that the judge did not approach our witnesses with impartiality and that he was leaning towards the prosecution. It was a startling application and one that needed courage, conviction and integrity for it to be made at all by a senior counsel to the presiding judge of the court, who was at the same time the Judge President of the Transvaal.

Bram Fischer made the application, and even though it proved unsuccessful, we admired and loved him more than ever for undertaking it for us. Judge Rumpff denied that his questioning of me amounted to cross-examination. He claimed that it was an example of "bringing the witness back patiently to a particular question . . . the witness did not give a simple answer." That might well have been true, but he did not ask simple questions. To me his questioning felt much more like cross-examination than anything Liebenberg achieved.

As the trial proceeded, several of my fellow accused went into the witness box. Nelson Mandela gave impressive evidence on the whole history of the non-violent policy of the African National Congress. It was inspiring to watch Nelson there, so completely at his ease, handling his cross-examination with calm confidence, based on his experience as a Congress leader for many years. Sometimes he was moved to anger, as once when Judge Rumpff suggested that to give the vote to people without education would be like giving it to children. We were all incensed at this suggestion for among the accused there were two greatly respected leaders, elderly men who had never been to school. They spent many of their detention days learning to read and write. We felt, as Nelson did, that this was a gratuitous insult to them and to us all.

Listening to Nelson, I realised again the grandeur and prestige of the African National Congress. Even though I was banned, detained and facing a charge of high treason, I wondered how I could ever have deserved to be so honoured as to be close to these leaders of the Congress Alliance. How could I really have come so far in less than ten years, after my fruitless existence during so many years of my life?

Soon after Nelson, Robert Resha went into the witness box. As soon as Trengove began the cross-examination, the tension was obvious. Robert was militant, contemptuous, and the mutual antagonism flared frequently. It was somehow not Robert testifying to the court, but Robert versus Trengove. There was never "My Lords" to the judges, as demanded by court protocol. Even Judge Rumpff gave up and suggested amiably that perhaps it would be better if this witness did not address anyone. But it made no difference; it was a contemptuous "Mr Trengove" to the end.

Robert admitted honestly that he had sometimes gone too far in his speeches. He acknowledged that he had then gone outside Congress policy and had afterwards accepted criticism from his leaders. But he had known what it was to come back to Sophiatown to find his home destroyed, his furniture out in the street and his family looking for some place to sleep.

He rejected the evidence of his speeches as reported by detectives. "God alone knows what I did say," he said. He had some grave doubts himself about the policy of non-violence in the face of government brutality. "Sometimes I feel that we too have the right to use violence." Yet he accepted that the ANC policy of non-violence was the only wise policy.

While Robert was still in the witness box, the Emergency came at last to its end. On 31 August, we knew that it would be over on the following day. We had been held for a full five months without a charge being brought against us.

Being already on trial for treason had nothing at all to do with our detention. Together with 2,000 others, we were simply the victims of the proclaimed State of Emergency after Sharpeville, where the violence had been perpetrated by the police, not by us. But the political climate had been created, the public thrown into a state of panic which made this violation of justice possible. For us, our trial had proved a partial relief from the confinement in gaol, but for all those others, detention had meant living under gaol conditions for endless weeks, allowed only limited visits from families, and deprived of access to news or knowledge of what was going on outside the gaols, or what the future might hold.

We did not know that this was only the partial shape of things to come. We could not foresee that the next decade would bring even harsher conditions of detention, that there would be those who would suffer unimaginable physical torture during interrogation, that there would be men who would die strange deaths in detention. We did not know that Caleb Mayekiso, a treason trialist, with us every day for all those years, would one day die in detention and the truth of his death would never be known.

Chapter XII

Can we be free?

The State of Emergency was over. Lilian and I came out of gaol together on the morning of 31 August and climbed into the police van for the last time, taking with us our many packages accumulated over five months. Mine had to include groceries, a scrabble board, jigsaw puzzles, books and magazines left behind when the other women returned home, for nothing at all could be left in gaol. It seemed bizarre that after five months, there must be no trace whatever of my ever having been there.

At the men's gaol, we found most of our friends waiting outside in the street for us, for the last ride in the "singing lorry". We had sung freedom songs every day, down to the court and back again. Our police driver had been delighted, encouraging us to "sing up, chaps". He was a friendly simple soul and he was genuinely sorry to say goodbye to us, but glad for our sakes that we were free again. So we sang loudly that day, triumphant as we trundled through the Pretoria streets.

Some of the accused had decided to walk down to the court, just to be able to walk in the streets again, they said. We met, outside the court this time, and went to the café opposite for a "freedom" coffee. I walked twice across the road and back, just because it felt so good to be free.

Yet of course we were not really free at all. We were still on trial, listening now to our own evidence, inspired by it, nearing the end of the trial, but not knowing what the next few months might bring — acquittal or conviction?

I don't think we listened very much that morning, even to Robert's evidence. Our eyes were constantly turning to the public gallery, rapidly filling up with the friends and families who had come to take us home.

Violet Weinberg came for me; we had last seen each other two months ago when she left our gaol with the other detainees on release. Humanity, for once, broke into the formality of the court and there was no afternoon session.

There were many friends to be seen on my return to Johannesburg. I first collected my car and then drove happily around the city. It was good that I had not had to leave anyone behind in gaol — that must have been very hard. I called in at the Medical Aid Society office to greet the staff and make arrangements to resume the early morning and late evening sessions the next day. Life had so quickly become relatively normal again that the memory of the past five months began to fade away.

The next day we were back in court. Nelson, Robert, Farid, Stanley and I had driven again along the Pretoria road, checking that "our" houses had been properly looked after in our absence! At court we were still catching up on the news which we had gathered only in snatches for so long. Judge Rumpff agreed to our request that the court should not sit on the Friday, so as to give the men from the Eastern Cape an extra day to spend with their families at the weekend.

We noticed Advocate de Vos, another member of the prosecution team, coming into court, inexplicably almost staggering under a huge pile of books, obviously law books. Just before four o'clock, when the court was about to adjourn, this little advocate with a Grecian profile, which we had had so much time to study, rose to his feet and stunned everyone by demanding that all the accused should be returned to gaol, because we were still legally in custody and no longer on bail.

It took a little while for this to sink in. Must we really go back to gaol? What did he mean about our bail? We saw it as a dastardly trick on the part of the government. We despised the prosecution counsel for being party to it. Was the government now afraid that we might be acquitted after the inept presentation of the Crown case? Were they determined to have us in gaol for many more months, in addition to the five we had already spent there? Was this part of the plan for ending the Emergency; to let everyone else go and keep us in?

I think our defence counsel were as angry as we were. Maisels argued vehemently that this could not be. Bail had fallen away when the first indictment had been withdrawn, it had in fact been refunded and we were merely coming to court on summons. Few of us had realised this and I thought again of what an extraordinary group of traitors we were, all coming to our trial without compulsion.

During the short, critical recess, while we were waiting for the judges' finding, we trooped across the road to the café for what might be our last cup of "freedom" coffee, so soon after the first. I don't think it even occurred to any of us to slip away while we were still free. Perhaps we were too conditioned to facing the trial to the end, perhaps it showed our complete and unbreakable solidarity with each other? I don't know the right answer, maybe a little of both.

By seven o'clock our anxiety was over. The prosecution had failed and we were still free. Maisels had cut the prosecution down to size. It all seemed to symbolise the whole structure of this unreal trial, becoming more abortive as the weeks went by. Our defence was growing in stature, yet the Crown would not let us go.

On our return to court, after our nearly wrecked long weekend, Professor Matthews, "ZK" as he was affectionately known to so many, the wise elder statesman of the ANC, came into the witness box. Thickset and powerfully built, sophisticated and urbane, he was academically head and shoulders above every other person in the court room. Our defence counsel led him through his illustrious career, from being the first African graduate of the University of South Africa, to the invitations to visit the United States as a visiting professor, through the many requests from overseas for attendance at various world conferences, some of which he had been unable to attend because of the withdrawal of his passport by the police. He had been a member of the ANC executive committee for many years and Cape President for ten years.

I remembered, almost with astonishment, that this was the man who, like us, had been held in gaol for three weeks at the beginning of this trial, had sat through the long preparatory examination and the first part of the trial in Pretoria, so was still one of the sixty whose fate depended upon ours and had been detained in gaol during the Emergency. It didn't fit in with his incomparable academic record.

Completely at his ease, the Professor sat with folded arms in the witness box, though of course on the black side. He might have been participating in some high-level world conference, or just sitting comfortably in his study, dealing with some undergraduate student — which was indeed the impression he created when replying to his cross-examiner, Advocate Hoexter.

In five days, Professor Matthews not only testified to the ANC policy of non-violence, but established it so firmly that the prosecutor could not make any dents in it. At the suggestion, once, that volunteers were being trained for violence, he exclaimed, "preposterous!" It was preposterous. "Not Africa for the Africans only," declared the Professor, "but Africa for the Africans too." He affirmed that the ANC feared that a violent revolution would leave an aftermath of bitterness like that which had followed the Anglo-Boer war between the Afrikaners and the British.

It was Professor Matthews who had introduced the idea of a Congress of the People at an ANC conference in the Eastern Cape in 1953. It should be a convention of all people, of all races, to draw up a charter for a democratic future. He said that he had been satisfied with the way the Congress of the People had been carried out; the motivation of the Freedom Charter had been the actual grievances of the people and each clause related to one of these grievances. Although he himself did not believe that nationalisation would be the solution to economic problems, he dismissed as entirely wrong any suggestion that its inclusion in the Freedom Charter might derive from communist influence. It was a world trend.

Listening to our star witness, I think some of us went into a state of euphoria. How could the Crown case possibly stand up to this? We closed our defence on this high note. Now only the last act was still to be played out on this strange stage, a synagogue which had become a court, yet so familiar to us that it had become part of our lives.

We had a strange feeling that there was nothing more the defence could do. We had given our evidence, defended ourselves and our organisation and affirmed our principles. Now the Crown must prove its case, once and for all. Our defence counsel would reply and then — the judgement.

It was a bitter experience to hear the prosecution condemn our struggle as violent, communist manipulated and indoctrinated, ruthless, subversive and treasonable. We knew it wasn't true, but we had to listen to weeks of Crown argument, smearing our organisations, before the prosecutor came to us as individuals. A good deal of this part of the argument was concerned with what the prosecutor assessed as our degree of communism or communist influence. The shades ranged from palest pink to rosy red, and there were quite a few surprises in store for some of us.

Because we were accused of being members of a conspiracy to overthrow the state by violence, the Crown had to show what knowledge any of us had of this alleged policy of violence. Sometimes it seemed to put us into a world of fantasy, of imagination, so unreal was it.

The prosecution could not do much with Robert Resha in the realm of communism. I never thought they could, and he came out only the palest of pinks, but the prosecutor relied on his fiery speeches to show that he incited the African youth to commit violence and was part of the conspiracy. His evidence was rejected, as indeed was the case with most of us who had been defence witnesses. It did not take long to get the point. When we disagreed with the Crown counsel, then we were simply untruthful or evasive.

When it came to my turn, the main point was that I was highly educated and had wide knowledge. I had, therefore, understood all the treasonable implications of the liberation struggle — and presumably also of the treasonable conspiracy. The prosecution counsel said that I was one of the most active members of the liberation struggle, and I felt that this was high praise indeed. He said that I had been untruthful in my evidence on the speeches I had heard at meetings, but he conceded that I was not a communist in the sense that I understood communist doctrine. I wondered whether I could perhaps be called an uncomprehending communist? My crime was that I had adhered to the conspiracy. I wondered too, whether the emphasis on my education, experience and understanding perhaps only meant that I was old enough to know better.

Nelson's powerful and positive evidence caused difficulty for the Crown, but he did not escape being painted red. The prosecutor insisted that he "KNEW" and accepted the communist doctrine of violent revolution. Because of his banning, however, he had made no speeches and the Crown could do little beyond allege his adherence to the conspiracy and his "hostile state of mind".

The prosecution did not get very far with Lilian either; she came out of it almost lily white. No argument on communism was led against her, despite her visit to the Soviet Union and to China. But, like Robert, she was alleged to have been an inciter to violent revolution and this was enough to include her in the conspiracy.

There we were, as the Crown saw us, all members of a conspiracy to overthrow the state by violence. The Congress of the People and the Freedom Charter had also been in pursuance of the conspiracy because the new state we envisaged was to be founded on the principles of the charter. We "KNEW" that our methods would lead to violent conflict with the state and we had intended to provoke it. We had no genuine belief in non-violence. This obviously made us a bunch of traitors, of varying shades of communism.

It had taken the prosecution team four months just to argue its case against us. Our defence counsel had argued in reply for only two weeks when the judges announced that they wished to consider the position so far and see whether it might be unnecessary to hear any further argument from the defence. The court was then adjourned until the following week.

We were all taken by surprise. Bram Fischer had prepared an argument on our speeches which, he said, would take a month to present, but he only got through a few days of it. Yet our counsel were actually triumphant, assuring us that this move of the judges could only mean acquittal. Despite what we had learnt of court matters during the past years, we were almost unwilling to believe it. We scattered for those few days, not knowing what to expect.

On 29 March 1961 we returned to court, and this time we all travelled together in the treason bus and came singing to the end of our trial as we had come singing to its beginning. It did not take long — only about thirty minutes for us to listen to the judgement. I found it difficult to follow and my hopes went up and down, uncertain of the outcome, until we rose to our feet for the verdict. "You are found not guilty and discharged and you may go." For us, some of the most beautiful words in the English language.

The Crown had failed to prove that the African National Congress intended, as a matter of policy, to achieve a new state by violent means. There was no conspiracy and there were no traitors. We could all go home. Yet, for more than four years of our lives we had been absorbed by this incredible, monumental folly of a treason trial.

Our defence counsel had been brilliant, had routed the prosecution. The ideas and the beliefs of our organisation had proved unassailable. Berrangé had said in his opening address, so long ago: "in the result, this trial will be answered in the right way, by history". It had been so. History had itself supplied the answer.

Yet it was a bitter and costly victory, after years of frustration, anxiety, deprivation, for so many. The state had failed to break our solidarity, it had indeed strengthened it, but there had been grim periods when our enforced personal inactivity had been hard to bear — the defection of the Pan Africanists, Sharpeville, the long months of detention when leadership was needed to keep the liberation struggle going forward.

For Lilian and me, especially, it had been almost unbearable that the great passive resistance of the Johannesburg women against passes had come and gone while we were still on trial. Now we were free again, but I was still banned, there were many others banned, and legal repression was mounting rapidly, year by year. The ANC Women's League had been banned along with the ANC, and it would take months of intensive organising to repair this damage to the Federation.

Our legal victory and the vindication of our organisations was celebrated nationwide, especially in Soweto, where it was said that there was a party in every home on the night of 29 March. We had carried our defence team, shoulder high, out of the treason court. We had taken our last ride in the treason bus, all of us together, not even remembering to look at "our" houses along the way. We thought sadly of Elias Moretsele, who had died only two weeks before, an old tired man. Perhaps it was those long journeys which shortened his life and deprived him of the joy of knowing he was acquitted.

It was good to be back in my office and have time in the evenings and at weekends to be with friends. It was a great relief to be finished with the trial summaries, but I missed my trial companions as we slipped back into our normal lives. Yet not all of us. There were several of us who had still to face months of unemployment, of further dependence on wives or families who had shouldered family responsibilities during those years. I realised how fortunate I had been to have kept my job. It had meant hard work, but others had not even had that opportunity.

March 1961 was the month of triumph, not only for our acquittal, but for the holding of the All-in Conference in Natal. In the last weekend of the trial, Nelson Mandela had slipped away to Pietermaritzburg. His five-year ban had expired, apparently unnoticed and certainly unrenewed by the authorities, and he was free, not only to leave Johannesburg, but also to attend and address a gathering.

The All-in Conference had been intended to be a widely representative gathering, but in the event it became almost a Congress assembly, with hundreds of former ANC members representing groups from all areas. The idea of broad participation, which had promoted the conference, had not been able to stand up to the enthusiastic support from the former ANC members. Indeed what else could really have been expected from a banned mass organisation? Former PAC members made only a token showing, due perhaps in part to PAC's immature organisation, even before it was banned, and in part to its unwillingness to accept that the ANC still dominated the political scene.

The conference was a great success, notable for its spirit of defiance and determination, calling for a national convention of all races to decide upon a representative constitution for South Africa. Nelson made a charismatic surprise appearance. It must have been an unforgettable experience for him after so many years of bans, but it proved to be his last public appearance in South Africa. After our acquittal he disappeared, to continue leading the struggle from underground, sacrificing any return to normal family life.

From that All-in Conference came the demand for a truly national convention of all races. If the government did not heed this call before 31 May, the date set for the proclamation of the Republic of South Africa, then there were to be country-wide demonstrations against the government and a call for a stay-at-home from work.

The government replied to this demand in its usual way, by a show of police strength, nationwide police raids on homes and offices, mass arrests for pass laws infringement, with nearly 10,000 people in gaol. This time the police action was on an unprecedented scale. Police leave was cancelled and the army rode around black townships in tanks in a demonstration of armed force.

All meetings were banned from 19 May to 26 June, thus carefully eliminating any celebrations of the Congress of the People on 26 June. There was also new legislation to provide for twelve days in gaol before any arrested person need be brought to court. Hitherto the maximum period had been only two days. White reaction was to hoard food and buy guns.

The National Action Council elected at the conference was undaunted, and called for a three-day stay-at-home on the eve of the proclamation of the Republic. The PAC took the shameful way of destructive opposition through leaflets issued from underground, calling upon the people to go to work and not stay at home. This political scabbing, by the very organisation which had brought about Sharpeville, aroused a new, deep and lasting resentment in the ANC.

Some of my white friends went into hiding as soon as the twelve-day detention before trial was legalised. Several of them had been detained in 1960, others feared their first detention, or feared that the twelve-day period might be extended. Hiding was not a possibility for me, even if I had thought it politically correct — which I did not — for I had to be at work, except for the three days of the stay-at-home. What then would be the purpose of hiding in the evenings? All the same, I dreaded detention and found myself listening to the sounds of cars stopping in the street outside my house, relieved when there was only the sound of one car door shutting, a little apprehensive if I heard two doors, because that might mean the police.

The Congress of Democrats took a militant stand, or tried to! We drafted a leaflet to be thrown over the fence into the Johannesburg Union grounds where units of the Citizen Force were now encamped. The leaflet told the men to go home — and told them why. Our legal advisers, however, clamped down on us, pointing out that this would legally be an incitement to mutiny. With great reluctance we gave up the plan.

The result of the stay-at-home was not surprising in the face of such intensive intimidation of all kinds. The protest had not achieved a national proportion, it was not a mass response, yet there was a positive response in many quarters and the call had by no means gone unheeded. Thousands of workers had stayed away from their jobs on that first day and many even on the second, despite propaganda from the media and armed intimidation by the police. In fact, the radio proclaimed it a failure at six o'clock on the morning of the first day, something which, at that hour, no one could have assessed.

It was not the national protest that had been hoped for, but it certainly cast a deep shadow over the celebrations of Republic Day and it posed a question that now required an answer. Was the peaceful protest of the past fifty years still effective or even possible in the face of the use of armed force by the state? The question had indeed been asked ever since Sharpeville. "As long as the grievances remain," said Nelson from underground, "there will be protest actions of this kind or another. If peaceful protests like these are to be put down by the mobilisation of the army and the police, then the people might be forced to use other methods of struggle."

Nelson's statement forced me to question my own position. I had affirmed in my treason trial evidence that I stood unequivocally for non-violence and against an armed struggle. And yet, in the face of all the armed might called up against a peaceful protest, was I going to be able to maintain my stand? Could I still be loyal to the ANC if it moved away from its commitment of non-violence? Could I still believe that non-violence could lead to peaceful change?

I had always relied on the example of India's non-violent struggle and its achievement of independence peacefully. Now I could see that the Indian government's response to non-violent protest, to passive resistance, had nothing in common with South Africa's brutal methods and use of armed force and nationwide intimidation.

The ANC found its own answer. It had been established and maintained on the policy of non-violence and it could not move from this standpoint, could not itself undertake violence. But it could no longer disapprove of properly controlled violence, nor discipline its members engaging in it.

Umkhonto We Sizwe, the Spear of the Nation, came into being to undertake sabotage of government buildings and installations because this did not involve loss of life. It might even avoid bitterness between the races and, hopefully, compel the white voters to think again. Umkhonto was to operate separately from the underground ANC, under its own high command. It would not be confined to Africans, although obviously many ANC members would participate in its activities.

The idea of destroying installations was a form of violent action that I could accept. In fact, I did not see it as actual violence because it was aimed at things, not people. I was in favour of attacking government property. Umkhonto solved my problem. It seemed to me that there might still be room for non-violent activities, protest, strikes, propaganda, meetings, and with sabotage support they might prove more effective.

The beginning of sabotage came at the end of the year, planned for 16 December, the Afrikaners' celebration of their Day of the Covenant and their victory over the Zulu King, Dingaan. Needless to say, Africans see this day differently. On the Day of the Covenant, government buildings in Durban, Johannesburg and Port Elizabeth were bombed and considerable damage inflicted.

Chapter XIII

Journey to the banished

At long last 1962 arrived and I could say to myself, "It's THIS year" — this year that my bans would end and I would be free again, free to leave Johannesburg, to attend meetings. The last year had brought home to me, more than any of the previous years, that I was restricted. Until that year the trial had gathered us all together in a sort of family circle which filled the greater part of our days; for me, my Medical Aid Society work and the treason trial summaries filled the other part. I really had not had time before to feel the true pinch of the bans, but once the trial was over, I found it galling to be so restricted, especially not to be able to attend meetings. It was becoming more and more difficult for me to maintain close contact with the Federation and the Congress of Democrats.

My efforts turned now to the banished African people, for in addition to bans there was another harassment of political leaders, especially in rural areas, but also amongst a few trade unionists and Congress leaders. The Nationalist government had chosen to invoke the power of banishment under the 1927 Native Administration Act, passed thirty years ago. This empowered the Governor General to order any tribe or native to proceed forthwith to any designated place and not to leave it again except by permission. The effect of this Act was that any African could be taken without prior notice from his home, with only what possessions could be carried, to be dumped anywhere within South Africa. The banishment order was sometimes served at the home, sometimes at the Native Commissioner's office, but the result was the same.

No specific reason for the banishment was given, only the statement that the removal was in the interests of maintaining peace and good order in the tribe. There was never any previous warning, nor any provision for the wife to accompany the banished man. When the order was served at the Commissioner's office, the banished man left with nothing but the clothes he wore. He was not even taken home to collect some belongings. His wife was not informed of what had happened, he simply did not return home.

Banishment was also inflicted on a few women leaders. One spent more than two years trying to be united with her already banished husband. Another had a husband serving a long gaol sentence. She was banished, together with her young son and daughter, who were both still at school. The girl was only sixteen, but nevertheless she received a banishment order saying that her presence was inimical to the preservation of peace and good order. At sixteen! Yet another banished woman was the widowed chieftainess of the Matlala tribe. Eventually I heard these tragic stories, so poignantly told, from the women themselves.

The wives of the banished men remained behind to gather up the tattered pieces of their lives, to bring up their children and to cling to their land in the tribal area. They dared not leave permanently to be with their husbands.

The dumping grounds were usually empty huts on remote government-owned farms, held in "trust" for some future allocation to the black population. The place selected for each person, obviously by design, would be where the language spoken in the area was almost foreign to the banished man. The opportunities, even for rough farm labour, were very scarce and ill paid, mostly non-existent. Neighbours were few and distant.

These banished people were indeed the forgotten people. Press reports, however, began to appear, telling of destitution, utter loneliness, bare existence on low wages or government allowances of £2 a month only, sometimes. The ANC called for a committee to find the banished people and to care for them when found. Lilian and I were asked to establish the committee and we found friends willing to join us. The Human Rights Welfare Committee was formed to help the few banished people we knew about through the press, and to find the rest.

Only the Department of Native Affairs knew where all these people had been taken. Enquiries for information brought a Chinese puzzle reply. Seventy-five men and five women had been "removed" (the official term for banishment) from twenty-six different places to twenty-seven other places. The names of the banished and lists of the places were given, but there was no information about who had been removed or where they had been taken. It seemed, at first, a hopeless task to sort this out and it took a long time.

Our first contacts with the banished people brought a shocking reply, "I have been banished to a remote area. I am thirty-nine miles from the nearest town and any transport. Before my departure I received £2. I have since received no assistance whatsoever. The nearest telephone in case of emergency is over the mountain. Life here is not worth living." As the contact grew slowly with the banished men and women, the horror of their lives became clearer. There was little we could do, even after both the banished man and his family had been located, beyond sending money, clothes and food.

Perhaps the worst aspect was the indefiniteness. The banishment order remained in force until the government gave permission for the banished man to return home. There was no term to this hell of desolation.

The banished people became very important to me as contact by letter grew through the committee and we gradually uncovered the whereabouts of these abandoned men. The message was slowly reaching them that there were people who had not forgotten them. "We are made people again" wrote one man in reply to my first letter to him. The task of finding them was no longer as hopeless as it had seemed in the beginning. Visits to some were being organised and the ugly picture was becoming clearer, the picture of banishment, how it operated and what it really meant to its victims.

The Act had been used against 116 people during the past twelve years, not eighty as claimed by the government. Over forty persons were still banished, some for more than eight years. Eleven had died in lonely exile and forty-one had been released and had returned to their people, but with the threat of re-banishment hanging over their heads. Six were still missing and could not be traced unless the authorities disclosed their whereabouts, which had not been done so far. A few had fled this unkind land and were struggling for existence elsewhere.

It was true, of course, as the government claimed, that there was nothing to prevent the wives from visiting their husbands — nothing but the fact that there was no money for food and education, let alone for travelling thousands of miles. The families of the banished were left destitute. Sometimes they were not even allowed to plough and the government-appointed chiefs took their land away or burnt or confiscated their huts.

The children of these people grew up without education because there was no money for school fees or books. When the families were not even allowed to plough, they lived on the charity of friends and relations. And even when some of the banished men were allowed to return home they found ruin and destitution and had to start again — with nothing.

For many of the wives there was no contact by letter with their men and they were not told where they were. There was nothing but silence. Some of the banished men were illiterate, sometimes barely able to write a few words in their own language and there was no one to write a letter home for them.

In Parliament, the Minister of Native Affairs said, when challenged about the banishments, "They are not prisoners." Yet when one of them was visited, his friends were not allowed to speak to him in his own language unless every word was translated for the benefit of the three policemen who remained throughout the visit. Not a prisoner?

Sometimes the banished men lived in exquisitely beautiful surroundings, waterfalls, mountain streams, luxuriant bush country, or maybe beside the blue Indian ocean. But the greenest of willow trees, the loveliness of the low veld, cannot ease the ache in the heart of a man for his home, for his children. "I want to see my children," they said sadly. "I want to go home."

My mind was full of all this. I had arranged a few visits for others through my contacts with the banished and I asked myself why I should not go too. My bans would end on 30 April 1962, and I wanted to see it all for myself. I wrote urgent letters to the addresses that I knew, made special arrangements about contacting the banished men when I reached their areas and planned a complete and comprehensive itinerary, covering the Northern and Eastern Transvaal, Swaziland, Natal, Lesotho (the British Protectorate of Basutoland, as it was then), the Transkei and the Northern Cape.

I invited Joe Morolong of the ANC and Amina Cachalia of the Indian Congress, for the tour. Joe had been amongst the accused in the first part of the treason trial, until the case was withdrawn against him at the end of the preparatory examination. He had already visited two banishment camps in the Northern Cape for us, with visitors whom we had sent. I knew that he was free to come with us for he was living in his home area, having been deported from Cape Town for his political activities. Joe was a lively companion for the trip, with valuable knowledge of African languages, though little knowledge, alas, of the mechanics of a car. I suppose he was in his thirties then. He was only too happy to come with us on this adventure.

Amina Cachalia was a member of the Human Rights Welfare Committee for the banished and also active in the Federation. She had herself served a gaol sentence when she was very young, in the Defiance Campaign of 1952, when she was included in the first batch of Indian women to court a gaol sentence. It is difficult now to describe how beautiful Amina was when we toured together. She is still beautiful today, with dark eyes and hair, a lovely smile that lights up her whole face. She seems untouched by time, but in 1962 she was at the peak of her beauty. Yet she was no delicate oriental flower, she was a sturdy comrade, ready for gaol or journey, full of laughter and fun, willing to face long tiring drives and completely undaunted by the accommodation problems of our racially-mixed trio.

As soon as we arrived, total strangers, in a Transvaal town, we would head for the Indian area, where Amina never failed to find friends or strangers who would offer us hospitality. Her husband, Yusuf Cachalia, was politically famous for his leadership in the Indian Congress and his name helped to open many doors for us.

I had bought a new car for the journey to replace the gallant "Treason Trixie" which had taken us on so many daily journeys to Pretoria for the treason trial. We left Johannesburg at dawn on 1 May after the expiry of my ban at midnight. It was only when we were safely out on the open road heading north that I became really aware that I was free at last, free to go anywhere I chose, with whom I chose, no longer confined to Johannesburg or banned from gatherings. I was excited about our tour and the adventures to come, but underneath there was a tremendous private joy. The bans were over and like the treason trial they faded into the past. I realised that they might be reimposed, especially in view of what I was doing in seeking out the banished people and their families, and I certainly intended to speak out about what I saw and heard when I returned. Somehow that did not matter as it was almost an occupational hazard and could not affect my present plans.

We had set ourselves a long trek for the first stage of our journey into the Northern Transvaal and then into Swaziland before going on to Durban. It took us almost two weeks. We met many people, the friends who offered us their generous hospitality, the contacts we made along the way, the banished men and, in other places, their families.

In Natal we met our beloved Chief Luthuli, President General of the African National Congress. He was restricted to the Groutville area, some miles from Stanger, where we had stayed overnight with Indian friends. Chief was banned from being with more than one person at a time, so we had to meet clandestinely by night, by special arrangement. We drove to Groutville through miles of sugarcane fields to stop on a curve of the road and wait for him.

Out of the darkness he came walking softly, and we heard him greet us. I could not see his face but to hear his voice was enough and to sit beside him as we crowded him into our car, always watching the road for the lights of any other approaching vehicle. Time was precious because Chief had risked disastrous consequences to see us and to hear our reports on the banished people whom we had seen. If we were all caught together then Chief could be charged with attending a gathering.

I told him of the Matlala people, deep in Northern Transvaal, hundreds of miles from Johannesburg, where we had visited the wives of men who had been banished eight and ten years previously. The sun had been shining brightly as we drove around the rocky hills to meet these lonely women. They had put on their brightest headscarves and their gayest beads to welcome us but as, one by one, they told us their tragic stories, with Joe interpreting, the sky seemed less blue and the gay colours only served to deepen the lines of sorrow on the dark faces. Sometimes tears trickled slowly down their cheeks as they spoke to us. Only one man had returned.

Mrs Sibija Matlala told us how an agricultural officer had come on a motor bike and told her husband to go to the police station at Sandfontein.

> Then he was taken away by train and I did not get a letter from him all the years afterwards. One day he walked back into the house. I thought it was a ghost and I got a shock. This was on a Monday. He collapsed on the floor and then he got up and asked, "How are you? How are the children?" He said he was well, but he was not well and he fell down again. He lay in bed for a week and then he died. He did not speak again after the first day.

When we asked how this dying man had reached his home, his wife told us that her husband had walked a few steps at a time and then sat down to rest. It had taken him nearly all day to walk the five miles from the bus to his home. We knew that Sibija Matlala had been released from the banishment camp at Driefontein, 1,000 miles away in the Northern Cape. Joe and our friends had visited the camp previously and found him there, even then too ill to move about. Yet that man had been put out of the camp to struggle home alone, only to die when he got there. We can only assume that the authorities did not want to have him die in the camp.

Another Matlala woman told us, "We were at home when the officer came in a government car and said to my husband, 'Stand up, let's go!' They wanted to take me too but when my husband knew that he was going to be sent far away, he would not allow them to take me. It was only after five years that I heard that he was still alive but now I do not hear from him at all." We said to her before we left, "Don't look so sad. We shall find your husband soon and you shall go and see him." Then she smiled for the first time.

We found him in the Eastern Transvaal, some hundreds of miles from his home and when we told him that we had seen his wife, he actually jumped for joy, this very little, very old man, well over eighty. He had served in the South African forces during the First World War in East Africa. He explained to us that he was a soldier and soldiers did not take their wives to war with them and that was why he left her behind when he was banished. Perhaps it was his age that had moved the officer even to suggest that his wife might accompany him. A tempering of cruelty with mercy? But Maema would have none of it.

I told Chief of others too, whom we had seen, of Chief Faku from the Transkei, now isolated on government property in the Northern Transvaal. His wife was with him but their little child had died. He wept as he told us how the baby had to be buried in the hospital grounds because the ground where he lived was too hard and stony to dig even so small a grave.

We had found Stephen Nkadimeng, a militant leader of his people, in Sekhukhuniland in the Northern Transvaal, but now living high up in the Pongola mountains on the border of Swaziland. It had taken us several hours to reach him and we had almost given up more than once. Then we found him, with his wife and children, many miles from the nearest village or any form of transport. His wife had followed him and I had seen her when she arrived in Johannesburg and put her on the train for Durban where other friends would put her on yet another train for Zululand.

This woman from the rural area was terrified of the city, and no wonder, for she had never even travelled on a train before, but she was quietly determined to get to her husband somehow. From the Zululand train terminal she walked up the mountain for thirty miles, her child on her back, her battered suitcase on her head. She could not speak the local language but somehow she made her way to Stephen.

There was no furniture in their hut except one wooden chair and a primus stove. Flattened cardboard cartons on the mud floor served as a bed and that was all there was. But Stephen's spirit was unbroken. He stood beside our car and said to me quietly as I left, "The struggle of my people goes on. I am satisfied."

There were others too, of whom there was no time to tell Chief. When I stopped he said quietly, "Thank you, Helen." It was enough. He had heard from us of the quiet courage of the banished men, of the bitter agony of their wives. Yet there was no bitterness in Chief, only compassion. He even rebuked me very gently for my angry desire to take revenge one day on those who had inflicted this dreadful suffering on others, so carelessly, so callously.

Then he left us again, fading into the darkness. We did not know that we should never see him again, that one day he would be struck down by a sugar train, perhaps even near the place where we had talked together by night in a car.

The next day we drove on to Durban to be with friends for a few days. I met the women of the Federation again, after five years, and some of our banned leaders of the Congress of Democrats. Amina left us to return to her family in Johannesburg and her place on our tour was taken by an overseas visitor, who almost reduced me to my old role of "wishy washy liberal" — so politically assured and well informed was she. Despite my years of association with above- and below-ground communists, I was still very vulnerable and aware of my deficiencies as an ideologue. However, Nan turned out to be a good-humoured travelling companion. We shared many jokes along the way despite my rather vain efforts to give her some in-depth understanding of the Women's Federation, what it was all about and why it had not developed along stereotyped separatist feminist lines.

We went on our way to Lesotho, to which some of the banished had fled, having been summarily "liberated" by well-meaning whites, moved by the press reports of suffering and desolation. Yet as refugees they were not materially better off, for Lesotho was a desperately poor country. I told Nan and Joe of Twalumfeni Joyi, banished to the dreary Kuruman country on the edge of the Kalahari desert. He wanted to take his few fowls along with him on his liberation journey, presumably squawking in the boot of a car as the border was crossed, silently, secretly, in the dead of night. It had been a hard task to persuade him to leave his fowls behind.

The banished refugees in Lesotho were poor, lonely and cut off from their families even more than before. I wanted particularly to see Elizabeth Mafeking, the militant trade union leader and Vice President of the Federation of South African Women. She had been banished in 1959, from Paarl in the Cape to a remote government farm in the Kuruman district. She had refused to go there, to take her eleven children to that desolate place.

In Paarl there had been a great outcry amongst the African and coloured workers against Elizabeth's banishment. There had been street riots and much police harassment. Elizabeth had slipped away at dawn one morning with her youngest child on her back and fled over the border, to hide at first in the Lesotho mountains. Most of her family joined her, but life was a hard struggle for existence, to feed all her children and herself. I remembered her so well from Federation days, barely forty then, always with her youngest child in her arms, but nevertheless a leader of women, and of men too, an eloquent speaker. It was sad to see her as a refugee, separated from South Africa, unhappy and homesick away from her people.

From Lesotho we went south to Port Elizabeth on our way to Cape Town, calling there again on our way back. The women had organised a great public meeting, solely by word of mouth; not a poster, not a placard, not a leaflet, no press announcement, yet the large hall was packed. The women wept at the tragic stories of the banished, but they sang for the freedom that would come to South Africa and all her people. Compassion and courage, these were the hallmarks of these women.

We had another 1,000 miles of our journey to do, but first back to Kingwilliamstown, to Kgagudi Maredi and another banished man from Sekhukhuniland, and also to Makwena Matlala, a banished chieftainess of the Matlala people. Maredi had been banished twice. He told us that when he was at the Royal Kraal in Sekhukhuniland, his banishment order had been brought by a colonel of the South African police, escorted by several vanloads of armed police. Like all the other banishment orders, it simply stated that his removal was in the interests of peace and good order — no details whatsoever. Together with his cousin, Maredi had at first refused to move from his land, but he had been overpowered by the police.

111

The police knocked me about very badly, I was bleeding. Then we were both put in leg irons and handcuffs. We were taken like this in a lorry to the nearest police station and from there in a closed van all the way to Ciskei (a journey of over a thousand miles). The leg irons were not taken off until we reached there and my cousin was left in one place and I was brought here.

A year later, Maredi was allowed to go back to Sekhukhuniland for a limited period, on condition that he would not hold or attend any tribal meetings and other such restrictions. After one year, he was told that he was the No. 1 Agitator and must return to banishment in Kingwilliamstown. He spoke sadly of his wife and children but he had no hope then of ever being allowed to return to them.

We had seen his wife in Sekhukhuniland, lonely and anxious. Her memories of the banishment of her husband were bitter and full of grief, for on neither occasion had he been permitted to come home to tell her of his removal. He had just disappeared.

From Kingwilliamstown, we went north into the Transkei to find another two men banished to the government farms in the foothills on the Lesotho border and then south to Pondoland on the coast to see the wives of some of the men we should find later in the banishment camps of Frenchdale and Driefontein, the last lap of our travels.

Our journey had not been totally without hindrance and police interference. That was to be expected, as all the banished people were in territory for which an official permit was needed for any entrance by a non-African. We knew that Amina, Nan and I would never have been granted such permits, so there was no need to waste time in applying for them. Risks simply had to be taken and we were extraordinarily fortunate to have been discovered only twice up to that stage.

The first time was in Zululand when we had just found the brother of Phikinkane Zulu, banished years before to Driefontein. We were standing on the road, talking to her, when I saw the police van coming towards us. There was no excuse, no escape possible. We were hauled off to the police station where Joe was locked up in the cells, while Amina and I spent a long, wet Sunday in the sergeant's office. In the evening the security police arrived to search our car and all its contents, which had in fact been taken to the police station.

After that, Amina and I were allowed to leave, with the warning that we had to appear for prosecution the following morning in the magistrate's court. Joe was held in custody, I think as a hostage, to spend an uncomfortable night in the cells.

Amina and I managed to find grudging accommodation in a white hotel, on condition that we took our meals in the bedroom, because Amina, as an Indian, would not be allowed in the public dining room. We had to swallow this indignity for it was Natal, not the friendly Transvaal, where Amina could so easily have found friends.

In court we pleaded guilty to being where we had no right to be, paid our fines and shook the dust of that Natal town off our feet. The incident had cost us more than money, however, for we had been delayed by a whole day. Worse still, the police had found our itinerary and warned us that if we were caught again in forbidden territory it would not go well with us. This meant that we had to change our time schedule but, despite this, from then onwards we were followed from time to time by security branch police cars, even as far as into Lesotho.

Towards the end of the tour, I was caught again in the Northern Transkei. We had found, almost by chance, a banished man whom we had been unable to trace. Douglas Ramakgopa was amazed to see us and to know that there were people who had not forgotten him and even wanted to help him. But I could only talk to him under the suspicious eye of the agricultural officer in whose charge he was. I explained my presence as truthfully as I could and thought I had got away with not having the necessary permit.

Later that day, however, the police came to the house where Joe, Mildred Lesia and I were happily meeting with former ANC friends from the Eastern Cape. Mildred, a black trade unionist, had replaced Nan when she returned to England. My car was searched again, and I appeared in court the following morning, a little apprehensive lest it had been discovered that I had been convicted for a similar offence only six weeks earlier. However, all went smoothly and I escaped with a relatively small fine. Within an hour we were on our way again to the next equally illegal assignment.

The final lap of our 8,000-mile journey was to Frenchdale and Driefontein, the notorious banishment camps in the Northern Cape. They were very small, these camps, not more than half a dozen men in each, but in stark semi-desert conditions of human isolation. We went first to Frenchdale, a government farm almost on the border of Botswana. We arrived there very late at night, after a long day's drive in a truck which we had hired for this part of the journey so that our presence should be less noticeable than in a car with a Johannesburg registration number. Joe had been there before and could guide us as we picked our way over the rough ground.

They were waiting for us, Chief Paulus Mopeli and his aged wife, and Piet Mokoena, all from far-off Witzieshoek, banished nearly twelve years previously. There, too, was Theophilus Tshangela, only lately brought from the Transkei, where we had seen his wife a couple of weeks before. Both Chief Mopeli and Tshangela were to die, some years later, in this place of desolation, where hyenas prowled by night and snakes lurked by day, and where there are no trees for shade from the relentless sun.

Tshangela died alone, the last of a long succession of banished men who had dragged out so many years in Frenchdale. He could have left when all the others had gone but he refused to leave without the animals he had slowly gathered around him, a few donkeys, sheep and goats. The authorities would not transport them with him back to Pondoland and so Tshangela remained in Frenchdale with his animals and a little deer he had found and tamed. "Babalazi", he had called her. But she died and he was then alone in those empty huts, his spirit unbroken until he too died. The story of his death is not known, nor ever will be.

In Frenchdale, once again we talked by candlelight. We sat on upturned boxes, there were no chairs. Yet we were made very welcome because we came from the Human Rights Welfare Committee which had found these lonely, abandoned people and cared for them. This welcome was reward enough for our long journey.

We drove through the rest of the night to Driefontein, another isolated government farm, 100 miles from the nearest town. It was just after dawn when we arrived, still in our hired truck. The five banished men were expecting us, but we could only stay a short while because they told us that police were coming daily, enquiring about a Johannesburg car. However, this was long enough for us to learn that here again were indestructible men, facing with courage the lonely years of barren land, empty huts and empty days.

We had recently seen the wives of two of the men. They had, like Tshangela, only lately been brought from Pondoland and had not expected to get any news of their wives so soon, so we were doubly welcome. For one man we could bring no good news. Mokate Ramafoku's wife had died without him during his banishment. Like Maredi, he was a twice banished man. He had been a teacher, respected in his community, and now he was old, banished and lonely; a stout heavy man, accepting his fate with dignity. He lived on in Driefontein for another eight years and then I heard from the other men there of his tragic death from an inoperable cancer of the stomach. He lay there in pain, wasting away, for several months before he was removed to hospital, already a dying man. For him there had been no doctor, no medication, no pain killers, to ease his agony during those last months. That he did not die on his dumping ground was due to the efforts of his fellow banished who called the police when appeals for the district surgeon brought no result. Ramafoku's end is a terrible testimony to the deliberate callousness and cruelty of the banishment system.

After Driefontein, our journey to the living dead was completed. Of the forty men and women still in banishment, we had actually seen thirty-six as we moved from place to place. We had talked to fifteen lonely wives and widows, but could bring them no hope of reunion or return, only comfort and compassion.

It had taken two months for us to see these banished people. It had taken nearly 8,000 miles of driving over good roads and bad. It had taken hours of searching, of asking the way, of retracing our steps until we found them, sometimes in the dead of night, sometimes in brilliant sunshine. We had found them waiting for the years to pass, the years, not the months, nor the weeks, nor the days. Or were they waiting for their lives to pass?

Each banished man's story was a dark testament to the violation of law, of justice. For not one of them had ever been brought to a court of law for their crime, if crime it were, which had led to their banishment. Joe and I had been on trial for our activities. We had been able to defend ourselves and our organisations and we had been acquitted. But the banished people had never been charged in court. Their only judgement was that the Governor General considered that their removal from their homes and their people would be in the interests of the "peace and good order of the tribe". For this they had been condemned to years of destitution and desolation.

In the years that followed, all the banished people, except those who died too soon, had been allowed, one by one, to return to their homes, but to poverty and hardship and a life under surveillance and restriction. Today the government no longer uses this dreaded weapon of banishment in the same way. There are other repressive and perhaps even more draconian laws that I suppose serve it as well, should rural leaders again show signs of resistance to new and unwelcome regimes imposed upon them and their people.

The Human Rights Welfare Committee fulfilled its promise. It helped with money, food and clothes right to the end of this punishment. We exposed the horrors of the system, the agony of the banished. Whether by this we stayed the hand of the government, I do not know, but should like to think so. This I do know, that Frenchdale and Driefontein now stand empty. Men no longer sit there in the desert sun and the dry hot wind waiting for death or release, whichever comes first.

Chapter XIV

End of an era

I drove back alone to Johannesburg, to my comfortable home in a white suburb, to my comfortable white life, my well-paid white job and it all seemed unreal. Lilian's bitter cry, "You are better off with your skin" was haunting me again. I had accepted my whiteness for so many years, ever since I came to South Africa. I had accepted that whites, simply because of the colour of their skins, lived on a higher socio-economic scale. It was for the eradication of this utterly invalid privilege that I was now fighting. The experience of the last few years, particularly the treason trial and the search for the banished, had begun to make me ashamed of being what I was and it made no difference that I did not choose to be white. I *am* white and I live a more comfortable life because I do not or cannot break out of my whiteness.

I had told Violet Weinberg that I should be back in Johannesburg on 30 June, but as she had not heard from me directly since I left two months previously, she stared at me, almost unbelievingly, when I walked into her house just in time for supper. There was so much to tell but I had to get back to my own house and rest before returning to work the following day, exactly on schedule. It felt strange after those two months of travel, adventure and companionship.

For our long journey not to be in vain, I knew that I must write and talk about those men and women, the forgotten people, whom I had seen for myself, those stories of injustice and suffering I had heard for myself, from their own lips. I wrote articles and letters to the press, I talked often at students' meetings, to Congress of Democrats members, to the women of the Federation — wherever and whenever I could get a hearing. It was good to be back and able to speak, even though I did not know for how long.

I had returned to Johannesburg only three days after the new "Sabotage Act", the General Laws Amendment Act, had become law. It spelt out the Nationalist government's determination to crush all opposition under the guise of preserving the safety of the nation. Not only did it create a new crime, sabotage, but it defined it so widely that it was the Suppression of Communism Act all over again, only worse, even more despotic. The new Act really perpetuated the 1960 State of Emergency; there would be no need for the government to proclaim another, for all the ingredients were there. "Sabotage" could mean almost anything, from blowing up pylons and buildings, to the illegal possesion of a firearm — and heaven knows how many thousands of unlicensed firearms there are in South Africa. It would now be for the accused to prove that the offence, great or small, was not committed with any hostile intent. No longer did the state have to prove a man's guilt, the accused must disprove it — and guilt carried a minimum sentence of five years.

Unlimited powers of prohibition were given to the Minister of Justice, power to ban people, to impose house arrest, to forbid people to be members of legal organisations, to require people to report, even daily, to the police, and to face a compulsory twelve-month gaol sentence for failure to do so. He had the power to forbid banned people to communicate with each other, even members of the same family, and to forbid publication of statements by banned people. All that was required for any of these drastic infringements of personal liberty was for the minister to be satisfied that the person was furthering the aims of communism or that his activities were likely to do so. There was much else in this tyrannical Act which no amount of opposition both inside and outside Parliament had been able to prevent. Like the banished people, the banned person's liberty of person, of association, of movement, could be in jeopardy without any trial, any recourse to a court of law.

The first blow from this repressive regime came in September 1962. The South African Congress of Democrats was declared an illegal organisation. We had held what was to be our last conference a few weeks before and I had been elected Honorary National Vice President. I was certainly proud to hold this high office in an organisation which had maintained its stand as a full member of the Congress Alliance, side by side with the ANC, the Indian Congress, the Coloured People's Congress and the Congress of Trade Unions.

"Side by side," we had pledged ourselves at the Congress of the People, "until these democratic changes have been won." We had been side by side with the Congress Alliance in freedom and in gaol, and now we were side by side with the ANC as outlaws. As an illegal organisation we could not call on our national executive committee members to meet together, yet there was one decision which had to be taken urgently. Should we try to continue working from underground, as the ANC was doing, or should we fold up?

Six of us sat one night in a car munching hamburgers, at a drive-in café, arguing until we came to what was really the only possible decision. We had been formed particularly to campaign politically amongst whites, and since we could no longer do that, certainly not from underground, we must fold up. It was our end as an organisation. In the nine years of our existence we had never mustered more than a few hundred members, but we had made our voices heard on many issues, we had been the spur to prod other organisations, especially the Liberal Party, into more militant stands. We could serve no purpose as an underground organisation, and in any event it was obvious that there could be no room for another secret organisation in addition to the ANC.

Another refinement of the Suppression of Communist Act was the "listing" of persons who had been members of any organisation banned under this Act. By this process the liquidator of a banned organisation places the names of such members, or even supporters, on his "list" and this carries various disabilities and restrictions, the implications of which became clearer as time went by. Listing did not apply to the ANC and PAC, which were banned under a different Act, the Illegal Organisations Act, passed at the time of the Sharpeville Emergency in March 1960. Perhaps the sheer magnitude of numbers and the absolute impossibility of tracing the membership of these two organisations saved them from the liquidator's list.

The banning of the Congress of Democrats gave the Federation of South African Women yet another blow by removing the affiliated white members of the COD — which of course really included me, but the committee members turned a blind eye to this. It was not to be for long.

The Federation had, of course, already been affected very severely by the ban on the ANC Women's League, declared illegal as part of the ANC. This deprived the Federation of the greater part of its affiliated membership. It was all too clear that we should be, to some extent, crippled by the loss of the African women.

There was only one thing to be done and that was for African women to start organising clubs for women, to be affiliated to the Federation. The white members must do this, too, but that would obviously not be on the same vast scale. It was a bold scheme, but once the 1960 Emergency was over, we set to work with suggestions for discussion clubs, co-operative vegetable clubs, sewing and knitting clubs, even running all-day training conferences for club leaders, much as we had done in the days of the Bantu education schools boycott.

On 9 August 1961, there had been Women's Day celebrations in all the main centres, clubs were flourishing, and it seemed that the Federation would be able to survive the loss of the Women's League as an affiliated body. After that we had moved on to our third national conference. It was already five years since that impressive gathering in Johannesburg after the Pretoria protest, but much had happened since then to prevent us from meeting together in a national conference.

The 1961 conference was held in Port Elizabeth in September. I had watched some of the Transvaal delegates leave, packed tight in a kombi. Spirits were high and the women went off singing for what must have been a very uncomfortable journey of over 600 miles. I was still banned and could not leave Johannesburg or attend the conference. Standing in their departing dust, I watched them go, angry that I must stay behind, proud of their defiant spirit.

The conference was a huge success with nearly 200 delegates from all the main centres and several hundred observers. It was clear that the Federation was as undaunted as ever and would not diminish its efforts to continue as a multiracial women's organisation, still part of the Congress Alliance and the liberation struggle.

Dynamic as ever, Lilian Ngoyi presided and was re-elected National President, but soon afterwards she received her first banning order, prohibiting her from attending gatherings for the next five years. I was re-elected National Secretary, despite my absence, a very precious mark of the Federation women's confidence in me. I was nearing the end of my bans, but Lilian was only beginning hers. I knew, only too well, how it felt to see five years of emptiness stretching ahead. A few months later her bans were intensified and she was confined to the Orlando suburb of Soweto. It was a bitter blow to both of us after being so close, almost daily, for more than five years. Now it would be extremely difficult to meet. I was a marked person and could not easily venture into Soweto without a permit.

In 1962, during our tour to find the banished Africans, I had been able to visit Durban, Port Elizabeth and Cape Town. In Port Elizabeth I had met the Federation leaders, the African women of the Eastern Cape, stronghold of the ANC during the Defiance Campaign and afterwards too. From this area alone, 5,000 volunteers had gone to gaol. Now the ANC was outlawed, but thousands of its former members were in Port Elizabeth and the Congress spirit was still very strong.

It was a great joy to meet Francis Baard and Florence Matomela again as we had been together during the first part of the treason trial. During the 1960 Emergency, we had all been detained, but had been gaoled in our own provinces and had not met. Now it was good to be with these two formidable women again. Both massively built, tall, their commanding personalities inspired confidence and courage. Francis was the Cape President of the Federation and had been President also of the Cape Women's League. Florence had been one of the most prominent of the 1952 defiers. At our first conference she was unforgettable as she strode to the platform to speak, Xhosa skirt swirling about her, beads jangling and headscarf piled above her head in Xhosa fashion. Warned by the chair that she could speak for only three mintues, she folded her arms and said "I am a defier! I shall speak as long as I like." I don't remember for how long she did speak, but it was much more than three minutes. These two women were also trade union leaders, and I am sure, too, that it was mainly Francis and Florence who organised that delegation of seventy women from there to the Pretoria protest, because they were the accepted leaders of the ANC Women's League and the Federation. As I had expected, they were busy building up new women's clubs for affiliation to the Federation.

From Port Elizabeth we travelled on to Cape Town, more than 600 miles away. I remember that we had managed to do it in one day, even in a relatively small car and I had driven all the way. Nan flew back to England and I spent a few days with the Federation women. They were battling to keep the organisation going, despite the prevailing reluctance of many women there to become politically involved after the 1960 Emergency and the many detentions. That crisis had certainly left its mark.

After my return to Johannesburg, the Federation held provincial conferences in Johannesburg and Durban. I was free to attend them. In Johannesburg my arrival at the conference was unannounced for fear of a last-minute new ban. I had a tumultuous welcome and I walked through the hall, past the security branch detectives, gathered there to take their notes as usual. The women sang for me as I went up to the platform for the first time in five years. There was no longer any need for me to wait around outside the hall, excluded from the meeting as I had been for those frustrating years of being banned.

It was exciting to be amongst women of all races again, amongst the women who had stood by their leaders on trial for high treason, amongst the women who had marched to gaol in 1958 and the women who had gone to Pretoria in their thousands in 1956. Winnie Mandela, still so young, made a gallant call to youth and was elected to the Transvaal executive. She was already emerging as a leader of women and it was then that I began to know her as a friend.

I went to Durban to open the conference there, again in a packed hall with a dozen security police in attendance, and had the same joyous greeting on my return to freedom. These conferences of women were the highlights of my first few months back in Johannesburg and I had great hopes for the Federation, despite the banning of our National President, Lilian Ngoyi. I spoke everywhere, too, of what I had seen on my tour to the banished people and the lonely agony of these abandoned people.

I had known, of course, at the end of the treason trial that Robert Resha would no longer be able to accompany me on our various campaigning expeditions, because he too had been banned and his bans would not expire until three years after mine. I missed his company and his guidance. It was a great shock when he walked into my office shortly after the end of the trial to tell me that he was leaving South Africa secretly that very night. He told me, rather grimly, that he had been ordered to go and he must obey. I knew he meant it for he was still the disciplined volunteer leader.

The ANC was already developing its external mission. Oliver Tambo, Acting Secretary General, was overseas, others would follow him and Robert was needed too. I knew that he did not want to go. He had often said that he must remain with his people, be with them until the end of the struggle. He was a man of his land and he loved it passionately. For me, Robert remained the independent-minded African nationalist, a true patriot, angrily resenting any suggestion that the ANC could be dominated by any white or any communist. "It is an insult to my organisation!" he had always declared. As he left my office, he said, "Helen, I shall come back." Years later, when I heard that he had died in exile, my heart was heavy for he was truly a man of his land.

In July 1962, I heard a horrifying rumour that Nelson Mandela had been arrested, driving to Durban disguised as a chauffeur in a private car. The report was soon substantiated. Nelson, the underground leader of the liberation struggle, had been arrested and would stand trial on charges of inciting workers to stay at home and of leaving the country without a passport. For eighteen months he had been underground and had also left the country to visit many other countries to obtain support for the struggle. He had returned to his country, from freedom, to face the danger of capture and gaol and he had been caught. I could hardly bear to believe that after all those months of hiding, of separation from his wife and children, save for occasional risky meetings, he had been arrested — I had seen him only once during those dangerous months and then only briefly in conditions of great secrecy at a friend's flat. Our meeting was precious indeed, joyful and loving — and so soon over.

Nelson's first appearance in court was to be in Pretoria on 15 October and mass protest meetings had been arranged in many areas for the previous day,

Sunday. Great crowds were expected at the meetings. I was scheduled to speak at one of them in Johannesburg and had made plans to be in Pretoria on the day of the trial.

Chapter XV

House arrest

On 13 October 1962, I became the first person in South Africa to be put under house arrest. The minister was "satisfied" that I was engaged in activities which were furthering or were calculated to further, the achievement of any of the objects of communism. Because of this satisfaction he could and did tear my life to pieces, set me apart from my fellows and deny me association with others, the very stuff of life itself.

It happened so quickly, no pre-warning, just a couple of men walking down my garden path that Saturday morning, to hand me a few sheets of paper, beginning, "Whereas, I Johannes Balthazar Vorster, am satisfied . . ." and ending, "given under my hand this eleventh day of October 1962" and signed J.B. Vorster. In between were the prohibitions which drastically curtailed my freedom and changed my life. All this was for five years.

No longer could I leave my house after 6.30 p.m. or at any time during the weekend, or leave the magisterial area of Johannesburg, or be in any black area, or factory, or communicate with any banned or listed person. Nor could any of my friends visit me in my home, or even walk down my garden path, nor could I attend any gatherings, social or political. Over and above all these prohibitions, I was compelled to report to the Central Johannesburg police station every day between midday and two o'clock, except of course on the days when I was confined to the house.

I thought at first that it related to the Mandela trial, due to start on the Monday and to the Sunday meeting at which I was supposed to speak. I telephoned one or two other speakers, but found that all meetings or demonstrations relating to the trial had been prohibited in any event, so it wasn't that. I realised unhappily that I should not now be able to get to court to see Nelson, although I did not know then that I should not see him again for a very long time. Even now, he remains incarcerated. Gradually I found out that I was the only person who had been put under house arrest.

I looked at the orders again and slowly the details began to sink in. The full implications took some time to be appreciated. Suddenly I realised that, as it was ten o'clock, I still had four and a half hours to get out of the house, to see people before the first weekend of house arrest started at two thirty. I drove quickly to Violet who lived nearby and we telephoned other people, the press, lawyers, our many friends. Nor had I realised that I could no longer speak to Eli,

Violet's husband, a trade unionist, because he was a banned man. The horror of this aspect struck me for the first time. There would now be so many friends from whom I should be cut off. Many of my friends were banned people, alongside whom I worked and shared my social life, for we stood together in our common commitment to our struggle for freedom and justice. They too, had been banned by the Minister of Justice for their political stand.

Defiantly we all had lunch together, despite this being a social gathering. Then I had to spend the precious last hour getting myself into the city to report to the police station. The police, rather like me, did not know what it was all about. They were totally disbelieving when they learnt that I should be coming there every weekday at this hour for the next five years. I had not been charged with any offence, I was not on bail. It just did not make sense to them.

I did not know exactly what I was supposed to do there. Did I have to insist on seeing the officer in charge, the commandant, to whom my orders said that I must report? But it was a Saturday and he was not there. We finally settled, a policeman and I, for a piece of paper which he signed to say that I had reported to him and then gave it to me. I doubt that I saw the comic side of all this at that moment as I was bewildered and becoming very angry. I left the press reporters, who had accompanied me there, and drove home from the first of many such visits to the police station.

I reached home to be greeted by more reporters. As I drove my car into the garage and walked back to close the driveway gates on myself, I did not realise that I was my own gaoler. That came later. I went into the house thinking that I should be totally alone for the next forty hours. However, I was wrong about that on two counts. First, the news of my house arrest had spread abroad. There were many telephone calls from friends and strangers. Friends came to my gate, not really believing that they could not come in, not then or for the next five years. And secondly, the security police came to my house at nine o'clock, pounding on the door to find out if I was there. That enraged me, but there was nothing I could do about it.

That weekend, after the initial shock began to wear off, I had time to think about what had happened to me and what my life might be like for the next five years. The astonishing part was that it was, in fact, only me. I found this impossible to understand and so, I am sure, did many other people. There were many others in the Congress Alliance who were far more prominent than I. True, I had been very active in the Federation, I was its National Secretary, I had been the National Vice President of the Congress of Democrats, but only for a few short weeks before it was banned. I had been detained in 1960, been on trial for high treason, but had been acquitted. Were these activities furthering the achievement of any of the objects of communism? Did the government really think I was so dangerous — a sort of mastermind? This could not be. Active I certainly had been. What had the treason prosecutor said of me? That I was one of the most active members of the liberation movement. But that was already two years ago.

I had indeed been making the most of my freedom after the five-year ban expired. I had toured the country to find the banished people, and I had written and spoken about them. I had written a book about the treason trial but it was not yet published. Were these activities crimes to bring such punishment upon me? And this time with no opportunity for a court trial where I could speak in my own defence. I could not even speak out in South Africa any more, for it was now illegal to publish any statement by a banned person.

All my political actions, except for a couple of arrests in forbidden areas, had been legal. If they had not been, I should have been brought to trial. I felt that they were all part of a legitimate non-violent political struggle for democratic rights for all the people of South Africa.

I thought about the past ten years and what my life had become, different indeed from anything that I had ever imagined. I had slipped easily, almost unconsciously, into this new political life which absorbed so much of all my days and nights. I had not made a deliberate choice. Bonhoeffer, the famous German pastor, executed in a Nazi gaol, had said, "I know what I have chosen." That was not true of me. I had not been aware of any specific choice. I had not been able to see what would be the result of this intense political involvement.

Certainly nothing in my early life had prepared me for it. My youth had been almost ordinary — a middle-class home, school, matriculation, university. I could not recall any serious discussions with my parents or even with my brother on justice or human rights, beyond the fact that England went to war against Germany for a just cause. Patriotism, therefore, was important. Our politics were respectably conservative and Winston Churchill was our MP. I had floated through university with no real social involvement, except a little dabbling in working-girl clubs. Even going to India was not really the result of any purposeful decision. I had to find a job; without a training, teaching was all that was offered to me, and travel appeared exciting. Coming to South Africa had been fortuitous, the result of a riding accident.

My air force career was more of an actual choice, and obviously my late political development had begun during my war service. The community service which followed it had pushed me further along a road which I still did not recognise as any particular road. Yet it was one, an important one for me, and in the 1950s my feet were firmly on the road of political struggle, never to leave it again.

Now I had to face the cost of those heady years of the decade of defiance of an evil and hostile authority. I had, with others, already paid a high price in the danger of the treason trial, in the months of detention, in a five-year ban. Yet through all those years it had been more than compensated by the knowledge of abiding solidarity, of achievement, of being part of something greater than anything else in my life. I had known and shared success in the building of the Women's Federation, in the organising of those great protests, in establishing the cultural clubs during the school boycotts, in seeking and finding the banished Africans — and in the great victory of the treason acquittal. Yet now, that weekend, I seemed to stand alone, impotent. The horrors of house arrest at first overwhelmed me. Would I be able to cope with the cruel lonely years that lay ahead? Telephone calls could not fill the empty hours, the empty house.

124

Would I be able to retain my job? And what could I do if I lost it? Who would employ me, house-arrested and banned? Could I adapt myself to coming home night after night to nothing but my own company, to lonely weekends — there would be 250 of those?

I did not suppose, of course, that I should remain the only one under house arrest. There would be others. The question was not really, "why me?" but only "why me first?" To that there is no known answer to this day. There was some bitter comfort in the unexpected public reaction, both national and international, brought about by my elevated position as the first "house arrestee".

It certainly seemed an incredibly stupid choice on the part of the government, to begin with an ageing white woman of fifty-seven, who lived entirely alone, who was not even seriously suspected of being a communist, and who had had only a short, if spectacular, political history. Genuine public sympathy and concern was aroused and expressed, though of course with it came execration, mostly in the form of obscene telephone calls, threatening, abusive, always anonymous.

The weekend passed quickly after all, although I felt like a caged animal on view, as people walked up and down outside, peering over the garden hedge for a glimpse of this very peculiar and dangerous woman. I soon learnt to replace the telephone receiver quickly on the abusive calls. I was glad when Monday morning came and I could go out again.

I learnt from the Sunday newspapers, which my friends brought to my gate, that my house arrest had indeed aroused enormous publicity, both here and abroad. It was termed "civil death" and I remembered the living dead, the banished people whom I had seen such a short time ago. I was far better off than they were.

John Vorster, Minister of Justice, declared to the press that when the General Laws Amendment Act was passed, which contained these new frightening powers, it was no bluff. A "certain person" had not heeded this warning and therefore the first house arrest had been ordered. He did not want to curb freedom of speech or the right to protest. Every South African was the child of protest, but the freedom of the state could not be violated. He warned that he could get even tougher. There was indeed some apprehension amongst the public indignation, that what had happened to me could happen to others. Intimidation was clearly part of the motivation of the house arrest. Nevertheless, the weeks that followed saw many demonstrations by the Black Sash, in Cape Town — where women stood silent in the pouring rain — in Durban, East London and Johannesburg, all protesting against this violation of human rights. Outside the Johannesburg City Hall, the Congress Alliance demonstrated at midday and I walked past them on my way to report at the police station. My Congress friends of all races cheered me as I passed. I could not stop or greet them, but it was a very good moment for me.

At the end of my first week of house arrest, there was a multiracial demonstration of young people on the Saturday afternoon, outside my gate. They held their posters aloft, defiantly. "The people are with you, Helen

Joseph!" ... "You will not be forgotten!" They sang freedom songs for me, while three police cars cruised up and down the road. As the young people walked away, still singing, the police told them they were in an illegal procession and must disperse. They were very, very brave, and they had come because they wanted me to know that I was not completely alone — a very precious knowledge then.

Nine days after he had dealt with me, the minister struck again. This time it was Ahmed Kathrada, "Kathy", of the treason trial. The orders were served on him outside the Pretoria magistrate's court where he had gone to attend Nelson's trial. House arrest orders were out for Walter Sisulu, too, the banned Secretary General of the ANC, but it took a few days before the police could find him. Our conditions were all the same, twelve hours' house arrest on working days and twenty-four at the weekend, no visitors at any time and the restrictions on attending gatherings, plus several other prohibitions.

I met Kathy one day at the police station when I went to report. We walked in side by side to sign our names in the house arrest book. We were not sure if we could even smile at each other — would that be communicating? But we did. From then on, house arrest orders and bans multiplied almost daily, although far more people were banned than house-arrested. I did not ever discover on what basis the minister selected certain people for house arrest, the preferential treatment! However, he had said that he could get tougher, and he did.

By the end of October, people were being put under twenty-four hours house arrest, not twelve. I had been promoted to the privileged class as I could be out of my house for twelve hours on every week day. Sonia Bunting, Jack Hodgson, Moses Kotane, all good friends, had to remain in their homes without ever going out, for five years, nearly 2,000 days. They were not entirely alone, as I was. Not even the Minister of Justice dared put a person who lived alone under twenty-four-hours house arrest for five years, but nevertheless these intensified bans shocked South Africa anew, almost as much as mine had done initially. As in my case, no prior warning had been given to anyone.

The South African Broadcasting Company suddenly produced a programme on me as part of their regular broadcast to schools, "Current Topics". Apparently I had become a prominent current topic, a subject of much controversy. "She proudly gives the clenched fist salute of the banned African National Congress, and recently toured the country visiting many people under restriction orders under the Suppression of Communism Act." The last part of the accusation was inaccurate; the people had been banished, not banned. It went on, "Whether or not the orders issued against her are too strict is therefore a matter of opinion." It was more than a matter of opinion to me.

This broadcast to the children was only a curtain-raiser, a prelude to the real thing, for a few nights later in the series, "We Present Facts", the SABC did a very workmanlike job of smearing, trying its damnedest, as the *Rand Daily Mail* editor pointed out, "to show that Mrs Joseph was a communist, or a crypto-communist, or at best a fellow traveller." Gobbets from the treason trial evidence, divorced from context, were presented, presumably as "facts", but what the broadcast did not quote was the prosecutor's concession at the end of the trial, "The Crown does not propose, in this particular instance, to direct any argument at the personal position of this accused as far as communism is concerned." I could not reply to the broadcast because, as a banned person, nothing I said or wrote could be published or quoted. It brought home to me how effectively I was gagged.

There was another demonstration outside my gate, this time by the women of the Federation. Violet Weinberg was there of course, the only white woman, the rest were black. Within a very short time the police had arrived and the women were carted off to the police station. Violet held out for a time, arguing defiantly, but she too, was finally ordered into a waiting police car and driven away.

I looked out over the gate and the road was very empty and quiet, until I saw Winnie Mandela and Adelaide Joseph, both of the Federation. They had come to demonstrate but they had been delayed. I told them what had happened to the other women and they went off to investigate at the police station. I felt very proud that they had all come to demonstrate for me. "House arrest can't intimidate us!" one banner had read and I knew it to be true. They could not be intimidated. Nevertheless, I was anxious for them. In due course they were brought to trial and fined.

In Pretoria, Nelson's trial was over and he had been found guilty of inciting workers to be absent from work, to stay at home illegally and also of leaving the country illegally himself. He was sentenced to five years' imprisonment. Was it for this that he had returned from other lands? He had told the court how his conscience had made it imperative for him to oppose laws which were unjust, immoral and intolerable.

Nelson's wife, Winnie, was at his trial to hear his conviction and sentence, to realise that she must stand alone, must bring up the two little girls alone, for the next five years. But she did not know then that it would not be just five years and that within two years her husband would be sentenced to life imprisonment.

I had received a letter from Nelson, from gaol, while he was awaiting trial:

My dear Helen,

I join the millions of democrats here and abroad in condemning the cruel and cowardly order of house arrest imposed on you by the Minister of Justice.

Courage never failed you in the past. It will not fail you now when all signs point unmistakably to the early defeat of all regimes based on force and violence.

You and I and indeed the millions of freedom fighters in this country cannot afford to take this challenge lying down.

With fondest regards,
Yours very sincerely
Nelson

I carried that letter with me everywhere during those first bewildering weeks. It brought back to me the journeys we had shared, back and forth to the treason trial, and the close and loving friendship that had grown out of those trial years.

The implications of "listing" under the Suppression of Communism Act very soon became clear, for the Act made it an offence to publish any statement made by a listed person, as well as statements by banned persons. The Minister of Justice published a list of 437 people "named" as communists. Neither my name nor Walter Sisulu's was amongst them, yet we had both been house-arrested under the Suppression of Communism Act. Some of the people on that list had left the country, some had died, many had taken no active part in politics since the Communist Party was banned in 1950, many others had been inactive for the past twenty or even thirty years. It was really the roll of the old guard, but it meant, for all of them, that nothing they said or wrote could ever be published or even quoted.

Another ban was to hit the Federation of South African Women — Violet Weinberg, Vice President of the Transvaal region, my friend and also my colleague at work. We could no longer speak to each other, nor could I go to her home, or she come to mine. Rowley Arenstein, too, in Durban, formerly active in the Congress of Democrats, was banned and house-arrested. He earned himself a special "first" within two weeks by becoming the first person to be arrested for reporting late to the police.

Rowley's actual sentence was for twelve months, the compulsory minimum sentence for this apparently most serious offence. The embarrassed magistrate found that it was merely culpable negligence that had caused Rowley to forget to report on time and his gaol sentence was therefore suspended for three years, except for seven days which he duly served in gaol. I found this ominous, realising that my own chronic forgetfulness might well bring me to the same fate. I was sure that I could not get through the next five years of this unpalatable and inconvenient duty of reporting to the police station every working day without ever forgetting.

The furore of publicity about me had long since died down. Those under twenty-four-hours house arrest were so much worse off than I was — and sad to say, the public soon recovered from the first shock of these bans and forgot about our twilight existence. The normal concept of freedom had once again been violated and loud protests had been heard from at least some of the whites. Yet the government remained unmoved, the protests had petered out and everyone was becoming used to living with the new laws. It formed a pattern, a kind of surrender by instalments.

I was trying not to think too much about Christmas Day and the sixty hours of solitude which would begin at 6.30 p.m. on Christmas Eve. However, to alleviate that thought, Christmas cards and letters soon poured in from South Africa and overseas, from friends and strangers, adding to the amazing number of letters that I had already received. Amongst the most precious of those was one from Bram Fischer, delivered to my house by hand within minutes of "lock-up" time on the first day. He said I deserved the honour of being the first to be placed under Vorster's vicious and inhuman house arrest. I did not think I deserved the honour, but it was good to have Bram think so.

The cherry on the top of the Christmas cards was the one with a snowy wintry picture of the British Houses of Parliament and inside the signatures of 140 Labour MPs. They were all there, Harold Wilson, Barbara Castle, Jim Callaghan, Joan Lester and many others. I was reminded by this of our "penny post" in treason trial days, when we too passed cards and letters along the rows of the accused to catch all our signatures. Other letters told me that I had been seen on television and I remembered the day when the TV man and I met secretly in a wooded park, using borrowed cars for fear of being followed by police, for the television interview.

There were so many Christmas cards that first year, more than 500, and letters and telegrams, telephone calls and flowers, until I felt more like a film star than a house-arrest prisoner. On Christmas Day itself, my friends came to the gate to greet me, one by one, almost all day long. We talked for a few minutes only, because no one was quite sure what constituted a visit or a gathering. Children had come with candles the night before to sing carols at my gate; the children of banned or listed parents, whom I could not greet, as they waited for their children a little way down the road. Christmas dinner came in a basket over the gate, turkey, plum pudding and champagne.

When all was quiet again that evening, I thought triumphantly how Vorster had failed, because he had given me the most wonderful Christmas Day of my life. There was soon more triumph to come, for Jack Hodgson had applied to the Supreme Court for the setting aside of his twenty-four-hours house-arrest order, on the grounds that the minister had acted unreasonably and also that a flat is not a "place" as defined in the Act. On 27 December, the judge ordered all the house-arrest orders to be set aside. Suddenly we were partially free, at least from house arrest, though not free from the other restrictions. At first we thought it meant total freedom and celebrated openly until sharply brought to our senses by our lawyers, who insisted that the judgement applied only to actual house arrest. We had had a couple of days of false freedom and then we returned meekly to life with the rest of our bans, thankful indeed to be able to come and go so freely from our homes.

As it turned out, the state did not accept the judgement and took it on appeal to a higher court. If the judgement were to be reversed, then we should all have to revert immediately to house-arrest conditions. The appeal took a few months to be finalised, and in any event we knew that, even if the state appeal was lost, it would not take long for the law itself to be amended in Parliament in order to close up this loophole. It was clear that we would not retain this new freedom for long.

For the past eleven weeks I had lived obediently to a strange solitary pattern, allowed out only to earn my keep for this "gaol on the cheap". By nine o'clock in the morning I would be in my office and the hours would pass all too quickly. I had always to be careful that I did not have discussions with more than one person, as that could be termed a "gathering". The Medical Aid Society had rallied nobly to the shock of the house arrest to their most senior member of staff, just as it had done to the treason trial, once it was clear that I should be able to do my work.

I went by car to work so that I could be ready for the midday scamper to the police station more than a mile away, and by five o'clock I would be speeding to friends for a brief visit before getting home by 6.30. Evenings were quiet, except for the radio and the telephone — and visits from the police. Friends telephoned often, strangers too, though they were sometimes too frightened to give their names. This was a welcome break from the silence, despite the many abusive or threatening or even obscene calls. At first the police came every night, once twice in the same night — "to check", they said. It wasn't pleasant to wait, night after night, for that knock on the door and the unwelcome intrusion into my privacy.

Weekends were long, even though there was plenty for me to do in my garden. My house had become an empty place and no longer really a home, for a home is the place you share with your family and friends, and this was forbidden. However, the lifting of the actual house arrest was a victory in itself, even if only for a few months. I think that only when you have lost it, can you know how precious a little freedom can be.

Part Two

Chapter I

Learning to live a half life

The 1950s had been a decade of protest, from the Defiance Campaign at the beginning to the Treason Trial victory and the resistance of women to passes at its end. There had been tough battles with the Nationalist government, there had been oppression, but the underlying feeling had been a sense of achievement, even of triumph, despite the setbacks along the road.

Now we came into a new decade — the decade of the worst legal oppression yet known. As the years dragged by, each new security law brought further inroads into personal liberty, into accepted norms of justice.

The 1960s became the years of political trials, of detention without trial, of torture and death under interrogation. The maximum security gaols filled up with hundreds of political prisoners, men who had committed no crime against society but had pitted themselves and their cause against the armageddon of the Nationalist state.

The first half of 1962 brought the General Laws Amendment Act, which had spawned house arrest and other intensified restrictions of personal liberty. December 1962 brought a sinister rider to this Act in Government Notice No. 2130. Its provisions had a devastating effect on the lives of many banned and listed people — the four hundred and thirty seven persons whose names had been published as having been members or supporters of the banned Communist Party. It affected even people who were neither banned nor listed but had once been members or even supporters of an illegal organisation, and this covered members of the now illegal Congress of Democrats.

The effect of the notice was far-reaching, drastic, as it forbade banned and listed people from belonging to any of thirty-six different legal organisations, some of which no longer existed, some of which I had never heard. What they all had in common was their opposition to the Nationalist regime. The Federation of South African Women was included and also the Indian and Coloured Congresses. The ANC, the PAC and the COD were, of course, already banned.

The notice then went much further. It contained a prohibition on being a member, officer or office-bearer of any organisation which propagates, attacks, defends, criticises or discusses any form of state or any principle or policy of the government of a state. It was so broad in its implications that it was breathtaking — once you understood it — for it was worded in such a cumbersome way that

I had to read it a couple of times before I understood it myself. It was also published very unobtrusively in the government *Gazette* so that it took a little while before even the people affected were aware that they could no longer work for an organisation which was political. Parliament was in recess and this notice was not even debated.

I was now totally excluded from the Federation of South African Women and had to resign as its National Secretary. This came as a very bitter blow because until I was banned in 1962, the Federation had formed possibly the most important part of my life. From now on I should be permanently cut off from it. Listing does not come to an end when a banning order expires. It is permanent and it still affects my life twenty years later. The earlier five-year ban in the 1950s, and even the more recent restrictions, had brought only difficulties that could be overcome and I was still the National Secretary. But that was over, for this notice undoubtedly covered the Federation — and me.

I also had to resign officially as the Honorary Secretary of the Human Rights Welfare Committee for the banished people. Its political nature was inherent in its very name but I had no intention of abandoning it. We had always held our discussions in private and my name never appeared thereafter in any minutes. After our journey to the banished people and their families, I could not tolerate the idea of giving up the close personal connections that had grown out of it. I continued my correspondence with the individual banished men and women, but only in my personal capacity.

I received a letter from the liquidator appointed for the Congress of Democrats after its banning in 1962. I was invited to show reasons why my name should not be included amongst those of the already listed people, on the grounds that I had been an office-bearer, a member and an active supporter of the Congress of Democrats. I had certainly been all of these and I was proud to have been so. I had also given sworn testimony in the treason trial about my position in the Congress of Democrats. In any event, nothing would have persuaded me to deny my association with my organisation. I ignored the liquidator's letter and my name was duly placed on the list. Now I fell under Notice 2130 on three counts. I was banned, I was listed and I had belonged to an illegal organisation.

Already in 1962, I had written to the Minister of Justice asking for the reasons for my banning and house-arrest orders. I received a reply as ludicrous as the one asked for at the time of my first bans in 1957. It added a few choice extras, for example, that I had associated with listed communists, but as the names of the listed people were published only after my house arrest, I could not see how I was supposed to know who they were. I certainly had not known that Joe Morolong, who had been with me for the whole journey to the banished people, was a listed person, until I saw that one of the reasons given for my house arrest and bans was that I had arrived in Cape Town in the company of this listed person. And I still could not see laughing, friendly Joe as a dangerous person!

At the end of March 1963, the Supreme Court of Justice upheld the minister's appeal against Jack Hodgson's legal victory which had brought us that precious three months of partial freedom. My taste of social life again had been brief but very good, but this time the minister had won and we went back to our half-life under house arrest. I found that I soon slipped back into the former routine. The first shock was over and it was not as difficult as the first time, especially as all the other restrictions had remained in force.

As I moved slowly through the first year of house arrest, it developed its own rhythm. The freedom to move out of my house as early as half past six in the morning didn't mean very much to me. This couple of hours before my office work began seemed a bit of a waste, until I started to call on my friends sometimes to have breakfast with them. I called on others on my way home in the evenings for a quick drink and some chatter — behind drawn curtains if there was more than one other person present, and always watching the time so that I could be sure of getting home before half past six.

For a time, one of my greatest joys was having the Cachalia family, Amina, Yusuf and their two little children, just around the corner from my office, not even five minutes away. I could and did go there often for a quick lunch with them, the kind of meal which only banned people know, always on the alert for a knock on the front door and the hasty retreat into another room with your plate, knife, fork and glass. It was not a violation of my bans to be found in the Cachalia home, but it would be if I were discovered with more than one person.

I had always known that Amina suffered from a heart condition, even from childhood, but the news that she was to undergo major heart surgery came as a great shock to me. I became deeply anxious and depressed over it, fearing that I might lose this precious friend. I suppose it was inevitable that during periods of enforced isolation, such as I had every night, anxiety affects one more severely. I reached the lowest level of depression that I had yet experienced. I could not sleep properly, I wept, I suppose mostly in self-pity, in fear that Amina might die and for my own feeling of being so desperately alone.

Amina recovered from her operation, but her family moved away from the little house around the corner from my office. It was no longer possible for us to share my lunch hour. We telephoned each other often until one night she said, "Hold on, Helen, there's someone at the door . . ." There was indeed — two security policemen who served five-year banning orders on her, while I was still holding the telephone. It meant that for the next five years, we should not be able to speak to each other, yet even this restriction could not destroy our friendship.

After that I could only look at her on Saturdays when she and her husband, Yusuf, also banned and house-arrested like me, would walk with their children to the police station to report. I would get there at the same time, just so that we could smile at each other as I passed in my car or walked in silence beside Yusuf to write our names in the house-arrest register.

Despite all my restrictions, I did not escape attention from the security

135

police. They suddenly instituted a vicious campaign of following me by car wherever I went. It was unreal, sometimes comic, mostly sinister. When I left my home in the morning to go to work, one or even two cars would be parked in Fanny Avenue, a block away, and would pull out behind me and follow me all the way to town. This performance would be repeated when I went to report at the police station too, whether I went there by car, or bus, or walked. When I returned home, they were there again.

For six weeks I went nowhere except to work, for I had no intention of leading these tailing cars to the homes of my friends. I think I drove the entire time with one eye on the rear-view mirror. I had two collisions with other cars during that time. Then this persecution stopped as suddenly as it had begun. Perhaps I supplied a useful exercise in training police recruits to follow suspect cars. Perhaps the police foolishly imagined that I was planning to escape from my irksome house arrest by leaving South Africa. I certainly did not have any such plans, then or at any other time. I had the right, as British born, to leave South Africa, but the bans prevented me from leaving Johannesburg to reach any airport or sea port. So perhaps they really thought I was going to make a dash for it.

It was a gruelling experience for me, but once I got a laugh out of it when my unwelcome escort got in front of me in a traffic snarl and I deliberately followed him, bumper to bumper, until he tired of this reversal of roles and drove away very fast. It reminded me of a time when Robert Resha and I were returning from a meeting one night and realised that we were being followed. We came to a traffic circle and I drove round and round it until it was impossible to say who was following whom. When it finally dawned on the police that I was not even trying to get away from them, but laughing at them, they drove off in disgust.

During the three months when house arrest fell away, I forgot one Saturday afternoon that I should have reported to the police before half past two. I was arrested a few days later and spent a few solitary hours in the police cells before being charged and released on bail. I was held in the same large cell where we had been detained three years before and I was delighted to see that our lipstick and eyebrow pencil scrawls, our defiant graffiti of Congress slogans, were still on the walls.

This dire offence, to forget to report to the police station and write my name in a book, carried an unbelievable minimum sentence of twelve months in gaol. I don't think anyone has ever really understood just why this offence should be considered so dangerous. Over the years almost every banned person has come to grief over this senseless obligation. To forget is not a planned defiance, as no one in his right mind would deliberately fail to report and court twelve months in prison for it.

Inevitably, I was convicted. It was held by the court to be blameworthy negligence. I should have taken adequate precautions to see that I did not forget this vital obligation. I did not of course know beforehand that I was going to forget but perhaps I should have plastered my office with notices, "Report to the police at lunch time!" It had not occurred to me to do that.

I was sentenced to the compulsory twelve months' gaol but the magistrate suspended it all except four days and I served my sentence in Johannesburg gaol. It ended up as only two days, thanks to the happy coincidence of a weekend and a public holiday. I handed myself over with a plastic bag containing my toilet things, which was all I was allowed to have of my own possessions, donned the prison garb and was released again the following morning. That part was over, but I still had eleven months and twenty-six days of gaol hanging over my head. This could be imposed, in addition to any new sentence, should I again forget to report.

There came a day, of course, when I did forget a second time. I was totally unaware of it and protested the next day that I had actually been to report, whether or not the house-arrest register had my signature. I persuaded the policeman on duty that I had been there. He believed me and reluctantly permitted me to sign the register for two days. On my way back to the office I tried to reconstruct the previous day, which I had taken off to attend to a number of private matters and do some shopping. Horrified, I realised that in fact I could not have reported to the police station at all.

I generally regard the police as enemies, even the uniformed police, for they are guilty of shameful acts of brutality towards black people. Yet over the years there had inevitably developed some friendly relations with the staff at the police station where I went to report. They had almost always been helpful and courteous. I felt ashamed that I had, even if unintentionally, deceived that young policeman. I was concerned lest his breach of duty might be held against him.

I drove back to the police station and demanded to see the station commander. I told him what I had done, that I was prepared to take the consequences. To my amazement he assured me that he knew about it already and that the police were not going to take any action against me for not reporting. I fancy the security police had not been informed of my omission. I went back to my office with a lighter heart. I knew that if I had been convicted again of failing to report, I might have to face the imposition of the twelve-month suspended sentence as well as any new sentence.

During 1964 I was arrested again, not this time for violating my banning orders, but on two other more serious charges, one for possessing banned literature and the other for furthering the aims of a banned organisation, the ANC. The banned literature charge developed a comic dimension. I had, in fact, thrown it into my office wastepaper basket, still unopened, but addressed to me. It had been "discovered" by a zealous security policeman who obviously knew where to look for it — on a recessed ledge in the men's cloakroom, where someone must have hidden it. When I protested in court that I had never set foot in the men's loo, the prosecutor accused me of standing in the doorway and pitching the magazine onto the ledge, some eight feet away. Not surprisingly, the magistrate acquitted me on that charge.

The charge relating to the banned ANC had to do with a sum of money repaid to the Federation of South African Women by the ANC in respect of a loan made from the Federation Bail Fund when the ANC was still legal. My defence counsel soon disposed of this allegation of furthering the aims of an organisation by accepting repayment of a loan and I was acquitted.

At this time, the danger of deportation was drawing rather close to me because, although I was a South African citizen, it was not by birth or descent. Conviction under almost every clause of the Suppression of Communism Act could lead to deportation, prefaced by a period in gaol. Fortunately, my only conviction so far was under Section 10 of the Act for failing to report to the police. Although this carried that ominous provision for compulsory imprisonment, it was almost the only clause which did not carry deportation. So I had to be thankful for small mercies and hope that I should be able to avoid any other offence under the Act.

After the end of the treason trial in 1961, I had written the story of the trial as we had known it from the dock. I called it, *If This Be Treason*. It could neither be published nor sold in South Africa because I was a banned person, which made it an offence to quote or disseminate anything that I had said or written.

The book was published in 1963 and a few copies eventually made their way to me. When I held one copy in my hand for the first time, only then did I feel that I was an author. I had a surprise telephone call from London one night, from the party held to celebrate publication day. My brother spoke to me and I think he too could hardly believe that this was all in honour of his sister's book. It all seemed very unreal to me that this should be going on so far away without me there. I felt isolated and elated, both at the same time.

Ever since our journey to the banished people, I had wanted to write the stories of these men and women we had found. We had listened to their stories, only one or two of which had ever been published. South Africa knew almost nothing about these forgotten people, about the stark horror of their lonely lives, the utter hopelessness of indefinite banishment.

My bans did not, at that time, prohibit me from actually writing, only from being published here, but I didn't want to risk the possibility of additional bans to prevent my writing at all. In 1965 I was able to take a few months' leave from my job and this helped me greatly towards writing another book — this time about the banished people. I called it *Tomorrow's Sun*. I had taken the title from Olive Schreiner's book, *Trooper Peter Halkett*.

> Tomorrow's sun shall rise and it shall flood these dark koppies with light, and the rocks shall glint in it. Not more certain is that rising than the coming of the day . . . here on the spot where now we stand shall be raised a temple. Man shall not gather in it to worship that which divides; but they shall stand in it shoulder to shoulder, white man with black and the stranger with the inhabitant of the land; and the place shall be holy for men shall say, 'Are we not brethren and the sons of one Father?'

Thoughout this period I worked at least one day a week at my office because I did not want to highlight my being on prolonged leave for fear of unwelcome police attention. I spent many days writing in the lovely peaceful garden of the

Community of the Resurrection, or in their quiet library. There I could work with a feeling of security, without listening for the opening and closing of car doors as I did at home. But I took care that I was not followed as I drove there and back.

I finished writing *Tomorrow's Sun*. I posted the chapters to London a few pages at a time, as friends completed the typing for me. I waited for the publishers' verdict. It came on a very wet Saturday when I was at home for my house-arrest weekend with no visitors allowed. The post brought the opinion from the publishers' official reader. I was devastated. The opinion was unfavourable, mainly because I had tried to put too much into the book; too many stories, too many people. He said, among other things, that I had produced an amorphous clump of people with unpronounceable names.

I found this accusation ridiculous, even an example of English chauvinism. What right had he, or anyone else, to reject names in another language simply because he couldn't pronounce them? At the end, however, he conceded that he had felt that I was standing at his elbow, saying "Listen, listen!!" and he had had to listen. The publishers urged me to consider rewriting the book, bearing the criticism in mind.

It was the day of Churchill's funeral, broadcast in all its sombre majesty. I thought miserably that I could also hear the death knell tolling for my book. It was a terrible afternoon and the rain kept pouring down. My gloom persisted right through that empty weekend. Write it again? Leave out so many of the stories about the banished people? That was what the book was all about — I had not wanted to write it for any other reason.

My first reaction was to abandon the book altogether. Then I consulted a couple of friends, themselves writers, finally taking their advice that I must try again. I owed it to the banished people, for there was no one else to tell their tragic stories as I could. Their stories would not be told unless I rewrote my book. I cut and slashed and I tried again. This time with success and the book was published. The stories of the banished people were told to the world, even if not to South Africa.

The advance publicity for *Tomorrow's Sun* appeared in London in February 1966. The government acted against me immediately. Within two weeks of the publicity I was served with additional banning orders which prohibited me from preparing any material for publication or even assisting in doing so. The connection with my book was clear enough. I was to write nothing more. This prohibition had not been included in my original bans because this particular refinement had not been thought up then. I could only laugh. The minister was too late, for the book had already been published in England.

When I read the orders more carefully, however, I realised that my laughter was a little too premature. There were other prohibitions, new to me, though often included in the bans of others banned after me. I was now prohibited from entering any building which housed the offices of a trade union or any organisation which produced a publication. I realised with a sort of sick horror that my office at the Medical Aid Society was in the building which housed the Garment Workers' Union and I could not enter it again.

With my usual confidence I was sure that I could find a way out of even this difficulty. It did not take me long to work out an interim plan while I waited for a reply from the minister to my urgent application to be allowed to enter the building where my office was. Meanwhile, I continued my work at home, keeping contact by telephone and fetching and returning work daily; just standing outside the building on the pavement. It wasn't a very dignified procedure but it was better than nothing.

The minister replied with a flat refusal. I realised that he had not only prevented me from writing again, but that my job was now in jeopardy.

Within twenty-four hours I was notified by the management committee that my appointment had been terminated. My suggestion that I might work in an office in an adjacent building was rejected. It was clear. My employers had had enough of Helen Joseph, despite my contribution to the Medical Aid Society.

I was stunned and humiliated, almost unbelieving. The Society was not ungenerous. It paid me a handsome honorarium, which I wanted to throw back, but commonsense prevailed over dignity. I had to live and I had more than earned that money over the years. It took me some time to see the whole affair in perspective and to accept that the patience of the Society had been sorely tried by this turbulent Secretary. It was not surprising that I had to go when the opportunity presented itself in that I could no longer even enter the building. I sometimes wonder how I managed to survive there so long, fifteen years, for there had been the treason trial, five months in detention and the house arrest and bans.

It was a new experience for me to be sacked. I had to accept that I was almost unemployable, despite my degree and diploma and my long administrative and social welfare experience. I was sixty-one, heavily handicapped by my political reputation and by these new banning orders with their prohibitions, not only on entering buildings but also on teaching or publishing of any sort.

Like so many other banned people, I abandoned any thought of employment at the executive or professional level, which I had enjoyed for so long. No welfare organisation would dare to employ me as a social worker for fear of losing government subsidies.

I went through a few disillusioning weeks of applying for advertised vacancies. Prospective employers would show initial enthusiasm over my experience and qualifications but freeze in silence on hearing who I was. It was necessary for me to say that I was banned because as both a banned and listed person I was compelled to inform the police of any change of employment. I knew from the experience of others that a new job was always followed by a visit from the security police to the new employers. It had happened to others. It would happen to me.

Until now my life had been cushioned by the security of my job, despite the problems of being banned and house-arrested. Others had not been so fortunate. Being banned had spelt financial ruin to some and to almost everyone intolerable anxiety over the future, with prospects of lengthy unemployment to be ended only with uncongenial and lower-paid jobs. This had already driven some banned people out of the country and well-meaning friends suggested that I too should go, return to England to be free, reminding me that I was at no age to start job-hunting with so many handicaps. Yet the thought of leaving South Africa was never in my mind. I was convinced I could survive somehow, even if I had to live very modestly, sell my car, perhaps even my home. But not yet. I could battle on.

I went on the dole. It had an almost comic dimension. I arrived at the Unemployment Insurance Fund Depot, my glowing testimonials under my arm, my unemployment insurance card in my hand, hoping to have some sort of job offered to me. I had to fill in various forms and when it came to the question whether I had ever been in gaol, I had to answer "Yes", remembering my one and only conviction, failing to report to the police. I was referred to the rehabilitation office, where I joined some weary men seated on hard benches. They gazed at me unbelievingly, almost resentfully, although I was simply ex-gaol and unemployed, just as they were.

The rehabilitation officer, after reading my testimonials from university, community centres and the Medical Aid Society, said despairingly, "Of course I can't find anyone like you a job. We just don't have that kind of job here." After that I drew my dole every fortnight and no one ever tried to find a job for me. I just went on trying on my own, unsuccessfully.

I wanted to do it myself. I didn't want to ask for favours, but I could not succeed alone. When my six months' dole was almost exhausted I went cap in hand to Fanny Klenerman of the famous Vanguard bookshop. I asked her for a job, any kind of job. I first had to make sure legally that selling books was not disseminating literature, as prohibited in my banning orders, but it was all right. Selling books is merely a commercial transaction. Before the end of the year I was working in the bookshop, though I never became a good saleswoman.

During the 1960s, the number of banned people ran into hundreds and included many who had completed sentences for political offences, only to face a further punishment on release, this time without trial. They too were house-arrested and banned, which effectively destroyed almost every avenue of employment. They were prohibited from entering factories, certain buildings, universities and schools. Bans and prison records sowed fear in the hearts of prospective employers. In this nationwide atmosphere of intimidation, so deliberately cultivated by the system under which we live, very few employers, even today, can be found to give jobs to banned people.

Banning orders were being imposed on all sorts and types of men and women, from university professor to housewife, from the man on the factory floor to the business executive. Joe Morolong, who came all the way with me on that long journey to the banished, Mildred Lesia and Mitta Goeiman, who had joined us for part of the way, they were all banned. Joe was confined to a radius of a mile and half around his father's dwelling in the lonely lands of the Northern Cape, with no other dwellings in sight.

All of us were now banned, Amina, Joe, Mildred, Mitta and I. We could no longer communicate with each other. I remembered those months of close companionship on our long journey and the tragedies of those we had visited together. My own loss of freedom seemed a small price to pay for the joy and hope we had brought to those lonely people. They had been forgotten. We had not.

Chapter II

More of the same

After almost five years of house arrest, I was eagerly but anxiously looking forward to 31 October 1967, when the restrictions were due to expire. I began to count the weeks and then the days, hoping, yet not quite believing, that the house arrest might not be renewed. There was no way of predicting what would happen, as I had been the first person to be placed under house arrest. Several other people were waiting almost as anxiously as I was, for then they too would know what to expect.

I stilled my own nagging doubts and planned for my freedom. I even sang to myself when I drive to work, to the tune of "Around the World in Eighty Days" but with my own words: "In eighty days I shall be free, and all my friends will come to tea!" Then I sang "seventy days" and fifty and forty, right down to "In four more days I shall be free!"

I planned a midnight party for the very moment when the bans expired and I could open wide my gate to friends for the first time in five years. They would walk right down the garden path and into my house. I had a great need to get out of Johannesburg after all that time so I planned to fly to Durban and then go by boat to Cape Town and back again. I even bought the tickets.

At about eight o'clock on the evening of Friday, 27 October, I heard the knock on the door. I knew who it was because no one ever knocked on my door except the security police. I opened the door to the two men standing there, but I did not invite them in. They handed me three sheets of paper — the mixture exactly as before. Traces of their evil aura seemed to float about so I closed the door on them before I looked at the papers — another five years of house arrest and all the other restrictions, another five years of reporting to the police.

The realisation of what this meant was like a dull pain in my chest. I felt stunned, unable to make myself do anything except sit in a chair and look at those damnably hurtful papers lying in my lap. I had of course accepted the possibility that this might happen, but being human, I had allowed myself to hope. I knew then how foolish I had been, but planning had been fun and I did not regret it.

Now there would be no midnight party, no holiday, no boat trip, no freedom, only the continuation of everything I had borne for the past five years. At first I was almost too shocked to be angry. Then I began to feel a bitter, deep wrath against the Nationalist government, against the security police, against the whole system. I had felt it often enough on behalf of others, now I felt it for myself. Yet not once did I feel that I could not go on. I had to. "Side by side . . . throughout our lives, sparing nothing of our strength and courage until this liberty has been won." That had been my promise twelve years ago at the Congress of the People. I had to keep that promise.

I went to work next morning. A great wave of sympathy and indignation engulfed me and bore me up at the same time. It came from all sorts of people, by telephone, by telegram, with flowers, in visits to the bookshop, for no one could visit me at home — all expressing horror at this cruel extension of persecution. I went home at midday to the first of the next 260 empty weekends. This magnificent support helped me to get through the coming difficult weeks.

The Black Sash protested on behalf of both Lilian Ngoyi and me, for her ban had also been renewed for five more years. Here we were again, the National President and the National Secretary of the Federation of South African Women, side by side in our restrictions, yet unable to communicate with each other.

At the police station, the policemen on duty when I came to report stopped counting off the days with me. "Only four more days, Mrs Joseph," they had said the day before I was re-banned. Now they were silent and so was I.

It did not make matters easier that soon after this a senior officer of the South African police bought the house next door to me. He and his family could look from their windows right onto my verandah and into my garden. I found this unbearable, yet I would not consider moving. Thanks to the Dean of Johannesburg, however, and his friends, within weeks a seven-foot concrete wall was erected, giving me the privacy I craved. Later I grew a forest of tall shrubs and trees in front of the wall, making my small garden even more private.

The policeman, interviewed by the press, asserted that he had bought the house "without the slightest knowledge of who his neighbours would be". This seemed strange in view of the state's decision to place me under a further five years' house arrest. He was, moreover, the second senior officer in command at the large and important police station in Norwood. It was hard to believe that he did not know where this "dangerous" woman lived. Did the police really believe that my home was a hotbed of intrigue, of conspiracy, of planning for insurrection? I did of course meet some of my banned friends secretly elsewhere, but with the threat of gaol hanging over our heads. That fleeting contact was simply to sustain ourselves through those awful years, not to plot subversion.

I soon settled down again into my house-arrest way of life, although I realised that I must plan some sort of constructive occupation for the weekends and the evenings. I no longer had the Medical Aid Society research to do at home, nor a book to write, as I had had in the first five years. I knew that even if I planned any reading or study course on my own, I would not keep to it without some form of external discipline. My thoughts turned to a university course. I realised how little I actually knew about the faith to which I had recently returned, so I registered for the external Bachelor of Divinity degree with the University of London. It was very ambitious of me, but I told myself that it would not matter if I failed the exams because they were simply to discipline me and keep me on course.

Thus, at the age of sixty-two, I became a theological student and had much difficulty in persuading people that I really had no ambition to become the first ordained woman priest in South Africa. The qualifying year was quite a struggle because I had to learn New Testament Greek. I used to write out declensions and tenses on cards and prop them up on the windscreen of my car, memorising them as I drove to work.

During 1968 I left the bookshop. True, I did not have much choice of alternative employment and I doubt that I should have gone far to seek it, but an opportunity presented itself. I was finding the bookshop a strain in many ways, grateful as I was to have a job at all. The daily reporting to the police took up almost all of my lunch hour. Parking facilities in the city seemed to move ever further from the bookshop so that I had less time to visit my friends after work.

Some friends owned a hotel in Roodepoort, west of Johannesburg, and therefore outside my permitted orbit. They offered me a job helping them with the office work and the management of the hotel. My work hours would be shorter and the fifteen miles each way would take no longer than it did to get through the city traffic from Norwood and then walk from the parking ground to the shop. It seemed to me that it would be a more peaceful life and although I turned it down initially, I finally accepted.

I had to apply to the magistrate for permission to leave the area of Johannesburg. The magistrate in turn had to consult the security police and all this took several weeks. Finally permission was granted and my restriction cage was doubled to include both the Johannesburg and Roodepoort areas.

I left my job in the big city and became a suburban hotel bookkeeper with occasional excursions into the supervision of the hotel bedrooms and the kitchen. Hotel housekeeping proved not to be my vocation so I arranged to work part time and restrict myself to the bookkeeping. The greatest disadvantage was that my friends could not contact me as easily as in the bookshop because of the distance from Johannesburg. On the other hand, reporting to the police was far easier than before as it took only fifteen minutes.

My interest in theology grew and my studies absorbed many evenings and weekends. I wrote my first examinations, in New Testament Greek, in June 1969, already sixty-four, very apprehensive of undignified failure. I was forbidden by my bans to enter any university premises so had to make private arrangements for the examination and for an invigilator. As always the Community of Resurrection came to my rescue. Their spacious Priory library was approved by London University as an examination centre.

On a bitterly cold morning I wrote the examination, wrapped in a heavy black monk's cloak, also kindly supplied by the Priory. Brother Norwood Coaker, a QC, but long since retired from legal practice, invigilated for me. We had to complete archaic forms relating to the circumstances in which I was writing the examination. One question read, "If the candidate is a female and the invigilator is of the opposite sex, was a third person present?" I found this concern for my virtue very amusing, especially since Brother Norwood was eighty and I was sixty-four. However, we truthfully answered "No" and I wondered whether this might disqualify me from the examination. It obviously did not. I passed and could go on to further theological studies.

Despite all this, the years were dragging. Many people were now under house arrest. Other bans had been renewed and there was always a question in my mind as to whether I should ever again be free, even when this second set of bans came to an end. A very influential friend from my pre-political years wrote to me to say that he was sure that if I gave an assurance of good behaviour and expressed regret for the past, he could persuade the authorities to set me free. This angered me so much that I destroyed the letter without replying. It did not, however, completely destroy our friendship of so many years and we are still friends today. Indeed, that was how many people regarded me, as an unrepentant sinner.

My brother in England asked me to consider returning but at the same time acknowledged that he was sure I would not agree. For me, to leave South Africa and return to England was unthinkable. South Africa is my land by adoption, even if not by birth. For me to leave would be the ultimate betrayal. I was not being a martyr about this. I wanted to stay in South Africa, to be side by side with my friends in the struggle, whether banished, banned or in gaol. Perhaps it might cost me dear. I did not know, but the greater price would have been to leave.

Sometimes it would be put to me that I could do more by going than by staying. It was true that in those sterile years I was politically hamstrung by my bans and house arrest, by the outlawing of the Congress of Democrats and the crippling of the Federation by the banning of so many of its members. The years seemed sometimes to grow ever emptier for me. Yet all I had to do was to ask myself the question, "Is there really anything that I could do overseas that someone else there could not do equally well or better?" I knew that the answer would always be "No".

It has always seemed to me that I can achieve something simply by staying in South Africa. I cannot articulate this clearly and I have never been able to, but in my heart it is as strong as any tenet of my faith. I could not see into the future. I did not know whether there would ever again be any political activity in which I could participate, or if I should ever again be free. I only knew that I had to stay. I could not take any easy way out.

I thought very often about William Letlalo. As an old man, he had been placed under house arrest for twenty-four hours every day. He could never go out of his tiny matchbox house in Soweto. It was a typical township house and there are hundreds of thousands of them, rows and rows of little hutches, with a million black people living in them. These houses have four tiny rooms, including the kitchen. The toilets are outside and there are no bathrooms. They are still there today, twenty years later, and there is an endless waiting list for them, for thousands of people who have no homes.

Perhaps William Letlalo was fortunate after all. He had a home and there were not twelve or thirteen people living in it. There was only himself and his wife. I doubt that in his loneliness he thought of that as good fortune. He remained in that little matchbox house for four years, walking only the few yards to his front gate for exercise and to look at the world and the people passing him by.

William Letlalo was seventy when this even more awful twenty-four-hour house arrest was inflicted on him. He was seventy-nine when the house arrest was lifted. He was eighty-three when the other bans expired. I knew him, a wiry old man, very active and a leader of his people despite his age. When I thought of those four terrible years of imprisonment in that small house, I found little room for self-pity in my own years of house arrest, free to move during the daylight hours, living in my comfortable home and in my comfortable white suburb, as I had always done.

By the end of 1970 I had already been under house arrest for 3,000 days. It didn't seem so much in later years, when others endured this gaol on the cheap for much longer, but I was the first to reach this point and the press took it up. It seemed to focus attention, not only on me, but on others. The editor of the *Rand Daily Mail* wrote,

> She is not the only one under house arrest or deprived arbitrarily of human rights. But somehow her case typifies all that is evil in this society. How old does she have to be before the State feels safe enough to stop persecuting her in the name of security?

I remembered William Letlalo and I thought I might well have to be another ten years older!

In his amusing political "gossip" column in the *Sunday Times*, Joel Mervis described an imaginary meeting of Nationalist Party supporters at which the speaker thundered, "We have the finest army in the world, the finest airforce, the finest navy — what do we have to be afraid of? (Voice from the back) 'HELEN JOSEPH'."

At the beginning of my house arrest I had received numerous abusive and threatening phone calls. Towards the end of 1970 a new manifestation of the evil that flourishes in our South African society appeared in my life. This plague was different at first. After it had died down I could see the comic side, but at the time it was acutely harassing.

It started off with a clumsy attempt to steal my car in broad daylight from the hotel yard and deposit it in a service station for unneeded repairs — where I should not be able to find it. This attempt was frustrated by the hotel head waiter, who warned me that mechanics were removing my car and he was doubtful about it because they didn't have the car keys and had not asked for me. As it happened the mechanics were innocent. They had simply obeyed a telephone instruction from a man who, it turned out, had given a false name and address. I reported it to the police but got little interest and less help.

That was the beginning of a stream of hoaxes that went on for a few days, all carefully worked out and no two the same. Lorry-loads of topsoil or coal or sand

147

or paving stones were delivered COD to my house, or dumped outside in my absence, and then I would find an invoice to say that I had ordered the goods COD. It took some time to explain to bewildered and indignant merchants that it was they who had been hoaxed. Eager salesmen called to take measurements for a swimming pool and gazed unbelievingly at my tiny garden where no swimming pool would fit.

Then came the first telephone death threat. It was after an agonising evening of trying to persuade some twenty or thirty would-be tenants that I had not advertised my home to let at a ridiculously low rental. I had difficulty in dissuading them from coming right onto the premises or to convince them that this was forbidden territory. Finally I went out and bought strong padlocks for the gates.

It was hard to make people believe that all this was a hoax and not my hoax either. I soon got very tired of that word, but it was the only way I could make people understand what was going on. It was even more difficult to convey any motive for it all because the hoaxed people were typical white South Africans, unlikely to feel any sympathy towards my brand of politics.

A very quiet English voice asked to speak to Mrs Helen Joseph. "Now don't put the phone down. I have a very important message for you." I waited. "I am coming tonight to get you and kill you." I slammed the phone down and called the police who said they could do nothing about it. They wanted to know why I was under house arrest and why my husband did not protect me. They finally conceded that they would tell the patrol to watch out. I did not find that very comforting. I padlocked both gates and the garage, made some supper and some strong coffee and went to bed. I left every light burning all night, both inside the house and outside. I closed all the windows, double locked the doors and slept in my slacks with my dog, Dinah, privileged for once, lying beside me. I memorised the flying squad telephone number. I prayed too from the Psalm, "Thou shalt not be afraid for any terror by night . . ." Then I fell asleep, waking once or twice during the night, but all was quiet.

I was left undisturbed at the weekend except for one telephone call with no voice, only maniacal laughter and another caller who, when I asked to whom he wished to speak, said threateningly, "To my victim!"

After press publicity and a prod from Helen Suzman, the Progressive Party MP, the police began to show some interest. A colonel called ceremoniously to see me, suggesting first that it might be my husband or some very personal enemy. I assured him that he was wrong on both counts. His next suggestion was that it might be my "former political associates" with whom I had severed my connection. That made me very angry and I reminded him that it was the government who had severed these connections and not I. I asserted that my political views were unchanged and that everyone knew it.

He then informed me that for two weeks my telephone would be monitored every day. I found this an amusing piece of news, for I had ample proof that my telephone had been monitored already for some considerable period, but I kept a straight face. He assured me that every effort would be made to trace the telephone calls. In fact there were no more at that time and I was duly notified after fourteen days that my telephone was no longer monitored.

It took me a little time to develop indifference to these nasty incidents. I half expected to find sacks of coal or loads of sand whenever I came home from work or angry would-be tenants awaiting me. In fact there had been another advertisement that my house was to let. This time my telephone number was given and I could deal with the numerous queries by telephone. That was often unpleasant, but it was better than having people come to the house for nothing.

My friends urged me not to live alone but to apply for permission to have someone else staying in the house. I did not want to do this, to ask for favours from the minister to alleviate a situation which he himself had deliberately imposed upon me. What I did not know was that I could in fact always have had boarders or lodgers in my house because once there was payment, they could no longer be termed visitors. Yet I doubt that I could have shared my house even if I had known this. I had bought it because I wanted to live alone. In any event I would have been reluctant to bring any other person into my house if there was really to be danger or violence.

One night in May 1971, I had been working late at my desk when I noticed that it was already after midnight and decided to retire. I let Dinah out into the garden for her last run. She rushed to the gate barking loudly and fiercely and I hesitated for a moment, thinking there must be a cat in the garden. As she persisted, I decided to investigate, but by the time I had reached the gate she had stopped barking. I looked up and down the road in the moonlight. All seemed quiet so I went to bed without giving it any further thought.

Early the next morning I went to open the drive gates. I saw an oblong packet with a lot of string attached to it lying in the drive. It looked like some sort of child's toy kite. I picked it up, turned it over and saw what looked like a couple of batteries in the open back. They were attached to a long piece of electric flex, not string as I had first thought. It seemed to come from a bush at the side of the drive near the gate. By this time I was suspicious. I put the packet down carefully on the ground. It was clear that it was no child's toy. I telephoned the police, who sent a bomb disposal team.

It turned out to be an amateur bomb which would have exploded when I opened the drive gates. It was very smart, but Dinah had been smarter, as she had startled the would-be bombers the night before and they had fled, leaving their contraption lying in the middle of the driveway, instead of hiding it. I asked the bomb experts how powerful it might have been and got the casual reply, "Oh, probably not lethal but you might have lost an arm or leg." I didn't find that comforting but I took some malicious pleasure in remarking to the security policeman in attendance, "How nice to see you in *my* service for once." He did not reply.

Dinah had certainly saved me from any possible injury. She had done more than that, she had brought me to my senses. For more than two months I had been aware of a growing lump in my left breast. I knew that I ought to have it investigated at once, but I deliberately held back, unbelievably on political grounds. I must have been more depressed by the house arrest than I realised. I was becoming obsessed by the idea that it would never come to an end. It would just be repeated every five years. I had already come through the first period and four years of the second period. When 31 October 1972 came, what then? The minister had the power to renew house arrest every five years, in fact for as long as he liked. He had done it to me once. What was to stop him from doing it again — and again — and again?

I was feeling very frustrated politically although I knew that I did serve some purpose, if only that I had become prominent. Anything that happened to me, as the first house-arrested person, was news. In this way I brought the plight of people restricted like myself constantly to public notice. Otherwise many of us would have become forgotten people, like the banished Africans.

I was very ignorant about the medical aspects of cancer, fearing that it would just mean being patched up to wait for the cancer to reappear in some other area. But, I thought, I was nearly sixty-six and I was not sure that I wanted to live to an old age in loneliness, especially in house-arrest conditions. Surely it would be better to let go now and face what might be coming to me, for I had no doubt at all that this was cancer. I actually hoped that my death from cancer while under house arrest might prevail upon the government to abandon this cruel persecution altogether. I knew that for me to die in this way, under house arrest at sixty-six, would have international repercussions.

I do not, of course, know how far I would ultimately have gone in this obsession, but it made me very happy at the time to think that I might be able to twist this cancer to political advantage. My death could be more significant than my life. I did not allow myself to think of what physical suffering I might be drawing upon myself.

The bomb escape made a deep impact on me — not fear, but the realisation that my way of thinking might be wrong. Perhaps Dinah's intervention was more meaningful than it had appeared, perhaps it was to teach me that I must go on living, that there was still work for me to do, that I could not give up, no matter how much use I thought I might be by dying. This was not for me to decide.

Within a few days I went to the General Hospital. The diagnosis was second stage cancer with a slight possibility of third stage as I had left it dangerously late. An urgent operation was necessary. It was only half an hour after I came back from the hospital, knowing now the folly of my earlier decision, that I had a call from Colonel Johann Coetzee of the security police. Such telephone calls invariably create apprehension because refusal to co-operate can lead to detention without trial with all its attendant evils.

For me, the whole horror of the security police and their power is somehow embodied in the personality and person of this man, who already in 1982, held the rank of lieutenant general in the South African police force and head of the security police. He has been in the background of my life since my very early political days, when he held the modest rank of detective sergeant, a shorthand writer in the police force. In the 1950s he used to appear at our meetings to take down our speeches in his competent shorthand, a dapper young man of medium height, with smooth dark hair and moustache. If it had not been for the sports jacket and grey flannel trousers, almost the uniform of the security branch, he might have passed for a young business executive, with his inevitable briefcase. However, he soon graduated to grey suits with pastel shirts and muted, subdued coloured ties.

Sergeant Coetzee's face was always expressionless, his movements controlled. He betrayed no emotion, even when some of us were deliberately rude to him, as we usually were to all security policemen. His effect on me was to turn me into a British iceberg, for his total lack of emotion evoked in me a deeply-rooted dislike and complete distrust. At the treason trial we once flared into open confrontation (if mute on my side), when he swore on oath in the witness box that he had been present at a meeting of the Federation of South African Women in the Johannesburg Trades Hall in 1955 and that he had taken his notes publicly. I knew that he had not been visibly present at that meeting. I had been on the platform throughout and knew personally the only two white men who had been there. They were press reporters and Sergeant Coetzee was not one of them. I don't know where he was, whether on the roof listening through the fanlight, or hiding in a cupboard, but I do know beyond all doubt that his claim that he sat through the meeting in full view is not true. It was a small meeting, not more than 200 women present, and I knew everybody in that hall.

Since then our paths have crossed occasionally. Our contempt and dislike is obviously mutual. It has been said of General Coetzee that his eyes never come alive, they are drained of expression. Yet a friend has said that she would not like to be in the crossbeam of mutual venom which shoots from our eyes if we are in the same place. Our eyes meet and hold, our faces are taut with mutual antagonism.

When Winnie Mandela was in detention in 1969, Johann Coetzee told her that he would get Helen Joseph behind bars one day. He had been trying to do this for fifteen years, he said, and he would do it.

Today this one-time shorthand writer has reached the pinnacle of success. He is now the head of the South African police. As such, I must hold him responsible for the indescribable cruelty and torture, even to death, which is meted out to political detainees, held incommunicado and without trial. I am old and banned and listed and unable to function politically as I should wish, yet I would not change places with General Coetzee, Commissioner of Police. I can live with myself. I do not know if he can.

In that telephone call, Colonel Coetzee, as he was then, said that there were a few matters he would like to discuss with me, including my failure to report to the police the previous month. It was true. I had forgotten again, now for the third time, and had been waiting to be arrested and charged. I replied as casually as I could that I had news for him, I was about to be admitted to hospital for an urgent major operation for cancer.

I certainly took him by surprise. After a noticeable silence, he expressed concern in his controlled voice and suggested that the discussion should be postponed. I replied that I should be interested to know what it was all about and would make an appointment before I went into hospital. But when I phoned again, the control was gone and he said angrily, "What I have to say to *you*, Mrs Joseph, will take a very long time. There is no point in going on with it now."

I had much to see to in those few days; my work at the hotel, arrangements for the house and my cat and dog. I had also to apply to the magistrate for permission to leave my house to go to hospital and to be excused from the daily reporting to the police. In retrospect, I regret that I so dutifully made these incredible applications. In the circumstances, I could hardly have been arrested for failing to do so.

On the day before the operation, the news came out in the press that I was in hospital for major cancer surgery. I had not, nor I am sure had the hospital, expected such widespread publicity and indignation as burst forth over the fact that I should still be technically under house arrest at such a time. I was deeply moved by the concern of all who knew me, and of many who did not.

My fellow patients in the ward were stunned when they found out who I was and I suppose the nurses were, too. Mostly they were very sympathetic, although not really understanding what it was all about, except that they now had a "Commie" in their midst, but a strange Commie who was visited by priests and even bishops and took Holy Communion in the mornings.

I am sure, all the same, that everyone was delighted by the masses of beautiful flowers which brightened up the large ward. There were even real lilies-of-the-valley brought direct from an English garden by a friend who carried them, wrapped in cottonwool in his sponge bag, throughout his flight from England. They were so delicate and pure, so exquisite, I can never forget them.

Visitors were a problem. I was still not officially allowed to be with more than one person at a time, but my friends crowded around my bed during the short visiting hours, regardless of my bans. Then the matron informed me that the security police had threatened to station a policeman in the ward during visiting hours if my visitors were not restricted. After that my friends queued up at the door, coming in one by one, rather as they came to my gate on Christmas Day.

In reply to my application to have a friend to stay with me on my discharge from hospital and also to be permitted then to receive visitors to my house, the magistrate, obviously under the instructions of the security police, had demanded the names and addresses of all of them. I was outraged by this and refused to comply with his request.

Helen Suzman, still fighting her gallant and lonely battle in Parliament as the lone Progressive Party MP, came to see me in hospital. She had approached the Minister of Justice for the lifting of my house arrest at this critical time in my life. He had commented that even if I lost both arms and legs I should still be a nuisance. He would not commit himself.

I had to have some radiotherapy after the very successful operation. This would keep me in hospital unless I could have some attention at home, so I had to resign myself to staying there. Meanwhile the scandal of Helen Joseph, sixty-six years old, still in hospital after a cancer operation, was growing, both in

South Africa and overseas. I am sure I was becoming an embarrassment to the government and it was not lessened by some pungent articles in the English press.

The London *Daily Mail* had said:

> Now she is sixty-six. She has had a veɪy serious operation . . . will she still be penalised? Still kept in the solitude of house arrest? If she is, the charge against the South African government will be one of slow murder.

Bernard Levin of *The Times* had written in his column:

> Without wishing to be indelicate, I must point out that she presumably has two breasts; if the operation she is at present having is for the removal of one, she could always, when she felt like a further spell of human society, pop into hospital and have the other off. After that, there is plenty more scope; here a hand, there a foot, anon a womb — she could pretty well have herself dismantled piecemeal before the South African government twigged what was going on and put a stop to it, and each time she could have anything up to a fortnight of the positively Sardanapalian luxury of talking to other human beings.

He added that since the house arrest had apparently failed to break me, "the torment has for years now been an end in itself".

I shall always believe that such articles and such widespread publicity played a large part in the sudden change of attitude on the part of the government. One afternoon two security policemen came to my ward, bringing a letter from the Secretary for Justice to say that my restriction orders were suspended until further notice. I was free — after nine years.

When the news spread, there was great excitement amongst the hospital staff. They came pouring in, including the matron herself, to congratulate me. I was allowed to have a champagne party when my jubilant friends arrived to share my freedom with me. Within two days I was permitted to go home, not to an empty house but to a house with people in it, people coming to it, all day, every day — to make up for the lost years. It was a new world.

Chapter III

The world outside

While I was living encapsulated in house arrest, the 1960s inexorably became a decade of disgrace, of repressive legislation. Sadistic incarceration, even torture by the security police to extract information from helpless victims, was the order of the day. South Africa was following the barbaric example of Nazi Germany and had learnt its lessons well.

Umkhonto We Sizwe sabotage continued and multiplied, always keeping to the policy of avoiding loss of life. Installations and buildings were the targets, not human beings.

During 1961, Poqo had emerged as a new underground sabotage organisation, formed by extremist members of the PAC, now itself underground like the ANC. Unlike Umkhonto, it did not confine its violence to attacks on installations but also planned and carried out violent physical reprisals on individuals, black and white, leading to injuries and death, sometimes in a kind of mindless violence.

In 1963, the government's response was another General Laws Amendment Act which went far beyond the Act of 1962. Detention without trial was introduced as a permanent feature, obviating any need for the declaration of a State of Emergency. This detention could be used against any person whom the police suspected of planning sabotage, or any offence under the Sabotage Act, or, and more sinister, anyone who, in the opinion of the police, could supply any information relating to it. Detainees were held totally incommunicado for up to ninety days, or released and then immediately re-detained for another ninety days. These were frightening provisions, opening wide the door for ill-treatment of detainees in order to obtain information.

The infamous Act became law on 1 May 1963. Within a week the first people were detained and by the end of 1963 there had been over 500 such detentions. There were horrifying reports of detainees' conditions, invariably solitary confinement, usually with no reading or writing material, although sometimes the Bible was allowed. There were reports of physical torture, especially electric shocks applied to sensitive parts of the body.

Some of my friends were detained very soon, others a little later, but the shadow of "ninety days" hung over us all. I listened, as many others did, I know, for the sound of a car stopping in the middle of the night, counting the number of car doors I heard closing, lest it should be the police.

The provision for ninety-days' detention without trial was suspended by the minister at the beginning of 1965, but not before it had cost the lives of three men. Official reports claimed suicide as the cause of all three deaths, but the doubts in the minds of many have never been laid to rest.

Babla Salojee was one of the "suicides". He was well known to us in Johannesburg as a lively member of the Transvaal Indian Youth Congress. After sixty-five days of detention, Babla, so often bubbling with laughter before his detention, fell to his death from a seventh-floor window of the police buildings while he was being interrogated. No one will ever really know what led to his death — unless you believe the police story. Nor is it really necessary to know the details, for his death, like others, lies at the door of the interrogating policemen.

More than 1,000 people were detained before the notorious Clause 17 authorising the ninety-days' detention was suspended, but it still remained on the statute book, to be invoked should the Minister of Justice deem it necessary. Within six months of the suspension, the ninety days was replaced by the provision for 180 days' detention without trial, this time to compel reluctant witnesses to give evidence. The minister was apparently not satisfied with the ninety days' results, even though one-quarter of the detainees had become state witnesses, betrayed their colleagues and their cause to escape from the horrors of gaol and torture. I should have thought the minister might have been satisfied with one in every four. But no, even harsher measures had to be devised to make a man sell his soul in exchange for his freedom. One hundred and eighty days became an even uglier weapon with the same terrifying background of isolation and torture, physical assault, thirty, forty hours of standing in one spot without sleep or rest, and electric shocks. This last refinement of torture seemed then to have been reserved for blacks. It is humiliating to realise that even in detention the white skin counts.

The year 1967 brought the new Terrorism Act. We had thought nothing could be much worse than the previous year's legislation, but we were wrong. The Terrorism Act spread an even wider net for those who participated in or even knew of terrorist activities, with a minimum of five years' imprisonment and room for the death sentence. Under the grim Section 6 of the Act, detention for interrogation became indefinite and the detainee completely incommunicado. South Africa had indeed become a police state.

Protest, whether national or international, made no difference. This sadistic compulsion remained enshrined in South African law, but the reality of it was hidden, high up on the top floor of police buildings, shut in by thick walls and barred doors, through which screams of agony could sometimes be heard. This barbarous method of extracting information has had different names, ninety days, 180 days, and now, even today, it is the dreaded "Section 6". It is still the same, but now not only for blacks. It can be the bag over the head, the total removal of clothes, shocks applied to the most private parts of the body. The miracle remains that so many are not broken on this rack of torture which leaves no physical mark. But other marks remain. "It has deprived me of my humanity," one detainee told me, "because I can no longer see these people as human beings. And I am angry at being deprived of any part of my humanity."

Much has been written over the years about this appalling attack on humanity which continues to this day in South Africa. The Nationalist government justifies it as a defence against encroaching communism. What white South Africa cannot see is that if anything can convince people of the advantages of communism, it is the poverty and exploitation that is firmly rooted in the apartheid system, supported and protected by a police state.

As these laws were passed, I became increasingly horrified and frustrated. Surely it could not be possible for human beings to stand back and allow these laws to be passed, to operate with all that goes with them in the detention cells? Yet white South Africa does. Almost the whole white population does nothing more than "cluck". The Western world equally "clucks" — and continues to enjoy the economic relations which benefit it and unashamedly bolster up this abhorrent regime.

I have already said how often I am — and still am — asked why I don't leave South Africa. Part of the answer lies in my utter hatred of the security and apartheid laws and practices of South Africa. It is my belief that by staying in South Africa, having suffered some of the persecution inflicted by the government, by being prepared to accept whatever lies in the future, I can make my stand clear.

By the end of the 1960s, seven years after the introduction of ninety days, eighteen black men had already died in detention. Only six were alleged by the state to have died of natural causes. Twelve were shamelessly claimed as suicide or death by hanging. Imagination shudders at what the dead men must have suffered to bring them to the state when death by hanging is preferable to life. Were they tortured beyond endurance until they made the statements demanded by their interrogators? Did they find death preferable to becoming state witnesses? Whatever the cause of death, these "suicides" must, like Babla Salojee's fall, lie at the door of the security police. Nor are there lacking proven cases of murderous assaults by the police upon their helpless victims. For Joseph Mdhluli and Steven Biko, for Neil Aggett, the full circumstances have never been disclosed, yet in these cases there can be no doubt that they died at the hands of the police. Were these indeed the only such cases?

As the trials began in the courts, so also came the triumphs and tragedies of the accused and the witnesses. The police bragged, "They all talk sooner or later." Perhaps they do. Human endurance must have its limits and gradually reports emerged of the sufferings of the detainees. Evidence was needed by the police for successful prosecutions. Statements from the detainees had to be obtained. Complaints to the courts of statements extracted under duress brought no relief. There were policemen a-plenty to deny any truth in the detainees' reports of violence or long periods of sleepless standing.

This decade of political trials led off with the famous Rivonia trial. Walter Sisulu and Ahmed Kathrada, my colleagues at the treason trial, had been dramatically arrested with twelve others at a house in Rivonia, a Johannesburg suburb of large houses and pleasant wooded gardens. Nelson Mandela was brought from gaol to join them while he was still serving his five-year sentence.

Only ten men stood trial on charges under the Sabotage Act. Four of those who had been arrested had made a dramatic escape from the Marshall Square police station. Their escape was hailed as a triumph in those dark days. Robert Hepple did not stand trial for he had made a statement to the prosecution and was released. He fled the country immediately and no one knows whether, had he not been freed, he would have become a state witness and faced his friends in the dock. James Kantor was discharged at the end of the state case.

Nelson Mandela spoke from the dock in words that have made history.

> The African National Congress is struggling for the right to live ... During my lifetime I have dedicated myself to this struggle of the African people. I have fought against white domination and I have fought against black domination. I have cherished the ideal of a democratic and free society in which all persons live together in harmony and with equal opportunities. It is an ideal which I hope to live for and to achieve. But if need be it is an ideal for which I am prepared to die.

South Africa had waited in tense expectation the day before they were sentenced. They had all been found guilty except one white. Would they live or die? The death sentence had been demanded and it was a possibility. I had not once been able to attend their trial in Pretoria because I was forbidden by my bans to leave Johannesburg. Even at this crucial time, I could not say goodbye to my friends.

On the day of the sentence I did not go to work. I felt that I could not bear to be sitting in my office when it came, whether life or death. I went instead to sort and prepare the food and clothing for winter parcels for the banished people. I took my transistor radio with me and when I heard the words "life imprisonment" I could only whisper "They live! They live!" Then I thought of the agony of the wives and the irony of it all, that they would be so thankful for the life imprisonment of their husbands which would make a mockery of their marriages. Life imprisonment for these convicted men meant just that. There would be no remission. Life meant for the term of their natural lives.

They left the dock, these leaders of their people, left their wives and their children and went singing down the steps into the underground cells below, singing into gaol, for the rest of their lives. Their wives came singing from the court to face the empty years. Winnie Mandela and Albertina Sisulu led them, both to face many years of bans and house arrest, in addition to the loneliness of the "Robben Island Widows", the women who see their husbands once a year through a perspex window in that forbidding maximum security island gaol.

Albertina Sisulu, Winnie Mandela: they were leaders in their own right, just as their husbands were leaders. Their dignity, their courage, their control, were beyond description. Winnie was already banned and we were forbidden to communicate with each other. One wife, Caroline Motsoaledi, could not be there. She had seven young children, the youngest only a few months old, born during her husband's detention. Caroline had been arrested and detained while she was actually in court during his trial and held in gaol for several months. She was not told until long after the end of his trial whether her husband had been acquitted, sentenced to gaol or condemned to death, and even then she did not know what to believe.

The Rivonia trial was not even a month over when another political trial affecting some of my friends flared up. From 4 July onwards there were mass raids throughout the country. I was raided as usual, in the middle of the night, relieved that it was only a raid and not an arrest. I lost some valuable material on the banished people and a few books. All these were removed by the police and I never saw them again. I sometimes wonder where and how all our documents are stored and if they have been properly filed by archivists so that at some future time we shall be able to recover them in good order. I doubt it.

In the morning I learnt that several of my friends had been detained and that the raids and arrests had indeed been nationwide. It seemed to have been a national crackdown and it led to many political trials of which the one involving some of my friends was the Communist Party trial. I knew that the former Communist Party had been revived as an underground organisation, because since 1960 pamphlets had been appearing sporadically over the name of the Communist Party. I had no idea who the members were. I supposed that they must be some of the old members working underground. I did not know that new members had been recruited, nor that some of them were former members of the Congress of Democrats. As a matter of fact, some of my closest friends turned out to have been Communist Party members. Some of these people had joined the underground Communist Party during the 1950s, including our president, Pieter Beyleveld, others only after the Congress of Democrats had been banned. Although these disclosures came as a surprise, I cannot say that they disturbed me greatly. The Congress of Democrats had conscientiously tried to do its work as a member of the Congress Alliance. It seemed irrelevant that some of its members had also been members of the Communist Party, for this was true also of the African National Congress and the South African Indian Congress, though admittedly in far smaller proportions.

Bram Fischer, our beloved advocate of the treason trial and the leader of the defence team in the Rivonia trial, was amongst those charged. He was detained first for a few days in June and then released again until a second detention in September. He was granted bail so that he could fly to London for an important civil case in which he was appearing as senior counsel before the Privy Council. He returned to South Africa to stand his trial with the other accused, but before the end of the trial, Bram went into hiding to work underground.

All except two were convicted in this trial, under the Suppression of Communism Act, and served sentences in gaol varying from one to five years. Most of them had been amongst my friends in the Congress of Democrats and I missed them very much, not only when they were in gaol, but also when they were released, because they all received house arrest and banning orders and we could no longer communicate with each other. That they held some political theories differing from mine was totally irrelevant to our friendship and to our loyalty to the liberation struggle.

It was during the 1960s that real treachery first raised it ugly head. In the Rivonia trial, Robert Hepple led the way. He had been arrested with the others but during the months in gaol before the trial began, he had been prevailed upon to make a statement to the security police and to agree to become a state witness. This was the first time in political trials that such a thing had happened and it came as a great shock. During the trial, Walter Sisulu said of Hepple in reply to the prosecutor, "He is a traitor. Anyone who gives information to the police is a traitor . . . Hepple will be ostracised to such an extent that he can do no further harm."

It was the first time that I had had to think about this and it seemed to me that Walter was speaking not just about Bob Hepple, but about any others who might fall in the same way. It has remained in my mind ever since. There have been many since Hepple, some tortured beyond endurance and for them there can be nothing but pity. There are others who have not been so tortured but have not kept silent. It must be a terrible burden to carry for the rest of your life and to be ostracised for it. When the Communist Party trial began later, it brought further shocking examples of betrayals of trust. Pieter Beyleveld, National President of the Congress of Democrats, a leader in the liberation struggle, appeared as a state witness against his former colleagues.

From the detention cells had come reports of ill-treatment of detainees, both black and white, long unbroken hours of interrogation without rest or sleep, and physical assault. Affidavits testified to the truth of these reports. The common pattern of detention was continued physical abuse in addition to total isolation and mental torture.

Pieter Beyleveld had been subjected to none of this. He decided, very deliberately, to betray his friends after only a short time in detention rather than face the possibility of a gaol sentence. This was the man who had been our leader, trusted and accepted not only by us but by the whole Congress Alliance.

I heard the rumours of his dishonour but I refused to believe them unless I saw him in the witness box — almost anyone else, but not Pieter Beyleveld. I soon knew that it was true, that Piet was a traitor. He had sold his friends to gain his own freedom.

I was appalled at this betrayal and I could not bear to see him again. A year later, however, I saw him coming towards me in a city street. There was no time for me to cross to the other side. We passed each other in silence but our eyes met. I have seen that same look in the eyes of my dog after some misbehaviour, but the difference is that I feel sorry for my dog.

On the other hand we also paid the price of our naïvety. Gerald Ludi, whom we had accepted fully as a member in all our Congress of Democrats activities, turned out to be a professional police spy. He had been very active with us and also in the underground cells and committees of the Communist Party. He testified in court as a paid infiltrator. It cost the accused dearly in their trial but although I hated Ludi I never felt the same contempt for him as for Pieter Beyleveld.

Against this agony of betrayal by those we trusted, there were those who refused to testify in court to the statements forced out of them by torture and they faced, unflinchingly, periods of imprisonment for their refusals. Amongst them were my friends, Violet Weinberg, Leslie Schermbrucker and Izzy Heymann. Leslie went to gaol for 300 days for refusing to testify against Bram Fischer, Violet was sentenced to three months for refusing to testify against Izzy. Izzy refused to testify against a friend and was sentenced to a year's imprisonment. There were many amongst the blacks too, but Izzy, Leslie and Violet were my friends and it came very close.

I thought often of whether I should be able to hold out against the threat of imprisonment, against torture. The pressure for a statement under physical duress is not something for which I can predict my own conduct. I have not been so tested. I do not know the limits of my endurance. I can only pray that I should be given strength enough for whatever might befall me.

Despite these heroic stands, the 180-days law was relentlessly succeeding with many in its vile purpose. Witnesses appeared, morally shattered, aware that they were betraying their friends and their cause, yet lacking the strength to face imprisonment and a broken life on discharge.

The claim is sometimes made that their evidence added little or nothing to the case against the accused. The judicial value of the evidence is set against the possible gaol consequences of refusal to testify. But this takes no account of the damage done to the witness, the shame that has to be carried for life and the ostracism that has been earned, the stigma of "traitor" that cannot be excised.

Some left the country, others remained. Some felt no shame. Yet most had been people of stature in the liberation struggle and this made their fall the more tragic, to have been so trusted and then to betray. This was a bitter period. No one politically involved felt safe from the menacing knock on the door. No one could get news of relatives detained for many months.

Even before Bram Fischer's arrest in 1964, tragedy had struck his family. Immediately after the end of the Rivonia trial, Bram and his wife, Molly, had set off for Cape Town for their daughter Ilse's twenty-first birthday. On the way, there had been an accident on a river bridge. Bram's car had fallen into the river and Molly could not be rescued from the car in time to save her life. Many banned people came to her funeral to say goodbye to her and to be there with Bram and his children. Yet with all our sorrow, there was also a feeling of triumph for us in being together with so many other banned people whom we had not seen for so long, to greet them with a clasp of the hand and a few whispered words despite our bans.

Bram returned from England to stand in the dock with his colleagues for the first part of his trial — no longer the eminent counsel in his robes, but an accused, still standing as upright, as fearless and dignified as on the day he applied for the recusal of the Judge President in the treason trial.

There came a day when Bram failed to appear in court. There was only a letter to his counsel. "I owe it to the political prisoners, to the banished, to the silenced, and to those under house arrest, not to remain a spectator, but to act."

He had gone into hiding in South Africa in order to oppose the policy of apartheid as long as he could. He believed that unless the whole oppressive system was changed radically and rapidly, disaster would follow. To try to avoid this became a supreme duty.

For months Bram succeeded in evading capture and led the lonely life of a fugitive, in heavy disguise, moving from place to place. His youngest daughter Ilse spoke of him with her own quiet dignity: "My father is a great, great man." Her mother dead, her father on the run, both within a few months, left a heavy burden for this twenty-one-year-old girl to carry. Her married sister lived in Rhodesia, a prohibited immigrant, able to enter South Africa only by special government permission; her younger brother was in very delicate health.

On 11 November 1965, Bram was captured by the police after months of hiding, but never far from Johannesburg. His trial began. His Communist Party colleagues were already serving their sentences. They had been convicted under the Suppression of Communism Act but Bram was linked also with Umkhonto We Sizwe and charged under the Sabotage Act which carried the death sentence.

Towards the end of his trial, Bram spoke from the dock. He had refused to give evidence on his own behalf because he knew that he would then be cross-examined and could endanger other people.

> I am on trial for my political beliefs and the conduct to which those beliefs drove me. The charges arise from my being a member of the Communist Party . . . two courses were open to me. I could confess and plead for mercy or explain my belief and my activities. If I were to ask for forgiveness I would be betraying my cause, I believe that I was right and I will explain my views to the court.

He spoke of the tragedy of the fine and loyal persons who turned traitor to their cause and their country, because of the methodology of the state.

In this, his final statement to South Africa and the world, Bram Fischer said,

> In confidence we lay our cause before the whole world. Whether we conquer or whether we die, freedom will rise in Africa like the sun from the morning clouds.

It was a translation of the inscription in Afrikaans on the base of President Paul Kruger's statue in Church Square in Pretoria, only a few yards away from where Bram himself stood that day. When I chose *Tomorrow's Sun* as the title of one of my books, I did not know that I was echoing Paul Kruger's words.

Bram was sentenced to life imprisonment on 5 May. His children were now alone and he gave them his last smile as he went down from the dock to the cells below, his hand raised in the Congress clenched-fist salute.

He had defended us in the treason trial and we were acquitted. He had defended the Rivonia trial accused and they had been convicted and sentenced to life imprisonment. Now he too was sentenced to life imprisonment. There was a press photograph of his children, Ilse and Paul, leaving the court. Ilse's head was held very high.

I could not be present at Bram's trial, just as I had not been able to go to the Rivonia trial, so I did not see Pieter Beyleveld standing again in the witness box, this time to testify against the man who had loved and trusted him.

During 1963 and 1964 there had been literally hundreds of political trials all over South Africa, wherever there had been centres of political activity. The Eastern Cape area had been the main target of the police crackdown. It had always been the most militant stronghold of the ANC from the days of the Defiance Campaign. With the national leadership of the ANC already imprisoned on Robben Island, the security police moved in against the rank and file membership everywhere and especially here. "We mean to have peace and quiet in the area for the next ten years," said a security policeman to a press reporter. His meaning was plain, but he did not spell out the cost to hundreds of men and women, mainly for membership of, or assisting, the banned ANC.

Almost 1,000 were arrested. Hundreds faced trial after months in custody, sometimes more than a year. The sentences were long, up to twelve years in some cases. There was sometimes immediate re-arrest after short sentences, sometimes even before the completion of the first sentence.

Trials were often held in camera, presumably to protect the state witnesses, and deliberately situated in out-of-the-way towns, making the provision of defence difficult at short notice. Sometimes there was no notice of a trial. Accused men wrote from police cells asking for legal defence for their trials and the letters arrived after the prisoners had already been sentenced and taken to Robben Island. The Eastern Cape was the area most severely affected, but this was the general pattern of political repression during those years.

It was during this time that the Federation of South African Women gradually ceased to function. At national and regional levels the executive membership was increasingly depleted by banning orders on our leading members, just when we needed them to organise and develop the new women's clubs for affiliation. In the Eastern Cape these clubs had initially been very promising, but this area was badly affected, not only by bans but by arrests of active African women. Several of them were gaoled under charges relating to the banned ANC.

Francis Baard and Florence Matomela were the outstanding leaders of women in the Eastern Cape, a formidable pair of fearless women. They endured years of political persecution, bans, detentions, solitary confinement and imprisonment, but nothing could break their spirit.

They were my friends. Francis is still alive, now living outside Pretoria. She was banished from her old home in Port Elizabeth, the centre of the Eastern Cape, on her return from gaol. Florence died within a year of being discharged. They shared indomitable courage and dedication, yet they were in many ways different from each other. Francis is tall and massive, dignified and reserved, a woman of authority, capable of immense personal and political loyalty. Florence was laughing and loving, warm and generous of heart. She sang her way through hardships, always leading and drawing others to her side.

Both these leaders of the ANC Women's League and the Federation were brought to Johannesburg for the early part of the treason trial. They returned to Port Elizabeth to continue their active resistance to passes for African women and their work in the trade unions, especially Francis. In the 1960s they both served gaol sentences. Of such stuff is the liberation struggle of the African people made.

In Johannesburg, the banned women included Lilian Ngoyi, the National President, Bertha Mashaba, Violet Weinberg, Amina Cachalia, Mary Moodley, Albertina Sisulu and myself, all national executive members, some of us also on the regional executive. There were many others. The Federation had needed time to compensate for the loss of the membership of the African National Congress Women's League and the Congress of Democrats. But we did not get the time we needed.

The government's repressive measures had also hit the surviving members of the Congress Alliance in the same way. The Indian Congresses, the South African People's Organisation, the South African Congress of Trades Unions, had all been depleted by bannings and arrests. There were some who had left South Africa. Not one of our organisations had dissolved itself, for that would have been to concede destruction and defeat.

It has been suggested by political researchers that when the government finally made passes compulsory for African women at the beginning of 1963, this marked the failure of the Federation as a women's organisation. Nothing could be further from the truth. As far as the anti-pass campaign was concerned, the Federation did not, at any time, stand or fall on whether passes were to be made compulsory in the end. Our task was to unite women in the struggle for freedom and justice. This we did.

For almost eight years, from 1955 to 1963, the Federation with the ANC Women's League undoubtedly delayed the issuing of passes to African women. The whole Congress Alliance saw this as a victory in itself. But in the climate of political repression in the 1960s, there was no possibility for the Federation to survive in the form in which we had known it.

At the end of July 1967, the beloved Chief Luthuli died, crushed to death by a sugar train near his farm. President of the ANC, winner of the Nobel Peace prize, he also held the highest ANC award, the Isitwalandwe, "one who has fought courageously in battle". Deposed by the government from his chieftainship, he remained "Chief" to his people and to all of us. I remember him in the treason trial, sorely wounded by Advocate Trengove's suggestion that he was not being honest in the witness box. Seven years later he was suddenly gone from us, killed by a train in Groutville where he had remained, a man of non-violence.

Some 7,000 people came to his funeral, millions mourned his death. His funeral became an African National Congress affirmation. Chief's body lay beneath the green, black and yellow flag. Men and women of the old ANC, the Women's League and the Youth League displayed their colours and their uniforms in tribute to their dead leader.

   Those bitter years of repression brought an exodus of people from South Africa. Some left by exit permit, that one-way door which lets you out but does not let you in again. Others went through the back door, without papers or permits and with this way there is no coming back either. I found it sad, a grievous disappointment, that so many should go. I knew and accepted that some were needed to play their part in building the external forces of the ANC, but I could find few valid reasons for others to go, to leave the struggle.

   Personal reasons for going were many and varied. None may sit in judgement on those who have made such a difficult and painful decision for themselves and their families. In some cases it was fear of interrogation and detention, of possible conviction and years in gaol. "You are useless in gaol!" I heard this very often but I didn't agree, for to me there is an enormous value in being ready to endure something of what our friends and colleagues endure, in keeping that undying pledge of the Freedom Charter, "Side by side, throughout our lives, until these democratic changes have been won."

   Some would say they must go for the sake of their children. I think then of the Mandela children, the Sisulu children, the Motsoaledi children and so many more. Yet I am childless, so it is not for me to question such decisions. Others were unable to adjust to banning orders and house-arrest conditions. This must depend upon the individual capacity to adjust, to accept what you cannot change.

   Whatever the reason, those who have left South Africa are not to be envied. Some have been materially or academically successful, others had to struggle to establish themselves. I think they all look back nostalgically to the land they left.

Chapter IV

A meaningful life

June 1971 had brought me freedom from all the frustrations of house arrest and the other onerous mutilations of my liberty. It had done more than that. It had set me free from the crippling fear of unending renewal of house arrest. I felt that I had moved into a new life. Here was a new decade. I did not know what it would bring to us in South Africa. The 1950s had come and gone, leaving great memories of resistance, of the Defiance Campaign, of the women's resistance to passes, of the Congress of the People and the Freedom Charter. But great scars remained too, the scars of the banning of the ANC, the long years of the treason trial, the scar of Sharpeville.

The 1960s, the decade of repression, forced us to the very sobering realisation that the security police had become an evil, sinister force. Succeeding Acts of Parliament gave them more and more powers of arrest and detention without trial. They were in reality answerable to no one but themselves for the treatment of their helpless victims, held completely incommunicado and beyond the protection of the courts. This power was a growing evil. The whole image of the security police seemed to have changed. No longer were they the bumble puppies at whom we had jeered. Within ten years they had become terrifying sophisticates, skilled interrogators, armed with secret methods of torture which left no physical marks, with the power to hold anyone in total isolation for months on end. I suppose it is true that forcing information out of detainees, both mentally and physically, is a cheaper, quicker, more efficient way of getting what you want than the old, outdated methods of investigation. It is an evil enshrined in South Africa's laws.

In the first excitement of being unbanned, I had not been able to assess the full implications of my freedom and how I could best use it. It had all happened so suddenly — I had been cut off from the mainstream of political resistance for so long.

The Congress of Democrats had been banned for nine years; the Federation of South African Women, though not banned, had lost too many members through bannings, gaol and exile, for it to become viable again. I was in touch with some individual women from the old days, but others were still banned and there could be no personal communication.

I did not take much account of the other disabilities of being a listed person until I was elected the Honorary National President of the National Union of

165

South Africa Students — NUSAS. This was such an unexpected and tremendous honour that I accepted immediately when the telephone call came from their national congress in Durban.

My joy was shortlived for suddenly I remembered my listing and hastily consulted my private and rather sinister file, entitled "Bannings and house arrest" and there it was. As a listed person, I could not become an office-bearer of any organisation that — the same old litany — "attacks, defends, criticises, propagates or discusses the policy of the government of a state". And certainly NUSAS does that, in its dedicated and principled struggle against all forms of apartheid and injustice. Thus it was brought home to me sharply that my new freedom was only partial. I could not join any organisation that was even remotely political.

I hastily sent a telegram resigning my office of Honorary National President. My resignation was not accepted and the office stood vacant for two years, during which I was the Honorary National "Un-President" of NUSAS. After that I became an Hon. National Un-Vice President. I still am.

Early in June, Father Cosmas ("Cos") Desmond, a militant Roman Catholic priest, was banned and put under house arrest, apparently because he had published a book, *The Discarded People*, about the abitrary mass removal of thousands of African people from areas on white-owned farms or outside white towns, where they had lived for generations. They were resettled on bare, undeveloped land in black areas. Cos had exposed the shameful conditions of these human dumping grounds. He had lived amongst the people, shared in the brutal hardship of lives which had been torn apart to fit the nationalist masterplan of a totally segregated South Africa. He had assisted, too, in the making of a film for overseas about it. These were his crimes. They were enough for him to be placed under house arrest and banned for five years. On the day before he received his banning orders, he had been with me and my friends, sharing with me my new freedom, unaware that he was so soon to lose his own.

The President of the Witwatersrand University Students' Representative Council asked me to speak at their mass protest meeting against Cos's bans. I knew I wanted to, but I wasn't sure that I could, because of the listing restrictions. I consulted a legal friend whose first reaction was that I could not speak. I was listed and that was that. We discussed a loophole which I thought I had found, that there was nothing in the listing provision to say that I could not participate in the activities of NUSAS or any other politically involved organisation. In my banning orders, such an embargo was included, but it did not appear in the clauses of the Act governing listing. I certainly could not be a NUSAS office-bearer, but I could speak on any political platform as a guest speaker, provided that I did not join the organisation. To my delight, there was legal agreement on this point.

The meeting was astounding. More than 1,000 students filled the Great Hall, sitting in the aisles, crowding outside the doors. There had been no announcement of my speaking until that very morning, for fear of a new ban, but when I walked onto the platform, the students rose in a standing ovation. They were on their feet again when I began to speak in protest against Cos's banning — who knew better than I what lay before him? I affirmed that I knew no gratitude to the government for my release, for it had only restored to me a part of the rights which ought never to have been taken away. It was no act of compassion. It was the fear that I might die under house arrest that had prevailed. It was expediency, not a change of heart.

I spoke of the banished Africans, recalling that the last public speech I had made in 1962 had been to an earlier generation of Wits students. It seemed fitting that after nine years I should come again to Wits University to make my first speech there, that I should re-enter public political life with this new generation of students, a new generation, but still part of Wits campus life and tradition.

I ended with my promise that I should never ban myself by keeping silent, for that would be to do the government's dirty work for it. If it wanted me to be silent, then it must ban me again.

The final standing ovation almost brought me to tears. I saw that Jean Sinclair, President of the Black Sash, standing close to me, was wiping her eyes. I looked again at the hundreds of young faces below me and saw that some of them too were wiping tears away.

The Wits students had brought me back to political life. How could I ever have doubted that some day, in some way, this would happen? I ought to have had more confidence, even in those worst days of depression. I ought to have known that any testimony of life would eventually be of more significance than any contrived testimony of death.

I was proud that I had been called upon to speak in public again after the long years of silence, but there was a difference. Now when I spoke, it could be only to those present, for, as a listed person, nothing that I said could be quoted, recorded or published. The press, aware of the embargo, would report only that I had spoken at a meeting, but not what I had said. Indeed, if it were taken to the legal extreme, anyone could be charged for repeating to another person what he had heard me say.

October 1971 brought the shocking news of the death of young Ahmed Timol, while in detention. He, like Babla Salojee, eight years before, had fallen to his death from a high window of the security police buildings. Did these young men fall? Were they driven by torture and despair to jump? These were unanswered questions.

I went to the home of Timol's aged parents, a stricken Muslim couple, tormented even before his death by security police telling them they would never see their son again. They were broken in spirit as their son had been broken in body, left to face life without him, never to know the truth of his death.

The Indian community called a protest meeting. More than 1,000 Indians, both Muslim and Hindus, with a few Africans and whites, came together on an Indian school playground, to register their anger at the violent death of this young school teacher while in the custody of the police. His was the twenty-first death in detention.

One of the Indian women leaders had telephoned me the day before to tell me of the meeting. I needed no urging to attend, but I did not expect the warm welcome which I received from a group of women who came to meet me, hands outstretched. They said, "Welcome back to the Indian community, Mrs Joseph!" I realised that it was many years since I had been in their midst.

On Christmas Day, for the first time in nine years, my friends crowded into my house again. It was a happy celebration and it went on all day, even into the night. It was no longer Christmas over the garden gate. We started a custom then of drinking a toast at midday to our friends in gaol, to the banned who could not join us, to those gone from South Africa.

Since then, many friends come every year to my house on Christmas Day. Over the years the party has grown, as new friends join the old. "Christmas with Helen" has become a tradition. Each year there are friends whose bans have expired and not been renewed, so they are free to communicate with me and join us at the Christmas party. Each year there are more who have served gaol sentences and been released, but there is no Nelson, no Bram, no Walter Sisulu, nor Kathrada. And there is no Winnie Mandela, for only once, in 1975, was she briefly free from bans and able to be with us.

When we drink the toast to our friends who are not with us, we are very close to them, for the message has been carried to the gaols that at midday our glasses are lifted in tribute and in hope.

The Dean of Johannesburg, the Very Reverend Gonville ffrench-Beytagh, came to that first party after I was free. He sat on my verandah looking around in amazement at my guests and then he said to me, "Well . . . Jews, Gentiles, Christians, atheists, liberals, communists, Indians, Africans, whites, coloureds . . . Marvellous!"

At the beginning of that year, the whole Anglican church had been shocked when this same burly Dean of St Mary's Cathedral was detained and then charged under the Terrorism Act. It sounded so absurd — what had terrorism to do with the Dean of a cathedral? His flat and offices were searched and then he was taken off to John Vorster Square, the enormous modern security building and police station which had replaced the old familiar Marshall Square. After a week in detention, he was charged with having participated in the affairs of unlawful organisations and also with incitement to violence. He was released on bail to await his trial.

This Dean was famous for his plain speaking from the pulpit against apartheid and for his compassion for people in distress. He was held by many, including me, to be one of the greatest and truest Christians in South Africa. For him to be detained, charged with political offences, was almost unthinkable, but it had happened and the whole Anglican church was shaken. Never before had so high a dignitary of any church in South Africa been subjected to police custody leading to a political trial. There had been Father Trevor Huddleston in the 1950s who had stood by the African people in the Sophiatown removals, but he had left South Africa. There had been Ambrose Reeves, Bishop of Johannesburg, who had stood by the people of Sharpeville in 1960, but he had been deported.

Dean ffrench-Beytagh had drawn many to hear his thundering sermons against injustice and had shocked the complacency of many Christians. He was known to have assisted many political victims financially, for that was no secret. For him to be charged in court under the Terrorism Act, dealt a savage blow to whatever political awareness or conscience was stirring in the Anglican church. Fear took over and the church withdrew to its citadel of "no politics in the church".

The Dean came to trial in August 1972. It was held in the Old Synagogue in Pretoria, where we had sat for so many years. I could attend his trial because I was no longer restricted to Johannesburg. I sat on the same bench where I had sat before, for it was no longer that large dock, but the public gallery. I looked again at the great Star of David over the judge's head. This time it was a Christian priest on trial for his conscience and his compassion.

He was found guilty of receiving welfare funds from the Defence and Aid Fund in London, banned in South Africa, and of encouraging others to support acts of violence. He received the compulsory minimum sentence of five years in gaol under the Terrorism Act. This dignitary of the church was now a convicted terrorist, but he was granted leave to appeal against his conviction and sentence and could remain out of gaol on bail. He won his appeal in a higher court on the grounds that the state had failed to prove its case against him.

The Dean's ordeal was over and within hours of his acquittal he left South Africa. I was not indifferent to his safety — how could I be? But I did not share the fearful insistence of those who advised him to leave immediately lest he be detained again by the security police. I saw it as a Nationalist victory that such a man was driven away and I realised that his going would seem like an act of betrayal to many black people who had had such confidence in him.

At the beginning of 1972, I embarked on a national tour of the English-speaking university campuses as their Honorary National Un-Vice President, accompanied by NUSAS President Paul Pretorius. I was to speak to the students on academic freedom, then threatened by the government-appointed Schlebusch Commission enquiring into the affairs of "certain" organisations, of which NUSAS was one. The Commission was a Parliamentary Select Commission which could and did call upon NUSAS to produce all its records and also its officials, to testify before the Commission. NUSAS had reacted strongly against these arbitrary requirements, seeing the whole issue as a new and sinister threat to academic freedom.

The student leaders went to the campuses for support in their demand for a judicial enquiry which would be held in public and not behind closed doors. They also sought support for their recommendation that University Students' Representative Councils should refuse to give evidence before this Commission unless compelled to do so by law.

Freedom, whether personal, academic or political, was a subject very much in debate and very important to me. To join this issue would give me a unique opportunity to talk about it, both from my own personal viewpoint and from a wider perspective.

Throughout the tour, I was apprehensive that I might be re-banned or searched by the security police and lose my speech. I even travelled with a tightly folded duplicate typescript concealed in my brassiere. That speech had taken me a quite a few days to prepare and I didn't want to lose it to the police and then try to rewrite it. I was certainly watched carefully and openly by the security detectives at every airport, but there was no interference.

This generation of students represented to me the questioning youth. This spirit had not been there when I was a student at Wits myself in 1947. Now the students were questioning the values of their own society, questioning their own roles and the moral values of the universities. I could not provide the answer to their questioning, but I welcomed it.

I told them something of what it was like to be banned and house arrested without trial and especially I told them, as I had told the Wits students the previous year at that first meeting, of my determination never to ban myself, never to do the government's dirty work for it, but to stand again to be counted, as they were standing. I told them of the things that had moved me, the tragedies of the banished African people, so well known to me through my journeys and my contacts with them. I spoke, as I have spoken ever since, of my sense of white guilt, which we must all share, the white guilt that has brought black rejection. Black consciousness, the assertion of black human dignity, was already strong on the campuses. I held this philosophy to be utterly right and inevitable. It was an idea whose time had come, was long overdue, but I knew it would bring hurt to many white students to be rejected as a body, even if not as individuals.

We started our tour in Durban, and again I was surprised at the long and enthusiastic ovation that the university students there gave me. It was a wonderful start to this speaking tour and did a great deal to conquer my nervousness, my fear of inadequacy and that I might have been cut off from political life for too long. I had been afraid that I might not be able to put across my thoughts and my hopes to these gatherings of the young. There was a gap of nearly fifty years between us. Would I be able to bridge it? Yet somehow it had been possible and I could feel, almost from the beginning of my speaking, that the communication was there. I had something to say to the students and they were not only prepared but eager to hear it.

At Pietermaritzburg University, that same night, the response, even the ovation, was repeated. A student came to the window of the car as I left, to say, "You have convinced me. I thought I should go and now I know I must stay." That would have been reward enough for me, without the long applause.

We moved on, to Rhodes University in Grahamstown, a campus divided in its attitude towards giving evidence before the Schlebusch Commission. Not all supported the NUSAS refusal to testify voluntarily. As I spoke, however, I soon became aware of interest and support, ending once again in a tumultuous standing ovation. Long afterwards one of those students told me, "If you had told us to burn down the Principal's house that night, we'd have done it!" I could only laugh, for I certainly had not delivered an incendiary speech of any sort. It was just that somehow I had bridged the gap and had been able to identify with these young students and to be completely accepted by them.

170

Cape Town University was the high spot of the tour. The students had organised a public meeting on the campus. It was Wits all over again. As I walked onto the platform, and then again as I stood up to speak, the meeting came to its feet to welcome me. When I had finished, they stood applauding for over five minutes, some even declared it was ten! I could not move, I could only stand very still, almost stunned, as waves of applause broke over me, for joy at my freedom and what I was doing with it.

There were several old friends in the audience whom I had not seen for ten years. One came to me to say, "Helen, I was sitting next to the only person in this whole gathering who did not need to feel ashamed after you had spoken." I knew she meant the Anglican priest, Bernard Wrankmore, who had fasted almost to death in protest against the death in detention of a Muslim priest, Abdullah Haroun. I knew, too, that what I had said about standing up to be counted had gone home to many people. I had ended my speech with Pastor Niemoller's famous words,

> In Germany, they first came for the communists and I didn't speak up because I wasn't a communist;
> then they came for the Jews and I didn't speak up because I wasn't a Jew;
> then they came for the trade unionists and I didn't speak up because I wasn't a trade unionist;
> then they came for the Catholics and I didn't speak up because I was a Protestant;
> then they came for me and by that time no one was left to speak up.

As I flew back to Johannesburg, I asked myself what I had done to deserve these great honours, these tributes. I found no answer, only a deep appreciation and love for all the hundreds of students who had given me this tremendous support. The nine years of house arrest were gone and I had a freedom and an opportunity greater than I had ever known before, despite being listed. I did not know for how long I should be allowed to keep this freedom, but the prospect of being re-banned held no fears for me. What I had endured once, I could endure again and the rewards were very great.

Later in the year, I was back in Cape Town, this time for the Civil Rights Week, organised by the university students. I found a mammoth programme, six speeches in five days. It was a tough assignment but somehow it was all fitted into the daily programmes. I spoke first to the university students; then there was an all-day seminar on passive resistance, a youth service at the Cathedral, a visit to a school to talk to the matriculation class. The attempt to have me speak at the Afrikaans-speaking University of Stellenbosch failed as I was not permitted to speak on that campus. Some Stellenbosch students, however, organised an off-campus meeting at which I spoke.

Monday night was intended to be the highlight of that Civil Rights Week, with a public meeting in the Rondebosch Town Hall. But our right-wing opponents had been busy before we got there, sprinkling sneeze powder on the seats. Spluttering, we closed the hall and cleaned the powder off. During the meeting a petrol bomb was flung into the hall from outside. This fortunately failed to ignite properly, though it went off with bang. That was followed by a sneeze-powder bomb which did go off, rather like a stink bomb, right in the middle of another speaker's address. The audience heroically remained in the hall while some of the effects of the sneeze powder wore off. I spoke next and sneezed my way through my speech on the United Nations Declaration of Human Rights. My sneezes didn't really matter because the audience was in as bad shape as I was.

We had laughed our way through the sneeze affair, but the onslaught from these right-wing terrorists had gone further than we knew. A petrol bomb had been thrown into the home of Geoff Budlender, President of the Cape Town University Students' Representative Council while he was presiding at our meeting and it had gutted part of his house. Slogans — "Communists live here" — and similar abuse had been painted on the walls of the house where I was staying with the Reverend Theo Kotze, Cape Director of the Christian Institute, campaigner for right and justice. He had already endured much of this kind of mindless violent behaviour and abusive painting on his walls and sundry other attacks both on his house and his office. I could not avoid the thought, nevertheless, that I had brought this latest attack upon him because I was his guest.

I flew back to Johannesburg the next day and read in the papers that a shot had been fired through one of the windows of Kotze's house. Hooliganism of this sort was appearing in Johannesburg, but it was mainly occurring in Cape Town. I had had nothing further since the bomb at my gate the previous year.

Almost a year had passed since Ahmed Timol's tragic death. There had been an inquest and the magistrate found that he had committed suicide and that no one was to blame for his death. No one? His friends and family knew whom to blame. Feeling ran high in the Indian community when it came to the anniversary of his death. The pupils at the Indian high school where Timol had taught hired buses and came to Roodepoort for a memorial meeting. They crowded along the wide corridor which opened onto all the flats in the building where Timol's parents lived. Almost a hundred of the schoolchildren came, and after the meeting we marched illegally through the streets of Roodepoort to the Muslim cemetery. We came to Timol's grave and I stood with the schoolgirls, a little apart, obedient to Muslim tradition. When I said to a young girl that I was guilty, with all whites, of Timol's death, she replied, "No, Mrs Joseph, we are guilty too, for we Indians have not spoken out because we have been afraid."

The two years which had passed since my restrictions had been lifted had been so full that I had not resumed my theological studies. I felt very guilty about it, and regretful too, for I wanted to go further in my quest for knowledge about my faith. The political and social world, so unexpectedly restored to me, had eaten into my life because my whole existence had come alive again with people.

There was only one thing for me to do — to give myself to concentrated study for several months and work for the first part of the Diploma of Theology of London University. I had enough sense to abandon the course for the Divinity honours degree and register for the less demanding Diploma. I announced to my amazed friends that I was putting myself under four and half months' "study arrest". No one must visit me except on Saturday afternoons and I should not go out at all except to work and to church. I would only relax this rule if I was called upon to speak at a meeting. I repeated this self-imposed ban two years later and finally obtained the Diploma in 1975.

Early in 1973 a law was passed in Parliament which filled me with forebodings. It provided for the removal of South African citizenship in the case of citizens who had also the nationality of another country, "when it appeared that it would not be in the public interest that such a person should continue to be a South African citizen". I was a South African citizen, but I was also a British national by birth. The minister stated that this provision was aimed at drug peddlers but conceded that it might affect other persons. This alarmed me, for the last thing I wanted was to be compelled to leave South Africa. This land was my adopted home and I belonged here. Yet the authorities might well not agree with me and the minister need not supply any reason for a decision to withdraw South African citizenship. If this happened to me I could be liable for deportation.

I went speedily to the British Consul and renounced my British nationality. I bought myself out of the British Commonwealth for eight rands and ten cents. Now I was safe. I could not be deported. The government might still do many things to me, but it had got me for keeps and I was satisfied.

Robert Resha died in London, in 1973. He would not be coming back to South Africa after all, not even when freedom had been won. I was aware of his resistance to the new policy of the external ANC of admitting non-Africans to membership. I knew this would have angered Robert deeply because of his inflexible African nationalism and his conviction that the ANC should remain the leading political organisation with an exclusively African membership. Other races should, as always, be welcomed in the struggle for liberation but not as members of the ANC.

Robert lost his fight against this new policy and died a tragic, lonely and embittered man, rejected by many of those who, for nearly thirty years, had been his leaders and his colleagues in the struggle to which he had devoted his life. He would never submit to what he thought was wrong and he paid a high price for his stand. A friend brought me a red rose bush and I planted it in my garden. Its flaunting crimsom blooms have something of Robert's arrogance in them. In a letter to me, his widow wrote, "A man's grave is by the side of the road he treads." Robert's grave lies beside that road to freedom which he trod.

April 1974 brought a parliamentary election. In a Cape Town constituency an active group of young people, mainly university students, past and present, was formed. They called themselves the Alliance for Radical Change (ARC), for they wanted change and were prepared to work for it. They put up their own candidate, Chris Woods, one of the recently banned NUSAS leaders, intending to expose the farce of South Africa's all-white elections, for no banned person could enter Parliament. They campaigned on a socialist platform and I was invited to speak at a mass meeting on the eve of the election in Rondebosch Town Hall, the scene of the earlier sneeze battle.

I was met at the airport by the ARC supporters, all wearing black gags to symbolise the enforced silence of their banned candidate. As we drove through the streets, I was confronted by large posters tied to almost every lamp post, "Helen Joseph speaks!"

Once again the hall was packed and once again a smoke bomb was thrown into the hall, but it was speedily removed before it could have much effect. I had been very dubious about my ability to hold the attention of such a large crowd for a long period, as I was the only speaker. Everything went well with even a little light relief provided by a heckler, notorious for the leading part he seemed to play in the violent attacks on the homes of NUSAS and Christian Institute supporters. He was not very effective for the crowd was against him and he could easily be dealt with from the platform, even by me.

Since I had started speaking in public again, I had always tried to keep the image of the Freedom Charter alive by quoting from the preamble or the ending: "This freedom we will fight for side by side until we have won our liberty" or " . . . to strive together, sparing nothing of our strength and courage until the democratic changes here set out have been won." For this meeting I had the green light to speak freely and fully about the Freedom Charter because its provisions were basic to the policy of the Alliance for Radical Change.

Vorster, the Prime Minister, had given a television interview, relayed to the USA, no doubt as part of the Nationalist Party's election campaign. He had been tackled on bannings and house arrest and had given some surprising answers about our "right" to appeal against our banning orders and obtain reasons why we had been banned.

I was delighted at the opportunity to deal with all this nonsense in a public speech. I could challenge him in relation to my own experience of house arrest and expose the half truths which he had fed to the American televiewing public and to the South African public, even if I could reach only the people present in the hall and could not be reported in the newspapers.

To speak publicly on the Freedom Charter was like a dream come true. For almost twenty years, a great cloud of unknowing had settled over it. There were fears about its legal position. Was it banned or not? I had argued that it was legal because only two of the organisations which had composed the Congress Alliance had been banned, the ANC and the COD, but not the SA Coloured People's Organisation or the SA Indian Congress.

Since that meeting, the government has attacked the Freedom Charter by banning specific printed issues of it. This can be done but the principles of the charter and the words in which those principles are expressed cannot be banned. The Freedom Charter can be, and is, reprinted over and over again.

There could be no doubt about how the audience received it. I was honoured with a standing ovation and I felt that I had done something, no matter how little, to put the Freedom Charter on the map. Predictably, our ARC parliamentary candidate lost his deposit. The Nationalist Party of course won the election. The only satisfaction was that the conservative United Party had to concede some seats to the Progressive Party.

In another area, the election day brought victory. When I came to the campus the next morning it was alive with reports that the Portuguese regime in Mozambique had collapsed and that it would be only a very short time before the liberation forces led by Frelimo would take over the government. This gave new heart and new hope to the black people of South Africa and to the whites who supported the liberation struggle.

Chapter V

Acts of conscience

One of the special joys of being unbanned was that although banned people could still not communicate with me, listed people could. This brought some old friends of the Congress of Democrats back into contact with me. Ilse, Bram Fischer's youngest daughter, was one. The very night that the bans were lifted she visited me in the hospital.

Since Bram's imprisonment, tragedy had struck his family again. Paul, his only son, died suddenly in Cape Town. He had lived his young life to the fullest, despite his delicate health, but his hold on life had always been precarious. He was dead at twenty-three and Bram had to bear his sorrow in prison, alone in his cell.

Not long after Paul's death, Ilse moved in with me and we spent three happy months together before she married and life began again for her. She wanted to be married in Bram's presence in the gaol. They asked very little, Tim and Ilse, only that a priest might be there, just for ten minutes to marry them where Bram could watch, even through the small perspex window that shuts the prisoner away from any physical contact with his visitor. But a priest was not allowed to come, even for this.

While Ilse was living with me, I went to visit Bram in gaol. It was a great privilege. I had half an hour with him on two occasions, talking of course through the perspex with three warders listening. At first it is a shock to see only the head and shoulders of someone you know, because that is all you can see through the window. Yet Bram was so natural, so much like himself, the same friendly, loving Bram, that the strangeness soon wore off. He asked about my Christmas Day parties — had the last one before my house arrest been in December 1961? Then he smiled and said confidently, "I'll be there again some day." This, from a man serving a life sentence, was almost too much for me.

Half an hour isn't long even when you can only speak of family and general affairs and not of the things that matter to you both. Yet those two short half-hour visits are among my most precious memories. I went twice to visit another political prisoner in the same gaol, Jack Tarshish, serving twelve years. On the one occasion Jack asked me, apparently inconsequentially, about visits to the moon. I asked one of the listening warders, "can I tell him that the Americans have got to the moon?" He shouted angrily, "No!" He was too late for Jack was laughing, he had heard what he wanted to know. After that I was never allowed

176

to visit my prisoner friends again. The next time I applied for permission to visit Jack, I was told, "You are not allowed into the gaols!!"

Before the end of 1974, distressing news had come from the Pretoria gaol. Bram Fischer had terminal cancer and was rapidly growing weaker and weaker. Appeals were made to the Minister of Justice to let Bram go to his daughter Ilse in Johannesburg for the last few weeks of his life. He was a dying man. Must he die in gaol? Must the end of a life sentence be the gaol hospital bed?

The minister appeared implacable. He would not commit himself, even at this very late stage. He even referred publicly to my own case. Helen Joseph had had cancer and the government had shown compassion towards her and released her from house arrest and other restrictions. Now she was speaking on public platforms. I was deeply grieved and angry for it implied that it was my conduct that was keeping Bram in gaol during the last weeks of his life.

Bram lingered for only a short time. It was only near the end that this dying man was allowed to leave the gaol and even then not allowed to be with Ilse in Johannesburg, but only in Bloemfontein, 300 miles away, with his brother. Presumably the minister thought that there he would be preserved from all political contact, but even so he was subjected to tight control of his visitors by the security police.

Even after this death the iron hand of the Prisons Department was not lifted. Bram's daughters were informed that his ashes would remain the property of the Prisons Department, but his family could apply for them if they so wished. Ilse and Ruth refused to accept this humiliating concession and Bram's ashes remain in the custody of the prison.

So passed a great and loving man, who had sacrificed his own freedom for the freedom of others. At his memorial meeting in Johannesburg, I paid my final tribute to the man I had known and admired so much, in the last words of Julius Fucik, a Czech political martyr, "People, I have loved you." Bram had had the gift of love.

June 1976 became another ugly anniversary for South Africa to add to its calendar of shame, another Sharpeville. This time it was the Soweto school-children who marched in protest and were met with police gun fire. They had been objecting for several weeks to being taught some subjects in Afrikaans — for them the language of the hated oppressor. The core of the protest, however, was against the whole basis of separate Bantu education. I thought of 1955, when Bantu education was first introduced, and of the boycott by the children then, when their parents had kept them out of school for more than twelve months. This time the scene was different. The children organised themselves, going from school to school in their mass protest on 16 June, 15,000 of them. No one had listened to them. Now they expected no one to listen to them. They marched, singing, determined, bearing defiant placards. Armed police met them along the road and a young boy was shot dead.

That boy was twelve-year-old Hector Peterson. The photograph of his dying body in the arms of another boy, his sister running screaming in terror beside him, went around the world. He was the first of over 600 black people to die within the next few weeks. Most of them were schoolchildren and students. The defiance spread from place to place and so did police retaliation. Soweto was soon on fire as arson spread and the horrifying reports came through. It was a night of horror, of violence. Thirty-one adults and two children were dead, shot by the police; 220 were injured. Other such nights were to follow.

A tragic photograph was published, of one man, an ordinary man of Soweto. Josiah Mlangeni had been called to the police station one morning and told that his son was dead. He was given a bundle of bloodstained clothes and he was photographed as he came out of the police station, a man in mute agony, clutching the bloodied clothes that were all that was left for him of his young son. The inquest finding was that no one was to blame. There were 575 such inquests and always "no one was to blame". No one?

The Wits University students came out in protest at the police shootings, proclaiming their solidarity with the Soweto children. A protest meeting was called on 17 June, the day after it all started. Bishop Desmond Tutu and I both spoke at the meeting. "The white man is stronger than you think," the Minister of Justice had blustered in Parliament. "The black man must not push us around." That was the reply of the government to the black children's demand for equal and effective education.

The Wits students marched out into the streets in protest. There they were joined by many black city workers, so that their protest became a mass multiracial procession blocking the streets. One of the student speakers had said, "Let us get onto the streets and if it brings a truckload of police to stop us then that will be one truckload less for Soweto!" It was in fact very soon stopped by police action.

When I reached home, I was telephoned by an Afrikaans press reporter saying he was coming to get a copy of my speech so that his editor could report it in full because I had incited the students to go onto the streets in an illegal procession, and as a white woman I ought to be ashamed of myself. I reminded him curtly that no one could publish any speech of mine.

The unrest continued and the death toll mounted. More and more young black students were being detained. Trouble was flaring up in other parts of South Africa, in black schools, universities and townships. White South Africa, as usual, reacted by parading a show of military and civil might, stockpiling food and buying guns.

Waves of unrest continued throughout the country for several months, in varying degrees of intensity. By the end of the year, the number of deaths rose to over 500, almost 4,000 had been injured and 6,000 people had been arrested and held in gaol. Of those hundreds of dead, 400 had been shot by the police. The black townships slowly became quiet again, battered into a sullen peace which was no peace at all, for the deep causes, the anger and frustration at injustice and racism, were all still there.

At the end of 1976 there was a renewal of that ugly dimension in my life — the telephone abuse and threats. Since the bomb at my gate and the hoaxes in 1969 and 1971, I had been almost free from this kind of thing, beyond occasional rock-throwing on my roof. Since it is a tin roof, the noise was quite frightening, but did no damage. Other friends in my neighbourhood had the same kind of thing, but more seriously, with broken windows. My windows were small and much less exposed and there were more sheltering trees and shrubs in the garden. I always padlocked my gates at night and I now had Kwacha, a German Shepherd bitch. I think all this helped to protect me to some extent from this obviously white urban violence.

On Christmas Day that year, there was no party at my house. We fell into a period of mourning for the hundreds of young dead. That night my telephone rang and a man's voice asked for me. "I'm coming tonight to kill you," he said. That was all. I put the phone down, not quite believing that it had really started again, after nearly six years.

It did not disturb me greatly then. My chief reaction was one of disgust that this could happen on Christmas night — the day of peace and goodwill to all men. However, it has continued sporadically ever since.

In the midst of all this, my sister-in-law, Lilian Fennell, came out from England to visit me. She met my friends and was welcomed by them, but I think she found it difficult to comprehend all the implications of the South African scene. She had endured the blitz in England during the war years, while my brother was serving overseas. She had met it all with quiet steady courage, but this did not prepare her for the realities of the struggle for freedom in South Africa, nor for my involvement in it. Yet I think she enjoyed her visit.

When she flew back to England, she was the only passenger to be called out from the boarding queue for an intensive search of her handbag and luggage. It must have come as a great shock to her, to keep a jumbo-load of passengers waiting for the plane to take off while she was still being cleared by the security police; presumably only because she had stayed with her sister-in-law, Helen Joseph.

I went to court for the day of sentence in the trial of nine members of the South African Students' Organisation, a black consciousness organisation. They were on trial for conspiring to commit acts capable of endangering the maintenance of law and order and were sentenced to five and six years' imprisonment. Their young wives and their little children were all in court that day and the public area in front of the dock looked almost like a park. The children toddled and scampered around, scattering sweet papers, even fruit pips and peel as they played, unconscious of the agony of their mothers on one side of the barrier, and their fathers on the other, waiting to hear the sentences.

When the sentences had been passed and the judge had left the court, the police stood shoulder to shoulder in the narrow no-man's-land between the convicted men and their families. The little children were lifted high up in the air and passed over the heads of the motionless policemen, into their fathers' outstretched arms for that goodbye kiss to last for so many years. The children were passed back again to their mothers and the young men went down to the cells, singing and smiling, to the years ahead.

In 1977, another glaring example of the white man's inhumanity to the black man had come to the forefront of public attention. This was the "squatter problem" (as the whites called it) of possibly a million homeless black people. Forced out of the rural areas and into the urban areas by unemployment and the need to survive, they tried to make for themselves the homes which were not there for them in the towns and cities. White industrialists needed their labour. White urban dwellers rejected them as human beings with families, accepting their men only as rightless sojourners, to be accommodated in dehumanising single-sex hostels.

Human nature is very strong and the women followed their men, brought their children out of the rural poverty to start family life again, somehow, in the cities. They built makeshift structures to protect the family from the sun and the rain, to provide privacy. It was an old phenomenon, not new. It had been going on for hundreds of years, a peasant family revolt against the evil system of migrant labour.

Squatter huts grew and multiplied every year. Large areas became squatter settlements, lacking solid houses and amenities. The squatters lived in depressed communities yet their spirit was strong enough for them to stand together and demand proper homes in the areas where their labour was needed. In some areas, especially outside Cape Town, the pressure became not so much a demand for non-existent homes, as a demand simply to be allowed to stay where they were; a protest against the inhuman bulldozing of their shacks. There was no place for the families to move to, unless back to the rural areas and starvation and separation from their men.

There were already 15,000 people in Crossroads, outside Cape Town; in nearby Modderdam Road, there were 7,000. They had constructed their shanties with whatever rough building materials they could collect. It was true that they occupied the ground illegally, for they had no official permits to be anywhere. Yet in these areas they had become communities, self-controlling, self-respecting communities. The South African government had declared these squatter dwellings to be health hazards, unlawful and, because they were increasing, they had to go. There was no answer to the question, "Go where?" Then, because the squatters did not move from Modderdam Road, the authorities sent bulldozers to smash the homes into the ground.

I knew, of course, that there were also squatter areas outside Johannesburg, as elsewhere. I went to see these for myself. I was ashamed and shocked, ashamed that I had not been there before, that I had been content to read the reports of others, shocked at what I saw, at realising how little we know of how blacks live.

The river in Kliptown doesn't flood every year when the heavy rains come. When there are no floods, Kliptown squatters are not news. They just go on waiting for houses, too long denied. There are people there who have been waiting for thirty years already.

180

Cosmos is a flower which has seeded itself over many parts of South Africa, and which grows high after rain, with delicate pink and white and crimson blooms. They were in bloom along the side of the road the day I went to Kliptown. The river had flooded after the heavy rains and the water had subsided, leaving sodden, mud-ringed, broken shacks. People still lived there and the washing danced gaily on the lines stretched between the houses, the defiant banners of the people who would still be living there when the river flooded again, because there are no proper houses for them. Since that day, the beauty of the cosmos has become obscene for me.

The students of Cape Town University had taken up this shameful issue, working actively amongst squatter families, protesting publicly. I went to Cape Town in April to speak at a meeting there. Kliptown was still on my mind when I addressed the meeting, for although the squatters' conditions were different in Cape Town, the agony was the same, the agony of insecurity and of no permanent home, not even the little matchbox houses of municipal African townships. Wherever the agony occurred it had been preventable: bulldozing was not the remedy. There is only one answer to the squatter problem and that is houses; houses which the state's coffers can afford — if it didn't spend so many millions on the defence of an indefensible society; an indefensible way of life for the few, dependent on the exploitation of the many.

It was good to be in Cape Town again, to be with these eager concerned young people who had organised this meeting, intent on exposing the evils around them, clamouring for redress. Part of the root of my hope for the future of South Africa lies in the thinking, questioning university students. They are not many, I know, compared to the whole campus. There never will be many in these radical groups, but they renew themselves year after year. It is true that when they go out from the university into the material competitive world, the flame dies down. It is small wonder that this society for which the university itself has been training them, conditioning them, engulfs all of them. Nor is there as yet any political home for this minority of radically thinking young people, where they can share their revolt against the perpetuation of this discriminating and unjust society.

Monday, 16 May 1977, was like any other Monday for me until a press friend telephoned at midday to tell me that Winnie Mandela had been banished to Brandfort, a small town in the Orange Free State. Her sixteen-year-old daughter Zindzi had gone with her. My first thought was that we must find her at once. Barbara Waite, a friend from the Cathedral, agreed to go with me to Brandfort. Father Leo Rakale, a black priest of the Community of the Resurrection and a friend of Nelson and Winnie, offered to take us by car.

We left the next morning soon after dawn for the 270-mile drive. When we reached Brandfort, Leo left us in the main street and drove off to look for Winnie in the black location. After an hour he returned to tell us that he had found them in a tiny three-roomed house with neither ceilings nor inside doors, with no water laid on and, for sewerage, only an outside privy.

We parked in the Brandfort main street until Winnie's car drew up on the other side of the road. Zindzi crossed over to be with Leo and me, while Barbara went to sit with Winnie in her car. It was a bizarre arrangement but Winnie could not be with more than one person for that would constitute a "gathering" and she could not communicate with me as I was a listed person.

All the restrictive conditions of Winnie's house arrest and bans remained. Only the place had changed. She could not leave that forbidding little house, surrounded by bare unfenced ground, at night or at the weekends. She could not receive visitors at her house, she must report daily to the police station — and all of this in a barren dehumanised cluster of 700 identical minute houses, a mile from Brandfort town, guarded by the superintendent's office at the entrance to the location.

We were not the only visitors to Brandfort; there was Winnie's family and the black friends who could visit Zindzi, though transport and the long distance made such visits rare. During those first months, however, I think that Ilona Kleinschmidt and Jackie Bosman were the only other whites who went there, except for journalists. Jackie and Ilona had been close friends of Winnie for several years. They were the first to be seriously harassed by the security police, when they were taken to the Brandfort police station to be questioned on their reasons for being in Brandfort. I do not know the details of that confrontation, beyond the fact that they both refused to answer any questions or make any statement because to do so might lead to their being called as state witnesses in some attempt by the police to bring Winnie to court on an alleged violation of her banning order. She was being continually harassed by the security police in their attempts to secure a conviction against her.

Under the Criminal Laws Amendment Act, any person who refuses to answer questions put by the police about an alleged offence by some other person can be brought before a magistrate. Failure to answer satisfactorily results in a gaol sentence. Jackie and Ilona were duly summonsed to appear before a Bloemfontein magistrate. They maintained their total silence, determined that there was no way in which they could be coerced into becoming state witnesses against Winnie. They received gaol sentences of twelve months each. They did not go to gaol then, but appealed to the Supreme Court against their conviction and sentence, remaining out of gaol on bail, pending the result of their appeal.

For Barbara and me this sounded ominous. Would the police try to do the same to us? We had been to Brandfort a few times already, but always taking care that we separated ourselves into two cars so that I could simply be visiting Zindzi and not Winnie. We completely endorsed the stand of Ilona and Jackie, agreeing that for us, too, there could never be any thought of replying to questions, making any statements to the police or appearing as state witnesses against our friends. We agreed, too, that we must not let ourselves be intimidated into staying away from Brandfort, for Winnie would need our visits more than ever.

On the morning of 27 September 1977, Barbara and I set out for Brandfort for a surprise visit on Winnie's birthday. We travelled through rain almost all the way. In Brandfort we parked outside a caravan ground to wait for Winnie and Zindzi. Zindzi had been a party to the plan about which she was supposed to tell Winnie that morning. After waiting in vain for over two hours we hit on the idea of Barbara sending a telegram to Winnie to say that she was waiting for her. The post office assured us that the telegram would be delivered in less than half an hour. We sat in the car gradually losing hope of seeing anyone until at last Winnie's plum-coloured Volkswagen came hurtling through the rain.

Winnie had come alone, for Zindzi had reached home only very late the previous night and was still sleeping. Winnie knew nothing of our visit, nor of the birthday surprise. She had come in reply to the telegram. After the birthday presents and cake had been unpacked, Winnie stood on the pavement, with her back to a hedge, talking to Barbara from the shelter of an umbrella. I sat in the car and saw, through the thin hedge, a comic little figure under a large umbrella, covered by a leather jacket, almost down to the nobbly knees atop the stockinged legs. It did not occur to me that it was Detective Sergeant Prinsloo until I saw his face, peering through the hedge, framed in leaves. It was rather like a cartoonist's caricature of a policeman doing his so-called duty.

I shouted, "There's Prinsloo!" as he scrambled through the hedge. He told Winnie she was violating her restrictions and instructed Barbara and me to drive at once to the police station. It was Jackie and Ilona all over again. We refused to say anything at all and were told by the station commander that we would be summonsed to appear before a magistrate, where we would be compelled to answer questions put to us. I replied loftily that he was mistaken as it would still be my decision as to whether I answered questions or not. For that I received a scowl and was told to go.

Winnie was waiting outside, anxious for us, furious with Prinsloo. We did not want to say goodbye outside the police station and drove down the main street, there to be hailed joyously by Bishop Desmond Tutu on his way back to Johannesburg from Lesotho. Brandfort was treated, not for the first time, to the sight of whites and blacks hugging and kissing each other in the middle of the town. I was happy that we could leave Winnie with a friend just at the moment of our going.

Barbara and I set out on our long wet journey to Johannesburg. I felt personally antagonistic towards the rain which seemed to have deceived us into thinking that there were no security branch men around, when in fact there was Sergeant Prinsloo.

We were completely at one on our stand of silence, yet it was clear that our personal situations and our obligations differed sharply. Barbara's husband was not in sympathy with her militant stand, and her children, one matriculating, the other soon to be called up for military service, were at a vulnerable age. I did not have such responsibilities and I was very conscious of this. We knew that we could expect twelve months in gaol if we persisted with our silence and there was no certainty that any appeal to a higher court would succeed in saving us from all or part of our sentences.

On the way back, we discussed it very seriously but I know that not for one moment did either of us feel that any course was open to us other than silence.

Barbara had to face the ordeal of telling her family at once of the possible consequences. She is a very beautiful woman but the classic serenity of her face was gone that night. Yet she still had her courage.

A week later we received the summonses to appear before the magistrate in Bloemfontein on 13 October. Barbara flew down and Leo Rakale drove me and an attorney to meet her there. I knew that we should have an opportunity to explain our refusal and I prepared my own brief statement, trying to make my decision clear to the magistrate and also to the public. Ironically, I could be quoted on this occasion in the press. This had not been possible for me for thirteen years. I had had to be brought to a court of law for it to happen.

During a court recess, the prosecutor informed my attorney that he could bring me back to court "again and again and again". I was aware that this extraordinary process could be repeated almost ad infinitum if I persisted in my silence. At the end of the legal argument, I formally refused to answer any questions and was allowed to make my statement in explanation.

Fifteen years ago today, on October 13th 1962, I was placed under house arrest. I know what it is like to be lonely, cut off from human society. I lived under such restrictions for nine years and what kept me sane was contact with my friends. They were my lifeline.

I find it impossible to answer any questions from the prosecutor or to make any statement which might be used against *any* house arrested person who is now suffering as I once suffered. Or indeed against any of my friends.

Winnie Mandela and her family are very near to me. Winnie herself is as dear to me as the daughter I never had. For me to make any statement which might lead to my becoming a state witness against her would be like a mother giving evidence against her own child.

I cannot do it.

I cannot participate in any way in this unremitting persecution of Mrs Mandela during her banishment.

I believe that God has guided me to this decision and I believe that He will give me strength to bear its consequences.

So I can only say with Luther, "Here I stand. So help me, God, I can no other."

The magistrate withdrew to consider his judgement and on his return commented on my "dignity" and also that I was a sincere Christian. He added, nevertheless, that my offence was serious and he must pass a sentence which, despite my age and health, must act as a deterrent to others. He then sentenced me to four months' imprisonment. When Barbara's case was heard, she, like Ilona and Jackie, was sentenced to twelve months in gaol. We, too, appealed to the Supreme Court against our conviction and sentences, and did not have to go to gaol immediately.

The difference between my sentence of four months and the twelve months for the other three, was very painful for me. I could find no comfort in the facts of my age and my heart condition. I did not want to be better off than the others. We had all taken the same decision and the cost to each of us ought to have been the same. I could only hope that on appeal we would all be acquitted or have our sentences suspended, or if we lost, at least have the sentences levelled out.

Appeals to higher courts of law can take many months in South Africa before they are heard. We had to settle down to a long period of waiting, not knowing for how long.

The simmering unrest in Soweto and the boycott of black schools in many areas had persisted into 1977. The spirit of the students and the schoolchildren had not been broken by the horrors of 1976, the hundreds of dead, imprisoned, injured, detained. Throughout the year, the long boycott continued and spread, deepening in intensity. Some 500 African school teachers and principals resigned their teaching posts in support of the students' stand. "A headmaster without pupils is irrelevant," said one principal.

The thrust of the boycott was against the whole system of Bantu education, against the separate and inferior education of black pupils. There was still arson, stoning, shooting by the police, arrests, violence of all kinds, despite the uneasy peace at the end of the previous year. Soweto secondary schools were taken over by the state and the pupils refused to apply for readmission. For these thousands of students, boycott, in addition to the unrest of the previous year, would cost them two years of their school education, yet most secondary schools stood empty, not only in Soweto and the Cape Province, but in many other areas too.

Detaining the leaders for six months in 1976 had not helped to subdue the unrest. Even police violence and intimidation could not force the children into the schools. The boycott was spreading both ways, upwards into the black universities and downwards into primary schools. Small children knew about "boycott" even if they didn't always understand what it was all about. My small black godson would refuse to put on his shoes, saying "Boycott. No school today, mum." He was five years old.

The boycotts went on until the year closed with a half-hearted kind of truce between the authorities and the school principals, and a promise that Bantu education be scrapped. It was too early to judge whether this was in fact a victory for the boycotters. Ministers had given promises before.

185

Chapter VI

A strange kind of gaol bird

The first anniversary of the Soweto shooting, 16 June 1977, was to be commemorated at St Mary's Cathedral in Johannesburg by a twenty-four hours' vigil, organised mainly by Barbara Waite. The programme for the twenty-four hours was highly imaginative and, for a cathedral, very unusual. It was not to be the customary denominational vigil of silent prayer. Its purpose was to give people of all faiths, of all denominations and of all races a venue and an opportunity to remember and pay tribute to all who had suffered and died in the struggle for truth, justice, freedom and peace in South Africa.

It was to be a vigil of tribute and it drew an enthusiastic response from political organisations and people of all races, particularly young black people. There were to be addresses, poetry and play readings, choirs and instrumental music throughout the twenty-four hours. The vigil was to begin and end with requiem masses for the dead, celebrated by the Bishop of Johannesburg. A tall candle would burn at the high altar for the whole twenty-four hours while the Black Sash would maintain a continuous stand of two women in front of it, wearing their black sashes. Below the candle would be the names of those who had died in 1976, those in detention or in gaol and those known to be banned or banished. There would be just one vase of flowers sent by Winnie Mandela, to be given the next day to the mother of Hector Peterson, the first schoolboy to die from the police bullets.

At the Witwatersrand University there was to be a mass meeting of commemoration at noon at which Helen Suzman, Bishop Desmond Tutu and I were to address the students. I was to address the people at the cathedral vigil at midnight.

On the eve of the vigil, the Minister of Justice warned the Bishop of Johannesburg that if there were to be any speeches at the vigil, the magistrate would stop the proceedings. The police had instructions to take action immediately if the minister's warning was not heeded. Both the Dean of the Cathedral and the Bishop immediately refused to preach if others could not speak and the Bishop decided that the vigil must be silent throughout.

It seemed that the vigil had been dealt a cruel blow. The element of spoken and sung tribute, such a vital part of the whole concept, had been destroyed. Yet the flame of the candle burned steadily on, the women of the Black Sash stood in motionless silence. Throughout that day and night, there were always forty or fifty people, black and white, kneeling in silent tribute and prayer. The dignity and the meaning of the vigil had not, after all, been touched.

I was at the opening mass of the vigil and remained there for a few hours until I came home to complete my address to the students. My midnight speech for the vigil had of course been discarded.

At half past eleven that morning one of the students phoned to tell me that all campus meetings had been banned for three days. At twenty minutes to twelve he phoned again to say that the ban did not actually take effect until midday, the students were already assembled in the Great Hall — could I get there in time to speak for five minutes before twelve o'clock? Fortunately Ilse Wilson, Bram Fischer's daughter, was at my house with her car and we drove at top speed to the university. I reached the platform with almost five minutes in hand to a great welcome, except for some boos from one corner of the hall. That was a new experience for me, but I was not altogether surprised, for I had already heard of an ugly act of vandalism on the campus. Some of the students had planted hundreds of black crosses on the campus lawns that morning in commemoration of the young Soweto dead. These had later been set alight with petrol and the crosses were burned — the work of right-wing students.

I spoke for five minutes, there was no time for more. Then the students sang "We shall overcome" and, as the meeting closed, exactly at noon, remembering the boos, I gave the clenched fist salute of the liberation struggle with a defiant shout of "Amandla!" (Strength).

I returned to the Cathedral for the rest of the twenty-four hours, moved, yet saddened, by the complete silence. The night hours passed very slowly for all of us. Most of the clergy and the whites went home for the night, except the gallant team of Black Sash women and the few who provided a continuous coffee service up in the Tower Room. Some forty black people had remained for the night, mostly women; they had brought blankets against the cold of that June night. They had come from work and would go back to work the next morning. At intervals during the night some would go up to the Tower Room for coffee and perhaps a sort of nap in a chair or for companionable talk amongst themselves, sometimes to sing part of those weary hours away — up there where they would not be heard.

The Cathedral itself was so quiet, so still, only a few lights burning high up in the roof, and the great candle, growing shorter as the hours passed, two women always standing beside it. I wondered whether the minister realised what he had done. He had killed a part of the vigil but he had totally failed to destroy its spirit. The very silence filled that great cathedral, poured out of the open doors into the dark night.

At five o'clock the next morning the black people began to sing, very softly, in quiet defiance. They sang hymns in lovely harmony; they sang for the last hour of the vigil, but the silence and the singing were each part of the other and it was a fitting end to an unforgettable night. I stood with Barbara at the door when it was all over and we had blown out the candle. It had not been as she had planned it, and we were still disappointed at the Bishop's insistence on total silence, but we both knew that the vigil itself, silent or sung, had proved indestructible.

The press coverage of my brief speech at the university and the Amandla salute aroused right-wing anger. There were a couple of death threats the following morning. "We're coming tonight to kill you, you communist bitch!" . . . "We'll bomb your house tonight!" with sundry obscene abuse. I telephoned the Norwood police and met with the usual lack of comprehension and just a vague assurance that the night patrol would be told to "watch out". I found out later that one of my friends had sat outside my house in his car until one o'clock the next morning, but he saw and heard nothing. This is a problem for all of us who are subjected to telephone threats. Should we ignore them on the assumption that nothing would happen on the night of the threat? . . . Yet some day it might . . . who knew?

The Suppression of Communism Act of 1950 had been renamed the Internal Security Act and its scope had been extended to cover, not merely suspected communist activities, but also those which "endanger the security of the state or the maintenance of public order". Its new name did not make the Act any less sinister or far-reaching and it made it even easier for the minister to ban organisations or persons.

In October 1977 these extended powers were invoked in the banning of seventeen organisations together with some of their officials. They included the multiracial Christian Institute, which, together with the South African Council of Churches, was keeping the banner of the struggle for justice and freedom flying in the Christian church. The bans also covered every black consciousness organisation.

The minister declared that the banned organisations, persons and publications had been a threat to the maintenance of peace and security. He had acted on the report of a committee consisting of a magistrate and two other jurists, but the banned organisations and banned people never saw those "factual" reports which in reality amounted to secret trials at which the accused could not appear. For good measure, the widely-read black newspapers, the *World* and the *Weekend World*, were also declared illegal, despite their enormous circulation — or perhaps because of it.

I saw a haunting press photograph of Theo Kotze, Director of the now banned Christian Institute, my Cape Town friend, in whose house I had so often stayed. He was standing in the doorway of the Institute. The photograph showed him flanked by two young policemen in full camouflage uniform. What for? To outlaw a Christian institution, did they need to appear in this garb? Was Theo, this gentle but determined minister of the Methodist church, so dangerous?

One policeman had the grace to bow his head, even to look ashamed, but the other was sharing a joke with a triumphant grinning constable in the background. Theo himself had just been served with a banning order, his life and work destroyed by a stroke of the minister's pen. I should not stay again with this warm, hospitable friend, for now Theo could not communicate with me.

In February 1978 a date was at last set for the hearing of our appeal against our conviction for refusing to answer questions about Winnie. Judgement was reserved but I was suddenly aware that I really had a possible four months' gaol sentence hanging over my head and the other three, Barbara, Jackie and Ilona, had far worse to face. There was no way of assessing the chance of any of our appeals succeeding and there would still probably be some weeks before we should know our fate. Nevertheless, I began to expect a telephone call, hour after hour, day after day, with a feeling of relief when each afternoon was over and I knew I could hear nothing until the following day. Then at last I heard that judgement would be given the following day, 13 April. Only a couple more days and I might well be in gaol for four months.

I decided that I must say goodbye to all my friends, so I telephoned, bidding them come to my "judgement party" the following night, although I did not yet know whether it would be a celebration or a "going in" party. I knew the next morning. My sentence had been reduced to two weeks and Barbara's from a year to two months. Jackie and Ilona had been acquitted because our defence counsel had discovered a flaw in the prosecution's case. I was delighted for them, but anxious lest they should be charged again and have to go through a repeat performance. I remembered what the prosecutor had said in my case, "I can bring her back again and again . . ." It seemed to me that there was no point in appealing further. The judge had upheld the conviction though reducing the sentence. Seeing that our stand was one of protest against any compulsion to make statements and become state witnesses, I felt that to appeal further would weaken our stand on principle.

Seventy of my friends crowded into my house for that "going in" drink with me, bishops and lawyers, priests and politicians, people who had already known gaol and bans, and those who hadn't, the young and the old, they were all there. Most of them had to stand for there wasn't room for sitting and it was gay, the way I wanted it to be, the way I wanted to go into gaol. Barbara was away on holiday at the time and would surrender herself to serve her sentence a little later.

Exactly what I was supposed to do next was not clear. I did not want to sit at home and wait to be taken into custody. I knew that I should have to report to the magistrate's court in Bloemfontein, so I arranged to drive down there on the Monday morning with some friends (provided I wasn't picked up by the police in the meantime). We should meet Zeni and Zindzi Mandela in Brandfort on the way, having a "going in" lunch at an "international" hotel in Bloemfontein where we could all eat together and then I would report to the court and surrender myself. Fourteen days still seemed an unbelievably short sentence. I took a few books, the Oxford Book of English Verse which a friend lent me for the occasion, a modern translation of the Bible and a couple of devotional books.

Zindzi and Zeni were waiting for us on the Brandfort bridge as we arrived (and so, we discovered later, were the security police, watching I suppose to see whether Winnie would join us!). Zindzi brought a huge knitted stole in ANC colours, black, gold and green, for me to wear for the occasion. Ilona joined us for lunch, as she was visiting her parents in Bloemfontein.

I reported to the court office and found a policeman at my elbow. "Come with me," he said, but I protested that I must first bid my friends goodbye and went back to them. They were standing together a little forlornly, not knowing what had happened to me, but there they all were, Zeni and Zindzi and her boyfriend, Ilona and the two Little Sisters of Jesus, Iris Mary and Valentine, my friends who had driven me down from Johannesburg.

There was laughter, and hugs and kisses, with the policeman still at my elbow until I was suddenly without my friends and on my way down to the dark cell below the court. My personal possessions were first taken from me and then returned when I was transported in the prison van to Bloemfontein gaol, where my reception was neutral but not unfriendly.

I was of course a strange phenomenon to the young wardresses, an old woman who had chosen to go to gaol rather than make a statement against a friend. I was taken to a cell, better than I had expected, far different from those dreary dingy cells high up in the rafters in the Pretoria gaol in 1960. Here there was a window which could open, even if barred, but I could see black women prisoners moving around in a courtyard. There was even a private loo in one corner — that was something I had not known before in gaol. I went to bed quite soon after lock-up time and slept peacefully on a rather hard bed, with sheets which were as usual too short for the bed, and enough blankets.

I was almost disappointed to discover the next morning that I was to serve my sentence in Klerksdorp gaol, about half-way between Johannesburg and Bloemfontein.

As I was driven into Klerksdorp gaol, high and forbidding, one of the newest prisons, I looked anxiously at the gigantic, monolithic concrete fortress. My spirits dropped as I clambered up three flights of noisy, steep iron stairs, holding rather desperately onto my issue of prison clothing, bundled together with my bag under one arm, grasping the iron railings with the other. I arrived at the reception office, panting, breathless, thankful to be allowed to sit, for prisoners usually stand. I was glad that with my papers there was a certificate stating that I had had a serious heart attack two years before and was under medication. I didn't fancy traipsing up and down those stairs very often.

The officer in charge of the women's section was young, cool, kind and serious. I discovered that I was the only white woman prisoner in the gaol. There were fifty or sixty black women serving sentences whom I never saw at all. Klerksdorp was in fact mainly a men's gaol and the women's section was tightly sealed off, a little world on its own. I, too, was tightly sealed off from the black women prisoners.

My cell was obviously part of a section specially designed for white women and it was like nothing that I had ever imagined a cell could be. It was light and bright and the afternoon sun was streaming in. I stood in the doorway and asked unbelievingly, "Is this for *me*?" There was a loo and a wash basin behind a three-foot dividing wall, windows, long and very narrow, from floor to ceiling, but the slit window of the top half could be swivelled open to let in the sun and the air. They looked outwards, beyond the gaol, right across the prison grounds to open country. The cells were high up, on the third floor and I had the feeling of being in a tower, like the Lady of Shalott, looking down on the passing world below, except that the only human life for me to see was a black convict labour gang working in the prison grounds.

Lights went out at eight o'clock so I had to learn to sleep early and long. I woke before five in the morning to watch the eastern sky slowly lighten and redden until the flaming sun came up on the horizon. For me that would mean that another day and night had passed. Yet I was not unhappy there. I could read and after a few days I had some wool and could crochet. All the same, it was a strange, sterile existence. My home and my life in Johannesburg faded away, although I thought very much about my friends.

As I came to each new experience, I thought of Barbara. How would the plain heavy starchy food affect her? I could not imagine her slim elegant figure, her tailored clothes exchanged for the loose heavy overdress, nor that classic head atop the tan jersey. For me it was all so much better than anything I had hitherto experienced in gaol. For her it was all going to be so much worse than anything she had ever known or imagined.

I thought very often of how my pink skin had made me better off as a prisoner. I could not doubt that black conditions had improved in the gaols in some ways over the years, just as white conditions had done, but the gap was still there and whites were still far better off.

When I was discharged, the officer came outside the gaol to see me off, saying, "I shall miss you," very sincerely. Thinking of a possible re-subpoena and a longer gaol sentence, I laughed and replied, "Don't worry — I'll be back!"

I returned to a gay, friendly welcome from my friends, but I wondered when the telephone calls would begin again. The day before the judgement there had been a particularly nasty one. Gaol had given me relief from this and I had felt secure in that cell, high above the world, the danger locked out.

As I had anticipated, the security branch were soon on my doorstep with a subpoena for a repeat performance. I must appear before the Bloemfontein magistrate again on 1 June, to answer questions relating to two alleged offences by Mrs Winnie Mandela on 27 September 1977 — the mixture exactly as before.

I accepted the subpoena in silence and they went away. I began immediately to make plans to go to Bloemfontein and to face gaol again. I thought I should handle it alone this time to save legal expenses. There would be no point in noting an appeal against the inevitable conviction. It had all been argued before and we had lost our case.

I was astounded a few days later to learn that the Attorney General of the Free State had dropped the case against me on account of my age. It seemed incomprehensible, for I was only a few weeks older than when I had gone to gaol. Although I was of course very relieved for myself, I was nevertheless very unhappy at being protected by age and thus levered into a more favourable position than Ilona and Jackie and Barbara.

I knew that Barbara had not been able to adjust to gaol conditions, that it was a continuous traumatic experience for her. It had not been so for me and I knew how fortunate I had been. I knew, too, that for me there never could have been any other way and never would be. It raised a question, however, to which I do not think I have yet found the answer. How far can you be held responsible for the sufferings of another? To some extent my example of not retreating from a principle had been followed. Barbara had taken her own decision, very courageously, but I could not escape from the thought that I had helped to bring this suffering on her.

Ilona and Jackie had also been re-subpoenaed, had again come before the Bloemfontein magistrate, refused to speak and this time had been sentenced to three and four months' gaol respectively. They had appealed against the severity of their sentences and were once again in that strange limbo of waiting for their judgement.

They were still waiting as Christmas approached and it seemed that they might still spend it with all their friends, but on 29 November, the judgement was given and they had lost. Their sentences were upheld and they had to go into gaol, not to Klerksdorp, but the Pretoria Central goal, where they were subjected to very harsh conditions and discipline. They were even kept in solitary confinement, separated from each other completely, for the first six weeks.

I knew that Joe Morolong's banning orders were due to expire in 1978 — the third five-year restriction. It had been inhuman, this confinement to within a mile and a half of his father's little house in Ditshipeng Reserve, a desolate semi-desert area in the Northern Cape Province. That was by day; by night, Joe's radius of movement was reduced to a little over fifty yards. During these fifteen years of his bans, Joe and I had not been able to communicate with each other.

We had been companions on that long exciting tour to find the banished people. We had both been put under stringent restrictions, but mine had ceased seven years ago. Would the Minister of Justice sentence Joe to yet another five years of that hell of desolation? I was in a state of both hope and dread as the third five-year banning order expired.

For the first few days, my hopes rose, for there was no report of any renewal of his ban, but on 4 April, the tragic news was published that Joe had been murdered five months previously. He had been found dead in the veld with a stab wound in his back. That is all that was ever known of the death of Joe Morolong. Today he lies buried in the place where he existed for fourteen and a half years of that living death, the man who had chosen to stay in South Africa.

Joe had been a laughing companion on our tour, but his laughter must surely have died during those lonely years. Photographs had been published from time to time of the stark isolation of Ditshipeng Reserve. Did the minister ever see them? Or did he ever care to know what he had done when he imposed those three five-year banning orders, one after the other, on Joseph Morolong?

I went to Pretoria a few times to attend the trial of eleven African men and one African woman on charges of ANC activities, training for guerrilla warfare and sabotage. Six were found guilty and on the day of sentence the court was crowded with whites, unlike all the other days when only the families and a few friends came there.

Security was always very strict at such trials and I often had the contents of my handbag examined. Once a policeman used his dog against us as we stood on the pavement to wave to the prison van as it drove the accused back to gaol. The dog was an Alsatian, as police dogs usually are, and I felt outraged that such a beautiful animal should be used for such a purpose. I had my own dog Kwacha in mind, but I knew that the blacks who stood with me to face that policeman and his straining dog did not share my view. To black people an Alsatian is a police dog, to be hated and feared on sight.

Some of the whites who crowded the court on this occasion were recognisable as security policemen, but there were other whites there too, and a few white women. All were grim-faced, expectant; they had come to hear a death sentence and to exult over the condemned men.

There were not many friends, wives and mothers, yet they had to fight their way into that crowded courtroom to hear the fate of their men. Two young women had married their men in prison during the trial. Would they be widows before they were ever wives? Their husbands were young men in their early twenties and it was for them that the state had demanded the death sentence. The judges, however, did not sentence them to death. Those waiting whites were disappointed. Anger was clearly to be seen on their faces as they left the court.

These two accused, Naledi Ntsiki and Mosima Sexwale, had made moving and inspiring statements from the dock before they were sentenced, not knowing whether they would live or die. They had declared their loyalty to the ANC and their adherence to the Freedom Charter. "As I look back," Naledi had said, "I cannot honestly say that I believe the decisions I took which led me to this position were wrong — what I regret most was that it was necessary and inevitable that these decisions had to be taken." As he went down the steps from the court to the cells to begin his eighteen years in gaol, I caught Sexwale's eye and he smiled at me. I blew him a kiss and the police had to restrain a white man from assaulting me. The next day, I would be seventy-three and I wondered whether I should still be alive to see these men, young and old, when they completed their sentences. Yet that did not matter, for they would live, not die. They would survive to be free again, whether it took the long years of their sentences or whether freedom came to South Africa before then.

In June, after I came back from gaol, the telephone calls started again but now more obscene than threatening, and only one which said, "We'll kill you tonight." I was becoming almost indifferent to them and they had little more than a nuisance value, until a rock the size of a tennis ball smashed through my sitting room window which, like my bedroom, faces the street, though sheltered to a great extent by shrubs and trees.

It seemed that the missile was thrown from the street as Kwacha had not been alerted, as I am sure she would have been had anyone climbed over the gate. I called the Norwood police and although fingerprints were taken and the rock taken away for examination by the police, I knew that it was unlikely that I should hear more of it.

Press reporters came the next day and while they were at my home the usual telephone calls started, threatening and abusive. I called one of the reporters to the phone to take the third call. What he heard was, "You dirty old bitch, we're coming tonight to cut your throat!" When the reporter asked who was speaking, he was told to ". . . off!" I assured him that this happened from time to time and felt satisfied that he had actually heard the threat.

No one can dispute a broken window and a rock, but I sometimes wondered whether people really believed me about the telephone threats. Until the reporter took the call, I had no way of proving that they had actually taken place. Once a woman telephoned and seemed quite pleasant until I asked who she was and then she said, "just another white who wants to break your communist neck".

Hoax harassment soon followed. I was amazed at the ingenuity which avoided repetition. A man came to collect a non-existent piano and another came for a garden roller, both of which I was supposed to have advertised for sale; there was a glazier to mend an unbroken window, paving stones for a garden already paved. Then a new, more sinister, macabre type of hoax. I was telephoned by a supposed hospital doctor to say that a friend had met with a motor accident. I was suspicious this time and asked for a number to call back, but when I did so there was no such doctor. The following day I had a call beginning "This is the government mortuary here . . ." I put the receiver down quickly. An hour later, a small closed van arrived at my gate with two men in white overalls. They said they were from the mortuary and had come for the body. That afternoon there was another call, "We're coming tonight to cut your throat, cut your throat . . ." screamed at me in a rising crescendo.

Nothing of all this really prepared me for what was to come. At midnight on 15 August I woke startled, to the deafening sound of gunfire and heard glass shattering in my sitting room. Kwacha only whimpered, she did not bark and I think the gunshots must have hurt her sensitive dog's ears. I heard a car engine start up and a car drive away. I thought there might still be a gunman lurking around so I did not want to switch on the light and become a target. I crawled across the floor to the telephone, only to realise that I did not know the police flying squad number and would have to put the light on to find it. I thought about that for a bit, sitting on the floor in the dark, then crawled back to put on the light. I waited and nothing happened, so I got myself onto my feet and went into the sitting room. I saw that almost every pane of glass had been shattered and there was broken glass everywhere. Only when the police arrived did I venture out to unlock the gate.

There was really nothing they could do except take a statement and scrabble around on the floor looking for bullets. The damage had mostly been done by a shotgun, except for one bullet which had gone through the glass pane of the front door and then through the wooden sitting-room door to lodge in the jamb of the bathroom door. I was thankful I had not been in the line of fire.

The next day there was first a call at midday, "What a pity! What a pity!" and then at three o'clock, "Next time you won't be so lucky!" Then, "Helen, the next one will be between the eyeballs." At four o'clock, "Are you insured?" and late that night, "What sort of wood do you want for your coffin?" A day or so later . . . "What about a date with death? Twelve o'clock is the time", and then a little later, "Tonight I'm coming to cut your throat, you old bitch."

For the rest of that year, there was little beyond obscenity, but 1979 brought more sinister telephone calls. "We're going to wipe you out . . . It won't be like last time, we'll do a proper job this time." On 8 February, at the usual time, 12.30 a.m., when I was not yet in bed but the curtains were drawn and the gates padlocked, I heard three ear-splitting blasts. This time I knew what they were, but I didn't hear any glass shattering, so I hesitantly looked into the sitting room but saw no sign of any damage. I made some coffee, put out the lights and went to bed. I did not fancy going out onto the verandah to investigate any further. At half past six the next morning I went out and was shocked to find a bullet hole in the wall only inches away from my bedroom window.

When the police came, they found a second bullet hole, this one in the roof just above the bedroom window and also two empty cartridge cases outside my front gate which established that nine millimetre bullets had been used. Yet I knew, as before, that the gunman would not be traceable, nor would the perpetrator of the telephone calls. The police suggested that I should obtain an unlisted telephone number, but I could not agree to this, for it would mean cutting myself off from the many visitors passing through Johannesburg, often strangers to South Africa, who wanted to see me.

Only a few calls followed this renewal of attempted violence, mainly laughter or just silence, repeated at intervals during the night. Then one, "Helen, don't go out tonight, we're coming with bullets."

Part of the horror of this protracted persecution and especially the shooting, was the realisation that I was actually so hated by other human beings as to make all this possible. A few friends were experiencing similar incidents sporadically, though not actual shooting, except of course the dreadful assassination of Rick Turner, who had opened his window late one night to investigate a sound on his verandah. He was shot and died in the arms of his young daughter.

I never met this brilliant young industrial sociologist who had lived his house arrest with courage and undimmed commitment, but after his tragic death, his wife Foszia became a very close friend. Whenever I went to Durban to speak at a meeting I stayed with her. I stood with her at Rick's grave one Sunday and loved her for her acceptance of this tragedy and her determination that life must go on.

In my case I found it hard to accept that these attackers were actually would-be assassins. Who were they? Yet Rick Turner was dead and I could not totally dismiss the possibility that even in my case it was attempted murder and not just intimidation.

Concerned friends urged me to build a high concrete wall, but I could not bear the idea of living behind it. Nor could I tolerate any idea of leaving the home where I had lived for more than twenty years, the little square house with the wooded garden which meant so much to me. Where would I go? Once I started to run, where would I stop? To share my home on a permanent basis, so as not to live alone, was equally unacceptable. I wanted to live alone. I had chosen to do so. I felt reluctant even to have casual visitors now, because I did not want to expose others to possible danger.

I realised, however, that I needed some form of protection and finally settled for a two-inch thick sheet of bullet proof perspex across my bedroom window. It gives me a feeling of security, even when I think I can hear a car stopping outside my house. I have become unconscious of it in the daytime and of the ugly need for it. I frame it in tall potplants and sometimes it reminds me of Prinsloo's face, framed in the Brandfort privet hedge.

Telephone calls increased in number at the end of the year, but hoaxes diminished, except for one outrageous and utterly incongruous incident. Two young men came to my door one evening to tell me that they had come to install and operate a discotheque for my party — as ordered by me. Anything looking less like a venue for a discotheque party than my quiet little home and this old lady at the door, can hardly be imagined. I tried to convince them that I had made no such order, that it was a hoax. But they were now two very angry young men and angry with me because they had refused another order for that night for which they would have been paid R100. They did not want to accept my explanation about the hoax because they could not understand how it had happened. It did not make any sense to them and they had lost 100 rands.

I tried to explain my political position to them and that only made things worse, for they could not see why they should suffer financially because I had stubbornly opposed government policies and actions — which they themselves probably supported. I had to concede a certain logic in this argument. If I had not been who I was, this would not have happened to them. It was all rather unreal.

Chapter VII

The 1980's

Two of our most loved women leaders, Mary Moodley and Lilian Ngoyi, died at the end of the 1970s. They had both dedicated their lives to the struggle for freedom, "sparing nothing of their strength or courage . . ."

Mary Moodley, a prominent founding member of the Federation of South African Women, died in October 1979. She had been one of the stalwarts of the Federation throughout its history. Coloured, she had also been on the executive of the South African People's Organisation and an active trade union organiser. It was not this that endeared "Auntie Mary" to us, it was her courage, her compassion, her boundless love for all around her — and her gaiety. But Mary would also weep with those who came to her in sorrow.

She told me once how when she was in gaol, in solitary confinement, she even danced in her cell to keep her spirits up. For the whole of her sixty-five years, she had laughed and loved her way through life. She knew no differences of race or colour, nor even differences within the organisations of the liberation struggle itself. Black consciousness supporters, Congress Alliance stalwarts, radical left-wing politicals, in some way Mary was part of them all. It was this solidarity that brought 700 people of many organisations together to wear the ANC colours at Mary's funeral. They paid tribute to her, crowding into a hall in a coloured location, together with the people of her own neighbourhood, now bereft of the beloved Auntie Mary.

When I came to the platform to pay my last tribute to her, I saw the Congress flags, black, green and yellow, on the walls, on the platform, draped over Mary's coffin. Women wore their Federation green blouses and black skirts. Before I began to speak, the women led the mourners in singing, not a funeral hymn, but songs to welcome me, for I had not been with them for many years. I knew then that the spirit of the Federation which had brought us together in the 1950s, was not dead. It would live on in the hearts of the women, it was recognised by the men ·and accepted by them as part of the liberation struggle. It would remain.

Banned for nearly twenty years, harassed continually by the police, detained, Mary had remained gallant and undaunted. We laid her weary body to rest to the freedom songs of her people.

Less than six months later, Lilian Ngoyi, our greatest Federation leader, died very suddenly. She had been ill for some months and in hospital for part of the time, but she had seemed to be regaining her health. She had visited me and I thought that she might soon be her old vital self again. But that was not to be. On 12 March 1980 Lilian died.

Lilian's earlier bans had expired in 1972 and were not renewed for three years. Friends brought her to me as soon as she was free and there we were, sitting together on my verandah, as though there had never been ten years silence between us. It had been a bitter time for her but she had survived it. She still seemed ageless; her vitality and her fire were undimmed. She told me of her plans to travel, to go to Durban, to Cape Town, to stay freely in other people's houses again, to catch up on what had been happening during her empty years. We were together again, but we were not going to be able to meet as freely as we should like because she had no transport and as a white I could not go into any African township without a permit. At least we knew that when the opportunities did come, there would be no barriers.

We had worked side by side in the exciting years of the 1950s, had been to gaol together, had been tried for four and a half years for high treason together and had been acquitted together. House arrest and bans had separated us on and off for the past twenty-five years. Only very occasionally had it been possible for us to meet, secretly, but the ties of our friendship had never been broken.

In 1975 Lilian was banned again, though less severely than before. She was still forbidden to attend political meetings but she could communicate with her friends and we met sometimes. The news of her death in 1980 was a great shock to me and I felt a sick rage when I received a telephone call only half an hour after I learnt of it. The voice was the usual one, "I hear that Lilian Ngoyi has passed away . . . I am so glad." I put the receiver down without speaking. Subsequently a friend answered the phone while I was out. "Tell Helen that Lilian Ngoyi is waiting for her."

Her death brought great sorrow to Soweto. "Ma Ngoyi" they called her there. "Ma" is a designation of great respect and love. In her little Orlando home, despite her bans, Lilian had remained a central figure.

I went to Orlando for her funeral, remembering that day we had led 20,000 women to Pretoria to protest against passes, the day she had called for thirty minutes of motionless silence and then led the women in the singing of "Nkosi Sikelele". At her funeral we sang it again but her voice was silent.

The large church was packed with people and bright with Congress colours. Six women of the Federation and the African National Congress Women's League maintained a guard of honour in their green blouses and black skirts, standing still and silent on each side of the coffin where she lay under the Congress flag.

It was a gathering of the old members of the ANC and the Federation and the Women's League, but they were joined by the young. As at Mary's funeral, all differences disappeared and young and old, black consciousness and Congress, joined together in tribute. I joined the guard of honour beside the coffin for a little while before the women carried it out of the church, Amina Cachalia's green and yellow sari brilliant among them. A moving announcement had been made. "Lilian Ngoyi lived a life of great simplicity and we shall bury her in simplicity. The coffin will be borne on a cart drawn by two horses."

A thousand people walked behind her, five miles to the cemetery. All the way, the people of Soweto came out of their houses to wave their farewell to her as she passed, giving her the Amandla salute, the clenched fist of strength and struggle. I did not try to walk the five miles. Father Leo Rakale drove me in his car, very slowly, at the back of the procession. I did not know then that within three months this kindly priest, my close friend, would be dead.

The campaign for the release of Nelson Mandela followed soon after, spreading far and wide. Thousands of people signed forms demanding the release of Nelson and the other political prisoners; hundreds of thousands had Nelson's name on their lips and in their thoughts as never before.

NUSAS arranged a series of meetings on different university campuses. The theme was political resistance. I went to Cape Town and Pietermaritzburg Universities to speak to the students on the history of resistance, particularly in the 1950s. To my surprise, Pietermaritzburg students also invited me to defend socialism against capitalism in a public debate. I agreed, but very hesitantly, because I am no ideologue. I know where I stand, unequivocally alongside the Freedom Charter, but I am not quite sure where this places me in the politico-economic spectrum.

I applied myself to intensive study and reading for a couple of months and found that I had simply come out "by the same door wherein I went". For me the door to the future of South Africa is the Freedom Charter and just as it had stood for over twenty years against all assaults from all sides, so it could stand against capitalist or free enterprise arguments.

I hold that the present system must go, there must be economic justice and the only alternative is the Freedom Charter, that amalgam of the hopes and the heartaches of the people. Nothing has changed. The hopes and the heartaches are still the same as they were in 1955 when the charter declared "Our people have been robbed of their birthright to land, liberty and peace."

Leon Louw, dedicated to the free enterprise system for South Africa, was my opponent. He was very articulate in the jargon of the political economist. On arrival on the campus I found the buildings plastered with notices announcing the debate, but there had been busy red paint brushes smearing right across my photograph — and even by mistake across my opponent's, too. "Socialism is Communism! Traitor!" The epithet of traitor didn't mean much to me, for I had once stood trial with many others on a charge of high treason and we had all been acquitted.

I proposed the motion that only socialism could satisfy South Africa's future and spent a few lively minutes damning the evils of the capitalist system before proclaiming Freedom Charter socialism as the only alternative.

A vote had been taken at the beginning of the debate and only ninety-one people had voted for socialism while 130 had voted for capitalism. I had a strong seconder in John Aitcheson, like me, a formerly banned Christian. We had agreed that we could not hope to win, for whoever had heard of socialism winning an open debate against capitalism in South Africa?

Leon Louw, replying to me, complained that all I had done was to quote a banned document. This of course was not true. The Freedom Charter itself was not and never has been banned. Various printed reproductions of it have been banned from time to time as they appear, but like a phoenix, it arises every time from the ashes of such banning of the printed word and lives on.

There was prolonged discussion from the floor before the vote was taken again, which eventually resulted in eighty-eight votes for socialism and only eighty-six for capitalism! John and I hugged each other, but we knew that we had not really won anyone over to our viewpoint. It was just that the socialists had more stamina and the capitalists had gone home to bed.

Six months later I was asked to repeat my socialism performance at Wits University, this time opposed by another strong supporter of the free enterprise system. Once again events brought me to unexpected victory. On the morning of the debate I had a telephone call from someone who said that he was the President of the Students' Representative Council. He informed me that the time of the debate had been changed. It would now take place at two thirty p.m. and not at twelve thirty as arranged. I was surprised, therefore, when a car arrived at midday to take me to the university. When the confusion had been sorted out, we discovered that the telephone call had not come from the SRC President at all and that the debate was still due to start at twelve thirty — in fifteen minutes' time!

At first I was inclined to dismiss it as some right-wing student prank. I changed my mind when I had a telephone call in a very familiar voice which said, "You old bitch, you're up to your shit again." What with all this, we reached the debate a little late but when the chairman explained to the audience what had caused the delay, I received applause before ever I said a word.

Almost all the audience were now clearly on my side and they had no time for my unfortunate opponent, who was hailed with hisses and boos. There was no need to take a vote at the end of this debate. Socialism had triumphed again, even if not by my eloquence.

In April 1980, I was seventy-five years old. I had the gayest of birthday weeks — not just a one-day birthday party — with friends and flowers, telephone calls and telegrams from all over, inside and outside South Africa, and all because I was seventy-five. For a number of years I had been thinking that it was time I bowed out from the political scene. The age gap grew wider every year, yet it had never become a generation gap and the students still called me to speak to them. But now, at seventy-five, surely I must accept my age, and the young must accept it too? These were my thoughts, but I was soon to be proved wrong. I was still needed.

Four years had passed since the revolt of the Soweto schoolchildren against Bantu education, in 1976. It was three years since they had boycotted their schools demanding that this inferior education go before they would return. Promises had been given and the children had returned to school but the promises had not been kept. After all, they were only promises to black children. Nothing had really changed and the resentment simmered on.

In 1980 it was all happening again as coloured schoolchildren rejected the shoddy education which the system handed out to them, and the conditions at their schools. The boycott began in the Cape and spread. In some areas black children joined in the boycott because they too still had their grievances. As the weeks passed, so the 1976 pattern re-emerged, restraint at first, then growing police violence, followed by violent retaliation from the students, evoking worse violence from the police.

Students on both black and white English-speaking university campuses boycotted lectures in sympathy, staging campus sit-ins for one or two days, even longer. So, seventy-five or not, within two weeks, I was speaking at Wits University on school boycotts.

Here for the first time I was the target of eggs and tomatoes flung by right-wing opponents. They were fairly far from the platform and their missiles didn't reach me. Bishop Desmond Tutu and I were the main speakers, just as we had been at that other meeting on the Wits campus four years ago, when the students marched out into the streets in sympathy with the Soweto schoolchildren.

I didn't mind the egg-throwing, for the audience gave me a standing ovation when I had finished speaking. Four days later I was back on Pietermaritzburg campus, proud to be identified with this expression of solidarity with the boycotting schoolchildren. The boycott was spreading and intensifying and the Minister of Justice took sudden and drastic action against the leaders of the people. It was 1976 all over again as leaders, black, Indian, coloured and a few white students, were detained without trial. In Natal, several Indian leaders were detained, including the President, Vice President and executive members of the Natal Indian Congress.

A protest meeting was organised in Durban by the Natal Indian Congress and I was asked to speak there. On my arrival in Durban I was told that a very large crowd was expected but I did not anticipate anything like the reality. A total of 5,000 people, mostly Indian, came to that meeting, many standing outside the packed hall to listen through loudspeakers. Archie Gumede, veteran ANC leader of the 1950s, was in the chair and the Roman Catholic Archbishop of Durban was one of the speakers. The wives of the detainees sat on the platform and each one was personally introduced to the audience. I was the last speaker and from the beginning of the meeting I could feel the excitement growing. I spoke of the great history of passive resistance and of the Natal Indian Congress, of the Freedom Charter and of the crime of detaining people without trial. I spoke of the need to speak out, to stand up and be counted. I ended, "And I do believe with all my heart that we shall overcome one day. That is my message to the detainees. Let it be yours, too."

All 5,000 people sang the American freedom fighters' song, "We shall overcome one day" with me. The sound poured out into the night and their hearts were in every line of it until they came to their feet in a great standing ovation. I was almost stunned, holding Archie's hand very tightly as we stood there, as we had stood more than twenty years before, in the days of the Congress Alliance. An Indian leader whispered to me, "Helen, you'll get banned for this!"

We sang "Nkosi Sikelele" and then it was all over. I had felt, deep in my heart, once again, that certainty that nothing could defeat the oppressed people of South Africa. I had felt it before at the Congress of the People and at the Union Buildings in Pretoria. Such moments are rare, unforgettable. I could not have gone on if I did not believe that freedom would come. But this is more than belief, it is unshakeable knowledge.

That was 11 June 1980. Exactly two weeks later, I was served with a banning order. Not house arrest, not the multiplicity of earlier bans, but a direct attack on my association with the students, with the young.

The Minister of Justice was "satisfied that I engaged in activities which endanger or are calculated to endanger the maintenance of public order". He had, therefore, prohibited me for two years from attending:

a) any political gathering, that is to say any gathering at which any form of state or any principle or policy of the government of a state is propagated, defended, attacked, criticised or discussed;

b) any gathering of pupils or students assembled for the purpose of being instructed, trained or addressed by me.

It would be two years before, if ever, I should hear "Nkosi Sikelele" sung again and I was back, perhaps where I belonged, in the shadowy legion of the banned. It seemed absurd that at seventy-five I should be banned again. That was how the public saw it. "The joke of the century . . . what does this government have to fear from Helen Joseph?"

I had to admit that it was well aimed. The only channel of activity left open to me had been to address and attend meetings. I could not be published or quoted in South Africa, nor could I belong to any political organisations. Yet despite my anger, this new "mini" ban was an award of merit, for it was proof that I was not wasting the years left to me.

The student youth wanted to hear what I had to say, and particularly what I could tell them about the 1950s, that great decade of protest and challenge. I had lived through those years, been identified with the political struggle. Some who were with me then are now in gaol, some are dead, many are banned or listed, many have left South Africa. There are few here now who can say, as I can, "I was there. I was part of it."

It was about all this that I spoke to students and others. I spoke also about the evils of our society and our duty to challenge them, resist them. I had not been charged with any offence arising out of my many speeches. Nevertheless I had been arbitrarily silenced. It was only for two years, but years are precious at seventy-five and there was no guarantee that the bans would not be renewed when I reached seventy-seven. Should I still be "dangerous" then? For that was what the ban said — that I endangered the maintenance of public order.

I wrote to the minister to ask for the reasons which had induced him to issue the banning order. He replied that this information could, in his opinion, not be disclosed without detriment to public order. For me it was a meaningless reply but there was nothing more that I could do about it.

What we have in South Africa cannot rightly be called "public order". It is a violent rule by force, intimidation and oppression, the oppression of the many by the few. We live in the violence of detention and death as much as in the violence of the streets. Certainly I do not want to maintain this system. I want it changed. To say this is no crime. Yet I was punished as though I were a criminal — except that I had no trial. I am not alone in this. There are hundreds of us, black and white, thrust into the shadows of a twilight existence.

I was banned for just over 100 weeks in all. Twenty of them I spent clumping around in plaster and more than that on crutches, from a broken leg. That accounted for more than a quarter of the time. I suppose it also helped make the time pass that, during these months, I was in any event physically prevented from doing what I was forbidden to do — attend political meetings and address gatherings of students.

I found it painful to be back on the sidelines again after nine years of relative freedom, of being a part of what was going on. I was more fortunate in these bans because I was not prohibited from social gatherings, though it was difficult to pinpoint where my kind of social gathering might end and a political gathering begin. Friends very often came to my house, the old and the young, my colleagues of the 1950s and the young and defiant of today. Inevitably we discussed what was going on. What else would we talk about? Perhaps I should have retired to my loo at such points in the conversation, but I never did and, thanks to my friends, I did not become isolated.

There were two Christmas Day parties during the banning period. My house and my garden were filled with friends. At midday, we drank our toast to those not with us, the banned, the banished, the detained and the prisoners. We drank to the end of oppression and the South Africa that is to come. We commemorated our dead heroes. Did that make it a political gathering, as we stood with our glasses raised and sang "Nkosi Sikelele"? I didn't know and I did not care.

In those two silent restricted years there was much of importance taking place in South Africa. For me, an exciting phenomenon was the re-emergence of women of all races to take their part, as women, in the struggle for freedom and justice in South Africa.

Perhaps Lilian's death and the great occasion of her funeral had something to do with it, for it was on 9 August 1980, our old National Women's Day, that this new strength of women began to appear. For almost twenty years we had remembered Women's Day only in our hearts and our minds, not publicly. But in 1980, suddenly, this day was being celebrated again openly in Durban, in Cape Town and in Johannesburg, with public meetings and a photographic exhibition. Press articles appeared commemorating that great protest of women to Pretoria, telling the history of the women of the 1950s.

In 1981 it was celebrated again, stronger than ever. New women's organisations had been formed during the intervening year and the name of the Federation of South African Women was once more on our lips. In April, Dora Tamana opened a large conference of women in Cape Town. Dora had belonged to the 1950s, she had been National Secretary of the Federation after

Ray Alexander had been banned and until she herself was banned. She had travelled with Lilian to Europe, the Soviet Union and the People's Republic of China. Bans expire with the years and Dora made her comeback with an unforgettable call to all women:

> You who have no work, speak,
> You who have no homes, speak,
> You who have no schools, speak,
> You who have to run like chickens from the vulture, speak,
> Let us share our problems so that we can solve them together ...
> I opened the road for you, you must go forward.

National Women's Day brought rousing conferences again in Durban, Cape Town and Johannesburg, and this time Albertina Sisulu was free after seventeen years of bans, to address the women again. Despite all her anxiety over her husband on Robben Island, her son under house arrest, her daughter in exile; despite the uncertainty of how long she would be allowed to enjoy the longed-for freedom, Albertina had spoken, and she went on speaking for the next ten months, to women and to men, carrying the message of defiance and commitment. "I cannot fold my arms and watch the situation deteriorating ... it has been going on for a long time and it must stop." She was banned again, but for those ten months she made her voice heard, loud and clear refusing to ban herself.

Students of the English language universities were neither silent nor idle. As always for the past two decades and longer, each generation of undergraduates produces its own radical core of young people, committed to the cause of freedom and democracy.

Just as there is a radical core amongst university students, so there is also a core of conservatives, calling themselves moderates, but they do not have a strong following. They invited Dr P.K. Koornhof, Minister of Co-operation and Development, to speak on the Wits University campus on the day before the anniversary of the Sharpeville massacre — a highly provocative date to choose, for feelings run high in South Africa on this anniversary.

This action by the moderates incensed the Students' Representative Council and its many supporters. They attended the meeting and interrupted and heckled the minister into silence, taking action on the ground that when Mandela and Sisulu and other imprisoned leaders were allowed to exercise their democratic right to speak on the Wits campus, then the students would allow Dr Koornhof, the Nationalist government minister, to speak.

An explosive situation followed on campus with the University Council taking strong exception to the student action and the SRC President becoming the whipping boy. The message was clear. The university authorities were concerned about any possible effect upon the university income from government subsidies and other major financial sources.

I remain one of the Honorary Vice Presidents of NUSAS. The students elected me every year even though I could not, as a listed person, accept the office. They came very frequently to my home, sometimes just to visit me, sometimes for serious discussion. Their presence always assured me of their loyalty and their determination not to leave me in isolation.

The government record of the past few years has continued to be as shameful as in the past. The minor cosmetic improvements for a few elite black people fade away before the onslaught of repressive legislation and action. Black people may now buy houses — at a price which very few can afford; more "international hotels" have been opened for racial social mixing. I usually still meet my black friends for fruit and sandwiches in a park, which is not frequented by the elite, black or white.

The shortage of houses for Africans in the cities and elsewhere is estimated to be rising steadily towards the half million mark. Before the end of the century, four million houses will be needed. The Nationalist government still seems to cherish the apartheid belief that Africans are only in the towns for the duration of their working life — maybe not as much in principle as before, but for sheer fright at the looming urban shortage of houses, a juggernaut which grows year by year.

The "fortunate" blacks still live in the little block township houses which are incapable of meeting the needs of a growing family. The rents rise ever higher but the wages do not rise at the same rate. Transport costs for these far-flung townships for urban dwellers rise too, as do food costs. True, there are some black workers moving into better-paid, more skilled jobs. There is a growing professional and entrepreneurial black class, but the higher incomes cannot match inflation. This is of course true for all races, but it is always the African workers who bear the brunt.

The Group Areas Act still brings the eviction of whole families from Indian and coloured homes, and the inhuman mass removals of Africans from white areas into black dumping grounds still goes on — for that is what it is, inhuman beyond description. In the past twenty years, three million people have been so removed, and there are thousands still to go before South Africa can present the "orderly" pattern of segregation so dear to the Afrikaner heart.

All of this has been going on for years now and there is scant change for the better, nor prospect of it. It is a sad and sorry picture of people waiting for what should be a fundamental human right — the roof over the head of a man and his family.

What of the squatters — our infamous squatter "problem"? The polite name now is the "Relocation of Africans". It is a rose by another name, but it has the same peculiar smell, for the war on squatters is being pursued with unmitigated severity, especially in the areas outside Cape Town. Pre-dawn arrests, raids, destruction of shelters — all this is the order of the day in the desperate attempt by the authorities to stem the flood of workless people and their families to the urban areas. "If you have a house, you may get permission to take a job. If you have a job, you may get permission to have a house." It is as simple as that, but it spells disaster to the work-seekers and the home-seekers who come from the impoverished rural areas, the "homelands". But "uncontrolled squatting is not to be tolerated". That is the government's policy.

There can be no secure family life as long as we still have 300 arrests daily for pass offences and influx control. A quarter of a century ago, 20,000 women went to the Union Buildings to protest against the issuing of passes to African women because they feared that African mothers would be torn from their families for lack of a pass. It has happened. Every year in South Africa 28,000 African women are arrested for some offence relating to passes. I don't know if they are all mothers; statistics don't tell you that, but probably most of them are.

It all makes nonsense of government claims of reduced pass raids, for the figures do not diminish year by year. In fact they rise — together with the population increase. In 1982 the Minister of Co-operation and Development announced a "new deal" for urban blacks. It was enshrined in a parliamentary Bill, pompously and cynically entitled, "The Orderly Removal and Settlement of Black Persons Bill". There was not much new about it, not for blacks, for it gave the minister power to override the few court decisions which had recently brought some remedy to the plight of black urban dwellers.

Sabotage or terrorism? It depends which way you look at it. ANC sabotage of installations and buildings has multiplied and continued. This left-wing political violence mushrooms overnight, goods trains are derailed, power stations and installations blown up, even police stations and a bank attacked, also a military base. Sometimes there has been loss of life, but the attacks are against the buildings, which are symbols of the oppressive regime. Political trials follow, horrific, even death sentences are imposed. I think always of the tip of the iceberg, that is all we can see, the tip, but the iceberg is growing and I do not know when it will surface.

There has been right-wing violence a-plenty, too; homes bombed and shot at, bricks hurled through windows and windscreens. I had a bullet again through my bedroom window, this time skimming the top of my perspex protection screen. It went into the top corner of the window and did little damage beyond a broken pane of glass. Policemen came disinterestedly, patently to look for the bullet, but they knew as well as I did that nothing would come of their investigations. Telephone calls, hoaxes, threats, for me and a few others, all these are a part of our daily lives. It is difficult to know what satisfaction they give to the perpetrators, for it disturbs us very little.

The horrors of detention without trial have manifested themselves sharply again, as students, student leaders, trade unionists and workers and others too, are picked up at dawn and taken away into the unknown, cut off completely from family and friends.

In 1982 there was a profoundly important and unprecedented development. Parents and friends of the detainees formed themselves into committees to affirm their trust and confidence in the detainees, to protest against the injustice of detention without trial, to demand external medical attention when required, to fight for better conditions for the detainees — yet not only each for his own but all for all and all for one, if need be.

There was need, tragic searing need. Dr Neil Aggett, still in his twenties, was found dead in his cell. Was it suicide? Was it murder? Did he really die by hanging? Neil was a doctor, but he had given almost all of his waking hours to the trade union movement. Many thousands came to his funeral in St Mary's

Anglican Cathedral in the centre of Johannesburg. They came from all parts of South Africa, trade unions predominant and, as for Lilian Ngoyi, the mourners walked behind his coffin to the cemetery — but this time defiantly through the city streets at the peak traffic hour. The traffic had to wait while the workers took their young hero to his grave. Neil Aggett was the forty-seventh man to die in his detention cell in eighteen years, but he was also the first white man to die in detention.

An inquest was held. It was the only current source of public information on detainees' gaol conditions, unless more came to light in trials of detainees. The government's reaction to this horror was to clamp down in terms of the Police Act and forbid the press to publish any information whatsoever about the helpless people in detention. Can we get any nearer to the Gestapo methods of Nazi Germany?

The Aggett inquest itself was a mirror held up by a fearless senior advocate, George Bizos, to reflect the unimagined depths of depravity, brutality and destruction employed by the security police.

All this and much else has been taking place, while I lived, frustrated, in a political twilight. I was able to do little beyond writing this book, the record of my thirty years of involvement in the liberation struggle. This helped to fill the days for me, and many nights too. Time did not hang heavily on my hands, but the frustration was indeed heavy on my spirit. When it was almost over I did not know what the morrow might bring. Freedom — or rather, what passes for freedom in this unfree society? Or another period of banning, at seventy-seven? But, after all, that is only two years older than seventy-five, so what difference should that make? I tried to be indifferent, but my ears were sharply tuned for the knock on the door and two men standing there with that deadly piece of paper. Or would no one come and the bans just fall away?

Chapter VIII
The Mandelas –
family extraordinary

The main street in a small country town in the Orange Free State, some 360 miles from Johannesburg; a few shops, a bank, a couple of filling stations and a hotel line the street. There are two Dutch Reformed churches and a police station. It is a place for whites. Blacks must enter through separate shop entrances to make their purchases lest they offend white customers by their visible presence. It is a place where the blacks who serve the white community must be herded to live in a small location, over the hill where they will not be seen by passing traffic. It is just like many another small town anywhere in South Africa.

On the morning of 17 May 1977, a mother and her daughter walked along that Brandfort street, looking as though they had stepped out of a smart hotel, elegant in high boots, polo-necked sweaters, slacks tucked into the tops of their boots. Brandfort stared in amazement. I think no one like this, black or white, had ever walked down that street before. Winnie Mandela and her daughter Zindzi walked very tall, their heads high, greeting with joy and grace the friends who had found them in their banishment.

I have known Winnie Mandela for more than twenty years. A deep and lasting bond of affection has grown between us, yet when I look back over those years I realise how little direct personal contact there has been between us, always sporadic except once for a few months in 1975. The circumstances of our lives, governed by our involvement in the liberation struggle, have held us physically apart.

I find that when I come to write about Winnie, the pattern is that of a series of vivid personal memories, held together by that affection which is rooted not only in her but in her husband and her children.

I am nearing eighty and I do not know how much longer I have left. Winnie is still banned and banished, for another four years. I doubt now that we shall ever know the joy of a fully shared friendship, such as others know. For us there are no frequent meetings, hours of talk, shared pleasures, not even the free exchange of letters.

When I recall the riches of our relationship with each other, the unforgettable moments of togetherness, then I realise how privileged I have been to have the affection of this woman who has transcended the hardships and persecutions heaped upon her almost beyond human endurance. She has emerged from it all as indestructible.

It will be difficult for me to convey a real picture of her, because of the rarity of our contact. I hope that what I have to tell of her from my personal knowledge and experience of her will describe something of those unique qualities of dignity, courage and commitment which have made her what she is today, the embodiment of both her husband's strength and her own. She stands as the living witness outside the prison walls of their joint survival.

My first clear memory of Winnie seems to be when she came to see Nelson on visiting days at the treason court in the Old Synagogue in Pretoria. That was during the 1960 Emergency when we were in gaol detention, but coming every day to our trial. Family visits were allowed there, but no provision was made for the usual prison conditions for receiving visitors beyond that small enclosed yard where we were herded for our meals and all court recesses. The visitors walked in past us, one by one, each to find her special prisoner.

Prison decorum and discipline were met by insisting that the couples walked together to an open shed to talk to each other through a window cut in a partition. We could see them as they walked past us and as they stood, one on each side of that ridiculous partition, there presumably to prevent them from embracing each other.

Two beautiful women stood out amongst our visitors, Winnie Mandela and Amina Cachalia, both so lovely, each so different from the other. Winnie was tall and elegantly dressed, she could hold her own in any fashionable gathering. Her classic sculptured features still had the smooth contours of youth. She was not yet twenty-five years old. Amina was small and exquisite in her Indian sari, glowing in her own radiance as she walked beside her tall husband, Yusuf Cachalia. The sight of these lovely women gladdened all our hearts and lightened our days during those dreary weeks of detention.

I wish I could remember how and when I first met Nelson Mandela or how I first met his wife, Winnie Nonzamo Madikizela. I can't. It is a long time ago now and there was nothing then to make me aware of what these two people were going to mean in my life. The treason trial brought me near to Nelson, the "gentle giant", as one of his contemporaries has called him. Yet that is not the whole story. Yes, he is gentle, slow-speaking, deliberate, his words are carefully chosen. He towered over the rest of us; his physique was commanding, that of a fighter. Over and above all this was the indelible impression of enormous strength of mind as well as body.

When I first met Nelson, he wasn't married. His first marriage had ended in divorce and he was a most eligible bachelor, a well-known attorney in his late thirties, in partnership with Oliver Tambo. He was handsome, popular and an established ANC leader, the Transvaal President until he was banned in 1953.

Amongst ourselves we used to speculate about Nelson remarrying but he didn't seem in any hurry. For a time he was seen about with Lilian Ngoyi, older than Nelson but looking far younger than her real age. Lilian, the attractive charismatic leader of the ANC Women's League and the Federation of South African Women — and Nelson! What a partnership that would be! The gossips were wrong. Nelson made his own choice. We soon heard about the lovely young social worker, Winnie Madikizela.

I must have met her first at a party, for I wasn't allowed to attend other meetings at that time because of my bail conditions. The actual meeting, of course, is not important. What is important is awareness of the young Mrs Mandela rapidly moving into political circles.

From its beginning the Mandela's married life was strange, bedevilled. Nelson was attending the treason trial, day after day, and, like me, earning a living by working long hours in addition to the monolithic demands of the trial. He used to join me in my car for the Pretoria run at eight o'clock in the morning. By then he had already put in a couple of hours at his law office and by five o'clock in the evening he would be back there again seeing clients, working late into the night before returning home to his bride.

During those first years there can have been little marriage companionship except during trial adjournments, yet that was all that Nelson and Winnie were to have. For the past quarter of a century they have been separated, first by Nelson going underground from the end of the trial and then by his arrest in July 1962 with the endless years of imprisonment to follow.

Dependent upon snatched meetings, an hour in secret here, a couple of hours there, never daring to meet in their own home, to sit at table with their two little daughters, what sort of life was that on which to build a marriage that must endure through twenty years and more of Robben Island widowhood? For widowhood it is, this pattern of thirty-minute visits at the gaol, through a perspex window, speaking through a telephone and always in the presence of a warder.

Winnie has not touched Nelson's hand for the past twenty years. Yet Zindzi, their youngest daughter, declares that they are still so much in love with each other that she feels she ought not to intrude on the togetherness that blossoms, even in the gaol visiting room.

Winnie was amongst the 2,000 women who crowded the gaol in 1958 when the pass-issuing units first came to Johannesburg. It was to be for her the first of a long series of arrests and gaol. She had married a banned political leader whose life already belonged to the liberation struggle, to the half life of the banned, to the shadow of gaol. It was the beginning for her of a life of persecution and harassment that was to persist for the next twenty-five years — and longer.

She was pregnant then with her first child. Eighteen years later, she wrote of it in a letter to me when she was detained in the same gaol: "thousands of us and me carrying Zeni, who was making all kinds of mute threats, protesting against sleeping on the cement floor at her embryonic age."

In 1960 Nelson came to my Christmas Day party in the last year of the treason trial. Winnie was in hospital for the birth of Zindzi. He brought the small Zeni, not yet two years old, very proud of her pale blue party dress and the wreath of forget-me-nots atop her little round head. She sat shyly and solemnly, a little princess, on Nelson's knee, looking around with wide wondering eyes at all these unknown people.

I remember Winnie at the conference of the Federation of South African Women in 1962 when she was elected to the executive committee. She had made a rousing speech (the only speech of hers that I ever heard). She called especially on the young to gird themselves for the struggle for freedom. Nelson was already underground — or perhaps even briefly out of the country. It was clear even then that Winnie was more than Mrs Nelson Mandela; she was already accepted as a leader in her own right. I remember that the older members of the Federation, including me, I must confess, were a little hesitant over the militancy of her speech, though at the same time inspired by it.

Nelson's first trial followed in Pretoria soon after that. He was charged with inciting workers to commit an offence by staying at home from work, and also with leaving the country illegally. By that time I could not attend the trial because of my bans and house arrest. It meant, too, that I could not see Winnie there, but I did not realise that this was only the beginning for us of a long separation, nor that we should draw so close to each other despite that separation.

I read the press reports of Nelson's trial, of his militant handling of his own defence in a court which to him was no court of justice but a court of discrimination. He was a black man "in a white man's court" facing a white magistrate, confronted by a white prosecutor, escorted by white orderlies . . . in an "atmosphere of white domination".

At the end of that trial, Nelson made his first historic court statement. The second was to come in the Rivonia trial. This first one, however, is for me the most moving. There are passages in it which I find deathless — and heart-breaking from a man who did not, could not know that two years later he would be condemned to spend the rest of his life in gaol. "If I had my time over again," he said, "I would do the same again, so would any man who dare call himself a man." And at the end of his trial,

> Not just I alone but all of us are willing to pay the penalties which we may have to pay, which I may have to pay for having followed my conscience in pursuit of what I believe to be right. So are we all. Many people in this country have paid the price before me and many will pay the price after me.

Nelson was sentenced to five years' imprisonment. He had worn tribal dress throughout his trial and so had Winnie. I wish I could have seen them, both proud and tall, proclaiming silently their unbreakable identity with their people. Beneath the outward dignity and splendour, their hearts must have been torn at the impending separation from each other in that marriage that had brought parting and sorrow alongside their joy.

During the year after that trial Winnie received her first banning orders. She was no longer free even to visit her husband in gaol. She first had to obtain permission to leave Johannesburg. At each stage of her journey she would have to report to the local police. For me it meant that there would be no further contact between Winnie and me for several years. We were now forbidden to communicate with each other.

Sometimes I used to see the little girls, but never Winnie, though I knew from others how she was struggling to bring them up, to keep them free from the taint of Bantu education. For a time, a coloured school accepted them and this must have been a relief to Winnie, for coloured children were not given a separate and inferior education. It was not to last. The nuns were visited by the security police and warned that it was illegal for African children to be admitted to coloured schools. The children had to leave.

Zeni and Zindzi were then sent to a convent boarding school in Swaziland, away from the racial discrimination which doesn't spare even little children. It meant that they had to be away from their mother. They had not seen their father since his arrest, for children may not visit prisoners in the gaols. Winnie remained alone in the little house in Soweto and the children endured unhappy homesick years at school while their mother struggled, as all banned people do, to find the employment which would enable her to maintain her children.

The years went by until an opportunity came for Winnie and me to correspond with each other. We wrote many letters, all illegal, about the children, about ourselves, about our friends. These letters became our lifeline for perhaps a year or more, until I went to work at the hotel in Roodepoort and I was too far away from Winnie for our secret "hand post" to continue.

Winnie was banned and re-banned. I was re-house arrested and our separation remained total. In 1969 Winnie and twenty-two others were detained in gaol for six months before they were brought to trial under the Terrorism Act.

These detainees suffered greatly during months of detention, especially during interrogation. Winnie described it years later in a speech during a brief period of freedom.

> . . . it means the beginning of that horror story told many a time . . . it means being held in a single cell with the light burning twenty-four hours so that I lost track of time and was unable to tell whether it was night or day . . . The frightful emptiness of those hours of solitude is unbearable. Your company is your solitude, your blanket, your mat, your sanitary bucket, your mug and yourself . . . All this is in preparation for the inevitable HELL — interrogation. It is meant to crush your individuality entirely, to change you into a docile being from whom no resistance can arise . . . There have been alleged suicides in detention; you keep asking yourself whether you will leave the cell alive for you do not know what drove those who died to their deaths . . . Here you have to enter into a debate with yourself. There are only two divisions; you decide whether you will emerge a collaborator with the system or continue your identification with whatever your cause is.

When Winnie and twenty-two others came to trial, the truth of her words were evident. There were some who had been their friends, their colleagues, who went into the witness box to testify against them. Only two had been able to hold out against the horrors of interrogation, had held on to their loyalty.

Acquittal for Winnie and her friends came in 1970. Within minutes, they were re-detained before ever they could leave the court, to spend another six months in solitary confinement. The state eventually brought them ludicrously to trial again on charges so nearly identical with those on which they had been acquitted that the state case was thrown out immediately and they were at last free.

Winnie could once again visit Nelson — her 471 days in gaol must have been well nigh unendurable for them both, nearly fourteen months without seeing each other in gaols almost 1,000 miles apart. Their children were still at school in Swaziland and during the school holidays they came home without sight or sound of their parents.

The acquittal brought an unpredicted consequence for Winnie. Her banning orders expired while she was in detention and it seemed that this had passed unnoticed by the authorities, for they were not renewed. On her first day out of gaol she came to me, to my gate, for she could not come in, not even onto my garden path for that moment of reunion after eight years of separation. I was still under house arrest and could not receive visitors.

I didn't have time even to open the gate before we were hugging each other. A picture was published in the newspaper the next day. It is mostly the back view of Winnie as we embraced over the gate, but it shows my face, too, with a very happy smile. Eleven years later I learned from an ex-Robben Island prisoner that this press cutting had somehow made its way onto the Island and into Nelson's hands. It went the round of the section, where all photographs must be shared. I was touched to know this. I still am.

Despite house arrest, I could leave my house during daytime, so Winnie and I went for a long drive in my car, just the two of us, to try to say in a few hours everything that had mattered in the past eight years. It wasn't possible, but I think that most of what was important was said. Winnie would not speak of what she had endured. She felt that pain should not intrude on our hours together.

After that the curtain of silence fell between us again for the next five years. Winnie was banned again and this time also put under house arrest. Zeni and Zindzi came to see me sometimes and I watched them grow year by year, Zindzi with much of her mother's sparkle, Zeni growing tall and like her father.

During those five years, I was able only once to be near Winnie and even then I could not speak to her. She had been sentenced to six months' gaol for violation of her bans by communicating with another banned person, Peter Magubane, "Uncle Peter" to the children. Today Peter is a photographer of international fame. In 1975 he too went to gaol for six months as a banned person for communication with Winnie. He was still establishing himself as a photographer after 580 days of solitary confinement during his detention without trial in 1969 and 1970.

A group of friends were present at the magistrate's court when Winnie surrendered herself to serve the six months in gaol. We followed her from her attorney's office, a little group of perhaps a dozen friends and students. We kept a little behind Winnie as she walked with the attorney so that she should not be part of our gathering. Tall and striking in a black high-necked blouse and long skirt to her ankles, headscarf in flaring black, yellow and green, the ANC colours, she was breathtakingly beautiful.

We stood together sadly as Winnie went alone up the steps to the forbidding door leading to the cells. She turned to face us and ran quickly down the steps to embrace each one of us, except me. Our fingers met and held for a brief moment,

213

that was all there could be for Winnie and me. Then she was gone, giving us the Congress salute as she entered the door, a black policeman behind her. Winnie Mandela was a prisoner again.

When my own bans and house arrest were suspended after the cancer operation, I still had not been able to see or greet Winnie, because she was banned. There had been so much rejoicing for me, but the face I wanted most to see was missing. It was a bizarre situation, comic if it had not been so heart-rending. There was nothing now to stop me from communicating with Winnie, except that she could neither write nor speak to me.

"Where else would I spend my first night of freedom?" It was Winnie's voice at last. Her five years' ban had passed. On 1 November 1975 I telephoned to her early in the morning, still afraid that her bans might have been renewed. To my joy I heard that she could speak to me at last, could even come to supper with me.

I waited at the door that night, listening for her car to stop so that I could walk down the path to meet her. She came running, arms wide open. The five years were gone.

On Christmas Day that year she brought her children to the party, radiant in her return to a full life, to people. That was a great party with friends who had been freed from their bans after years of restrictions, sometimes after gaol as well. Other friends were still under house arrest and bans but they sent their children instead.

From the moment her bans expired, Winnie plunged into political life. I think one of her greatest moments must have been the enormous welcome she received from the women of Durban within the first weeks of her freedom. That was when she made her moving speech on detention. The prospect of re-banning did not deter her, even after so many years of restrictions. Her attitude was always, "being banned and unbanned is really one and the same thing . . . I really do not regard myself as any freer than I was yesterday." She knew her "liberty" could be taken away from her at any moment, nor could she really be free while others were still unfree.

"I'm still a part of Nelson," she said. She would not accept that she had any real freedom. "Nothing changes in my mind," she said, "because the orders have been lifted. The situation in the country remains the same, my views remain the same, there is really no freedom as such." I knew she was right. I had been speaking too lightly myself about my "freedom". The lifting of a ban is not real freedom because it affects only the person concerned. Perhaps it is because there is no real freedom here that we have cheapened the word.

"In there I have seen the future we are fighting for," Winnie said, on Ascension Day 1976 when she joined me in St Mary's Cathedral for the first time — for there the Mass is totally integrated. I knew that she would be moved deeply by this, as well as by the fact that we could kneel side by side, be together in this mixed congregation, with the mixed choir, with the priests of different colours administering Holy Communion. As we walked out together I saw tears in her eyes. For a few Sundays after that we shared the Mass at the Cathedral with its lovely ritual of lights, incense and music and we took Holy Communion side by side.

214

I had had no idea that her thoughts were turning this way, towards a return to church worship, although I knew that she had never abandoned her faith, even in the hardest times. It had been something that she had carried in her heart, not dependent upon church services, but now she felt the need to take it further.

A month later came the agony of Soweto. As the news came over the radio hour by hour, I tried to reach Winnie on the telephone. I got through only once, to hear her say, "Orlando is on fire. Keep telephoning." Soon there were no longer any telephones in Orlando. We could not meet again in town for a few weeks because she was rushing back from work every day to Orlando to be with her people and also all through the weekend.

Events moved swiftly. On 18 July Zeni and Zindzi came back from school for the holidays. They came back to an empty house for that was the morning that Winnie and many others had been detained in gaol. Uncle Peter Magubane moved into that desolate home to care for Winnie's children together with his own teenage daughter.

Once again Zeni and Zindzi had neither father nor mother. It is almost impossible for others to understand what that must have been for these two teenage girls, sixteen and seventeen years old. Even the small security of being in their own home was to be for only a few weeks before Soweto exploded again and very near to them.

I came home one day to find a note on my front door, "Uncle Peter says we must come to live with you. We'll be back soon. Zindzi." On the verandah was a small mountain of boxes. They came very soon, Zindzi, Zeni and a friend who had been living in their house with them. Peter came to tell me that it was no longer safe for them to be in Orlando. I learned much later word had come from Nelson that they must come to me.

We expected Peter the next night for supper, but he didn't appear. His driver came instead with his cameras and a whole pile of his precious photographs. Peter had been detained.

I was more than a little embattled by the prospect of three tall lively teenagers in my little house and in my solitary life. Somehow we all fitted in together and settled down to a shared life, surmounting even the cistern disaster, when gallons of water descended onto my kitchen floor. We endured almost a week of endlessly boiling kettles and pans of water on a two-plate gas stove for baths.

Cooking for us all on that little stove wasn't easy, but friends rallied to our help with cooked chickens and tasty pies. Like all families we quarrelled sometimes and I felt guilty and inadequate until Zeni consoled me by saying, "Oh, that's just how families live!" She herself was living in her own dream world, waiting for the daily telephone calls from the young Prince Thumbumusi Dlamini of Swaziland, son of King Sobhuza II.

Weekly highlights were the children's visits to Winnie in the grim Johannesburg Fort prison where she was detained, bringing oranges and sweets for her comfort. I asked for permission to visit her but it was refused. Once we managed to exchange a few words through a barred and wire-meshed window at the side of the forbidding gaol doors. We were abruptly interrupted by a stormy matron who literally chased me off the stone steps onto the pavement, threatening to call the police to throw me out if I did not go. I went. She called me by my name and I knew that made it worse because in fact she had been a gaol officer on both occasions when I had been an inmate of that gaol. She obviously thought I ought to know better than to try to communicate with a prisoner.

Zindzi and Zeni had both been allowed to visit their father during the school holidays, the father they were not allowed to touch, to kiss, but only to look at through a perspex window. These meetings must have been strange and exciting yet desperately sad for these two young girls, seeing their father a prisoner in prison garb, behind bars.

Zindzi said that he still looked young and strong. She had even "seen him walk once" and he had walked "like a young man". He must inevitably have seemed something of a stranger that first meeting, trying to capture some of the lost moments of their childhood, the family life that neither he nor they had ever known. Zindzi had seen her father "walk once" — for me that sums up the searing tragedy which miraculously has not destroyed this family.

It was not illegal for the girls to stay with me in my white suburb. In any case I realised that I could not hide three black teenagers from public view nor from being heard either. My police neighbours stared in disgust, receiving visibly hostile looks from us when we saw them alighting from police cars, father and son, carrying their guns. We knew they had come from Soweto and to see them with their guns brought this horror nearer.

The girls went back to Waterford, their new school in Swaziland. I was relieved of the responsibility for the time being, yet I missed the noise and chatter, even the crowding and the non-stop radio.

I wasn't allowed to visit Winnie so I wrote her a letter, not very optimistic about whether she would be allowed to receive it, but she did. Another precious exchange of letters began, and this time I could preserve them. I hadn't been able to do so in 1967 because we were corresponding illegally since we were both banned. I knew that if I were raided by the security police and her letters found, it could bring dire consequences upon both of us, probably a gaol sentence.

Gaol letters, both in and out, are always difficult to write because they are censored, because they may not contain any political reference whatsoever and because they are supposed to be restricted to family matters — and I wasn't officially family. Within a few days a loving reply came and several other letters followed. She wrote of our going to Mass together — "the first few days it was hard to take it. Anyway I know we shall have many more . . . indeed we shall walk side by side to receive Holy Communion . . . I look forward to being with you once more."

She reminded me that gaol letters are "as you know from experience, a fantastic sedative, that little link with the outside world . . ." She worried over how much I could take of the "teenage explosion" and over my health. "Please take things easy. You have to be eternal and you know why." She dreamt of "our garden and its tranquilising beauty in which I found such peace of mind". Once she wrote, "I feel bad about the fact that it took me so long to know your true self — anyway Someone decides our fate and He knows why."

Winnie was echoing my own regrets about the wasted years when we didn't get to know each other when we had the opportunity. Recalling that one Christmas Day party at my house, she wrote, "I cannot help thinking of that last year's party in that lovely garden where I met so many old forgotten friends. Little did we know it was to be a relic of the past. I doubt if we shall ever have such a lovely time in the near future."

Many of the detainees were released just before Christmas, some with banning orders as a sort of Christmas present. Winnie and a few others were only released on the morning of 30 December 1976. As she left the gaol she received a new banning order, another five years of house arrest, of no visitors, of daily reporting to the police. Other detainees also received banning orders on release, but only Winnie was subjected to house arrest.

It meant that we were separated again and could no longer communicate with each other. In every letter from the gaol she had looked forward to our reunion. There would have been so much to say that would not go into letters and now it could be only me writing to Winnie, never Winnie to me.

These new banning orders must have been very hard for Winnie to bear. She already knew from experience over ten years the life of a banned and house-arrested person. Now there was an added bitterness because in her eight and a half months of liberty, she had been able to move out into the political field. In addition to the new Black Women's Federation, she had been on the executive of the Black Parents' Association in Soweto, the organisation which she had helped to bring about during the June unrest. Her time to serve on it had been short. She and several of its officials had been amongst those detained in July.

My contact with Winnie was gone except for kneeling side by side in silence sometimes at an early morning weekday Mass. A friend would tell me when Winnie was coming to the Cathedral so that we could be there at the same time. It was tempting to exchange a greeting but there might be strangers in the church, no one knew from where. These glimpses of each other were deeply important as the first few months passed.

Nothing had prepared Winnie for the shock of 16 May 1977 when she was banished to Brandfort in the Free State. Only she and Zindzi know the real agony of it. When they finally sat alone that night in that cold dark little Brandfort house with their unpacked suitcases, what were their thoughts? Did Winnie pray then as she had prayed during those endless days of interrogation, of solitary confinement? Did she pray for physical pain as a relief from the torture of the reality of five years to be lived out in the loneliness of banishment? I do not know, for from that day to this we have not been allowed to communicate with each other.

As I drove to Brandfort the next day with Father Leo Rakale and Barbara Waite, we passed through Winburg, where African women had won their place in history for their resistance to the issuing of passes to African women in 1913 and again in 1956 when they defiantly burnt their passes at the municipal offices. I remembered them as we drove through the little town. On a stony slope outside the town I saw a huddle of dilapidated buildings, obviously part of an African location of some sort. My mind recoiled from what I saw. Was it to anything like this that Winnie had been taken? For the next thirty miles I dreaded to reach Brandfort for fear of what we might find.

I watched them come across the road to us, Winnie and Zindzi. Our meeting was warm and exciting despite the horror that had brought it about. Zindzi told me what had happened, simply, almost stoically, with no tears. She was quiet, still a little stunned, the usual bubbling vivacity of this child of sixteen was gone.

Four car loads of police had arrived before six in the morning to take her mother off to the police station, together with Uncle Peter and a cousin. They had been staying in the house quite legally as Zindzi's guests, not Winnie's, but they were all bundled off. Zindzi was left alone with the police, not even allowed to telephone anyone, while her home, the house where she had grown up, was dismantled, stripped of everything. Furniture, personal possessions, clothes, everything was loaded into a furniture van. Only when this ruthless four-hour operation had been completed and the little house stood empty, was Zindzi taken to join her mother. Only then was Winnie presented with the document which was designed to change her life, destroy everything she had built up for her family.

I don't know how Winnie and Zindzi spent that first night in that place, hundreds of miles from their home, with no light except the candles supplied by the police, no heat, no water laid on. I can only imagine dimly what it would be like if my furniture and the things I live with were suddenly jampacked into three rooms the size of police cells, dark and cold, empty of all the amenities which I accept as essential.

They found themselves totally isolated. The African people in the township had been intimidated, warned by the police to keep away from Winnie. They were already under surveillance from both black and white security police. There would be many informers among the township residents. They had been made social lepers by their banishment.

Their only link with the outside world was the public telephone booth outside the Brandfort post office. From there they would try to get through to Johannesburg. They would spend many hours waiting hopefully for calls from their friends. This was to be the highlight of their lives for the next five years and longer.

As we were leaving, Winnie came to the side of our car to speak to Leo. She put her hand inside. From the back seat, I held it for a moment. That was all. Then I kissed Zindzi and we drove away on our journey back to Johannesburg and our comfortable homes. We had found them. We had seen and talked to them. We should come again. I knew there would be others coming after us but could even this help much in this desolate banishment?

A week later, Leo and I and two other friends returned to Brandfort. This time we parked under the tree outside the post office. There is nowhere private in Brandfort for us. As before, Zindzi and I remained together and the others went one by one to spend time with Winnie in her car. Security policemen watched us from their cars, this time taking our names and addresses.

Leo was undaunted by the name-taking. He held a brief Holy Communion service for Winnie as she sat alone in her car, while the rest of us and the security police watched and waited. I longed to join them but I knew that once it was realised that I was a listed person, there would be attempts to charge Winnie with communication with me and I did not want to involve her in that.

On another visit, of course, this actually happened. Barbara and I eventually served gaol sentences for refusal to make statements to the police. Two other friends met with the same fate. It became almost impossible for me to get to Brandfort again. I wanted to go, to talk to Zindzi again, to support Winnie if only by my silent presence. I could not drive myself to Brandfort. It was understandable that, after the police harassment and our convictions, others were apprehensive lest the same thing happen to them.

I managed to get to Brandfort only once more, with an overseas press representative. Winnie was always so welcoming, like a gracious hostess, when she came to us under the post office tree. We shared the transferring of gifts from one car to another. Winnie and I could then exchange secret smiles, secret because Sergeant Prinsloo of the security branch was always watching us from his car only a few yards away. He always knew when we were there. Obviously the local informer service was very well organised.

My hopes of helping Winnie to endure the loneliness of her banishment were fast fading. I had not been able to talk to her on these expeditions to Brandfort but she had known that I had come to her, perhaps six or seven times in all. Now it could not go on.

As the months went slowly by, part of Winnie's life was taken up with prosecutions for alleged violations of her banning orders. Ironically, she had to be given permission to leave Brandfort to travel to Bloemfontein to the magistrate's court there. On two occasions I was able to be present at her trials. I could then see Winnie in court and be very close to her during recesses, both of us always of course under the watchful eye of Sergeant Prinsloo. In fact every one of these prosecutions was Prinsloo-contrived.

On the first occasion Winnie was facing five charges. I found a great gathering of pressmen there, both South African and international. She was tall, proud, elegant in black from head to foot with a headscarf of ANC colours. The prosecutor tried to interpret this as an act of defiance. Winnie reminded the court, "One of the very few rights I have left is the choice of my wardrobe."

During every interval of the trial, the court was locked. We crowded into the corridor, Winnie and I always careful to keep Zindzi between us, while Sergeant Prinsloo, crouched a little distance away, was doing his best to keep an eye on both of us at the same time. It was not an easy task and it made him look somewhat like a malevolent frog.

Under cross-examination in court, his reply to questions on his harassment of Winnie and Zindzi was always, "I was doing my duty." His duty led him into strange positions. I remembered his face, framed in the dripping privet hedge on our fateful visit to Brandfort. Here he was again, screwing up his eyes lest he should miss a gesture or a word between us. He was enraged when his picture was taken by a press photographer while he was in that undignified crouching position.

Winnie was acquitted on three charges, but sentenced to six months in gaol on two, the sentence suspended for four years. This trial and everything about it exposed the petty vindictiveness of the state's treatment of Nonzamo Winnie, wife of Nelson Mandela. It was not enough that she had been forced out of her home to live amongst strangers 360 miles away. Forced even here to live under cruelly restrictive house arrest and banning orders, she was exposed to the prying by the security police which had brought her to trial.

To trial for what? Talking to a neighbour about the price of chickens or coal? Refusing to debar her daughter from having visitors to their home? Speaking to her own sister in her own home? Such actions are the stuff of our ordinary life. For banned and house-arrested people they are crimes. This criminality and the consequent appearances in court were fast becoming the stuff of Winnie's ordinary life.

Eventually Nelson applied to the Supreme Court for an interdict on Sergeant Prinsloo's harassment of Zindzi, who was not subject to any ban or house arrest order. The application was granted and the persecution of Zindzi ceased, but that of her mother has continued ever since.

Winnie's eldest daughter Zeni had married her prince and was living in Swaziland. Her first child was to be christened in the Bloemfontein Cathedral so that Winnie would be able to be there. Nelson had said that he wanted both Dr Moroka, onetime President of the ANC, and me to be godparents to the baby. It was a great honour and I went to Bloemfontein for the baptism. Dr Moroka was there, upright at ninety years old.

I waited in the Cathedral that morning for the family party to arrive. Winnie came first. Carrying the baby, she moved past me to the end of the pew. Our hands touched for a moment. Zindzi followed to sit between us and then came Zeni and Prince Musi. Winnie and I walked together to the altar rail for Holy Communion. We knelt side by side, in silence but in deep and true communion with each other.

After the Mass, Winnie led us out into the centre aisle. Then I saw in Bloemfontein, in the heart of Afrikanerdom, the whites come out from their pews, greeting Winnie as she walked down the aisle, welcoming her, glad that her grandchild was to be baptised in their cathedral. I saw Sergeant Prinsloo at the back of the Cathedral, leaning against the wall, arms folded, watching and waiting. I found this utterly sacrilegious, despicable. As we gathered round the font, Prinsloo drew a little closer, fearful that he might miss something — what? A whisper between Winnie and me? He followed us out onto the Cathedral steps where Winnie and I stood apart from each other. I went to stand on the pavement as she drove off with her family. I called out, "Goodbye, Winnie!" and I heard a soft "Goodbye" as her car pulled away.

As I flew back to Johannesburg I thought of Nelson in the Sunday afternoon lock-up in his cell on Robben Island. He would soon be sixty. How much longer must they all endure his captivity and the separation? Yet neither he, nor the men with him, were separated from the struggle for freedom. They were a part of it.

I wrote to Nelson for his sixtieth birthday. I had sent telegrams in previous years but had never known whether he had received them. I told him about Zaziwe's christening, what a wonderful occasion it had been for me. To my amazement and delight I received a reply. It wasn't the first letter, of course, that I had ever received from him. That had been sixteen years before when he wrote to me from his police cell about my house arrest.

He said in this letter that right from the time when he had had to leave Winnie all alone, the fact that I was still there had comforted him. He wrote with delight that he now had a picture of me in his "family album". It was one of those taken of all of us at Zaziwe's christening.

On Nelson's sixtieth birthday I received a telephone call from someone asking to speak to "Aunt Helen". The nameless voice said, "Nelson Mandela is dead. Ha! Ha! Ha!" I knew it could not be true, not if I heard it like that, but I had almost believed it for a moment.

Black as I am. This is the title of Zindzi's book of poems, all written before she was sixteen years old. They are as startling as the title, the outpouring of a young, proud, sensitive girl for whom there could never be any compensation for the frustration and agony of her childhood, yet the warmth and capacity for love and joy are there. Peter Magubane provided the photographs of Soweto life which set the perceptive framework. The poems reached Nelson. How proud he must be of the daughter he did not see for so many painful years, the daughter who could write:

A tree was chopped down
and the fruit was scattered

I cried
because I had lost a family
the trunk, my father
the branches, his support
so much

the fruit, the wife and children
who meant so much to him
tasty
loving as they should be
all upon the ground
some out of his reach
in the ground
the roots, happiness
cut off from him.

The years moved slowly towards 31 December 1981, when Winnie's bans and banishment orders would expire. Meanwhile the international stature of the Mandelas was growing steadily. 1980 brought Nelson the Jawaharlal Nehru award from India for his staunch support of freedom and individual liberty,

221

justice and peace. He could not go to India to receive his award, nor was Winnie allowed to go in his stead. Nor was Zindzi given a passport to go. It was Oliver Tambo, President General of the ANC, who finally went to India.

Other honours followed in quick succession from Glasgow, from Austria, from London. Nelson became Dr Mandela with an honorary doctorate from Lesotho. Because I want to be sure that my letters reach him, I don't address them to Dr Mandela but to 466/64 Nelson Mandela when I write to him in gaol.

White Brandfort became restive, appealing to the Minister of Justice to take Winnie away because her presence was "causing such unhappiness in the community". Was it because she used the white entrance to the shops and other black people were following her example? Yet the same whites took themselves so seriously that they talked of "improving the quality of life" in the location. They were not, however, prepared to face the implications of integration if they were to remove the evils of segregation.

The attitude of black Brandfort was naturally very different. Winnie had become the mother of the township in a very short time. The people had soon realised that far from being a threat to their well-being, as the police had indicated, this woman not only loved them but really worked to improve their "quality of life". She did so both by her example and her generosity. She helped the people, despite their poverty, to grow vegetables, even in those barren patches of ground on which their houses stood. Despite her own difficulties, Winnie brought them together as a community, learning to understand the struggle for liberation.

Shortly before 31 December, I wrote hopefully to Winnie about perhaps being with her on New Year's Eve. Like all of us who draw near to the end of a banning order, she didn't know what to expect. That is all part of the petty sadism of the banning system, to keep the victim in a state of anxiety for the last few weeks. She wondered whether the police would come to load her furniture and possessions as they had loaded them five years before when they brought her to this place. Would they take her along with her goods back to Orlando? She didn't know, so she packed and waited.

Two days before the expiry date, the police came with new orders for another five years. There would be no New Year celebration for Winnie Mandela, not for another five years. And then what? How long would it go on? It is her fifth banning order and it will not expire until 1986. By that time she will have been banned for twenty-five years, and she will be fifty-two years old.

Brandfort location must have wept for Winnie but I think they also rejoiced that she would remain with them. She used to say laughingly that if she were allowed to go back to Johannesburg she would keep No. 802 Brandfort as her country cottage, keep her loving links with the people there.

There was only one concession in the new orders. Winnie could receive bona fide visitors (whatever that might mean!) one at a time in her home. This she could not do before. But not me. I am still a listed leper and she may not speak to me.

Arrangements had been made for Winnie to pay her first "freedom" visit to Nelson. She could not go for the New Year weekend for there would be no time to obtain permission from the magistrate to leave Brandfort or be relieved of the house arrest. She must have hoped that all this would not be necessary. It was, and there was no freedom visit. I remembered what she had said years ago when her bans were lifted. "There is really no difference between being banned and unbanned." I wondered if she felt the same way now.

Winnie's life is lonelier than before for Zindzi is grown up and must live her own life. There are now four grandchildren. Zeni has two daughters and a son. Zindzi has her own little daughter, Zoleka, who lives mostly with Winnie. Sometimes the other three children are in Brandfort and then it must be crowded in that small house, but what joy they must bring.

Nelson has been in prison for more than twenty years. He spent eighteen years on Robben Island in that great company of his fellow political prisoners, even though he has not been allowed to be with all of them. In April 1982, in the middle of the night, Nelson and three other leaders from the Rivonia trial, Walter Sisulu, Raymond Mhlaba and Andrew Mlangeni, were suddenly and secretly transported to a maximum security gaol on the mainland. They were not allowed to say goodbye to the comrades they had suffered with, lived with and, I am sure, laughed with too. It was a vicious and cruel move that as yet remains totally unexplained. Or was the ANC leadership too powerful to be contained on Robben Island?

In 1982 Winnie was awarded an honorary degree from Haverford College in the USA. Needless to say, she wasn't allowed to go herself to receive it. Zindzi could not get a passport to go instead of her mother, just as she had not been able to go to New York to receive her own Tanus Korczak prize for her poems.

Zeni has diplomatic status as the wife of Prince Thumbumusi of the royal house of Swaziland and she can snap her fingers at a South African passport. She doesn't need one and thus she was able to go to the USA to receive her mother's award.

Not only Winnie and her children but black South Africa waits for the return of Mandela, as it waits for the freedom that must be fought for, to which there is no easy walk. Soweto waits for the return of Winnie Mandela as I too wait for her to come again down my garden path.

I know, too, that as surely as night follows day, these two, Nelson and Winnie Mandela, will return to us, for they have proved themselves indestructible, far stronger in their pride and their integrity than those who try to destroy them.

What I have written about the Mandelas is neither their triumph nor their tragedy alone. It is the triumph and the tragedy of all the prisoners, the detained, the banned and the banished. Nelson and Winnie and their children are closer to me than any other family in South Africa and they have made me a part of themselves. That it why I have written so much of them, of what they mean to South Africa and to me. Dr Manas Buthelezi once said of Winnie that she had tasted what redemptive suffering means. It is so. She has accepted this suffering for the sake of her people and her land.

There are others. Especially there are families who have handed down the tradition of redemptive suffering from father to son, from mother to daughter, even to three generations.

I think of the Naidoos, with an unbroken record of three generations of gaol and sacrifice. First came Thambi Naidoo, a President of the Indian Congress and also close to Gandhi. He was gaoled fourteen times for passive resistance. His wife gave birth to a child during a period of imprisonment. His son, Naryan Naidoo, also a former President of the Indian Congress, went to gaol twice during the 1946 passive resistance campaign. His daughter-in-law, Naryan's wife, served two gaol sentences during the same campaign. Their eldest son, Indres, the first of the third generation to go to gaol, left the path of non-violent civil disobedience to serve a ten-year sentence on Robben Island for sabotage. Their daughter Shanthi, detained and persecuted, is also from this third generation of commitment and courage. "I don't want to give evidence," she said in court, "because I will not be able to live with my conscience if I do."

Shanthi proclaimed her refusal to become a state witness against her two friends, Winnie Mandela and Joyce Sikhakane, both accused in the 1970 trial of Winnie and twenty-two others. "It has been a good friendship," she said. That was all, but she also told the court of what she had endured during the continuous interrogation of several days and nights without rest or sleep until, "My mind became muddled and I lost touch with reality." Whatever statement may have been thus barbarously extracted, Shanthi would not testify to it in court. She was sentenced to two months' imprisonment for her refusal.

Prema, the youngest son, has come to the end of a year's gaol — for finding shelter for one night only for a political gaol escapee. It was only for one night but it cost Prema one year of his liberty in addition to the five months he first spent in detention before his trial. He testified to days and nights of savage torture at the hands of the security police.

I think of the Cachalia family, the grandfather in gaol at the beginning of the century in Gandhi's passive resistance campaign, his sons Yusuf and Molvi in the 1946 and 1952 campaigns. I think of Amina Cachalia, my companion in the journey to find the banished people. She served a gaol sentence in 1952 and she and her husband Yusuf endured many years under banning orders. And Cachalia children of this generation know detention and banning orders.

Walter Sisulu, General Secretary of the ANC until he was banned in 1953, is now a life prisoner. Like Mandela he has been taken from Robben Island to another prison. Like Mandela, his commitment is carried on actively by his wife. Seventeen years of continuous bans and house arrest failed to daunt Albertina's spirit and she was back on the platform addressing political meetings within days of the expiry of her bans. In 1982 she was banned again, punished for her courage and her commitment, not convicted of any crime.

Their children carry on the Sisulu tradition. Lindiwe, the eldest daughter, was detained for a year in solitary confinement before she was twenty-one but never charged in any court of law. Zwelakhi, the youngest son, is banned and under house arrest. He too spent many months, solitary in a gaol cell, detained but uncharged.

The Weinberg family lived close to me, Eli, Violet and their daughter Sheila. Gaol claimed them all in 1965, the parents for involvement in the Communist

Party and Sheila at eighteen for painting ANC slogans. On release from gaol Violet and Eli lived through years of house arrest and bans. Ten years later, Sheila was also banned and house-arrested. Eli eventually left South Africa, to die after a few years in his exile. Violet had followed her husband and now lives lonely without him, far from South Africa but unable to return. Sheila has remained.

I wonder whether for the youngest generation of such families, the little children only beginning to grow up now, there will still be need for them to sacrifice themselves and their liberty?

Chapter IX

Return to my faith

Forty years is a very long time to be away from the faith into which you were born and baptised, the faith in which you were brought up and confirmed. Yet it happened to me and I cannot really account for it.

There was a period of about two years between leaving convent school and going to university, because I matriculated at sixteen and could not be accepted at London University until I was eighteen. During this period, away from the convent, away from any familiar church, because we had moved to a new area, I became very apathetic about going to church and very spasmodic in my own devotions.

By the time I started at King's College in 1923, my faith had been pushed to one side, where it remained for nearly forty years. I was never an atheist and I do not think I could even have been called an agnostic. It was complete indifference, although I would never have denied the existence of God.

Once while I was in India and a few times when I first came to South Africa, I did go to church to please friends, and it would have been embarrassing not to accompany them. In church I would go through the forms of prayer and make some sort of apology to a god in whom I suppose I still claimed to believe. Thereafter, I made no further effort towards any prayers nor to go to church on my own. Yet, probably like many a "lapsed" Christian, I would pray desperately in times of anxiety or distress, "please, God, help me to bear this . . .", whatever it was.

Once I was married, I moved into a new society in which I no longer met any practising Christians and I moved even further away from my former faith. It took gaol to jolt me out of my indifference — gaol and Hannah Stanton, even though we spoke only once of my lack of faith.

It seems to me, in retrospect, that it would have been impossible to share a cell, as I did, with a committed Christian like Hannah, and not be moved by her example, almost to envy of the joy and strength her faith brought her. I had to admit to myself an emptiness in my life, but I remained obdurate, behind the wall that I had built between myself and all things spiritual.

Perhaps I had been more affected by those first weeks of solitary confinement than I had realised at the time. Gaol indeed strips you of everything that belongs to your normal life. If you are alone it is worse and I had suddenly been removed from the daily close contact of my fellow accused.

I know that Hannah's example brought me to the recognition of faith as a real dimension of living. I always acknowledged it in the religious life of a convent and also in the church congregational life. I did not deny the value of the church ministry, but I deplored its failure to go beyond this, to take up the struggle for freedom, for justice, for the full recognition of human dignity.

I once, only once, tried to express this feeling to Hannah, but it was with bitter words about what I saw as the failure of the church. One day when Hannah and I were together in the exercise yard, the commandant of the gaol came to us to inform Hannah that a priest would be coming to give her Holy Communion. Turning to me he said, "Not you! He says you're a heathen."

Quite unreasonably, I felt outraged and insulted though I said nothing to Hannah about it. However, when the other women detainees arrived, they wanted the padre to visit them on Sundays. I was amazed for there wasn't a Christian amongst them but they still accepted his visits even after Hannah had gone. I think mainly because it broke the monotony of the gaol weekend and because they had established a pleasant, if non-religious, relationship with the chaplain.

I was still smarting under the epithet of heathen and refused to join the other women for the chaplain's visit. For this I was called to the matron's office, where I gave my reason that since he had said I was a heathen, I need have nothing to do with him, adding defiantly that I would rather fight on my feet than on my knees. The matron informed me a few days later that the "heathen" had been the commandant's touch, not the chaplain's, but I still would not accept his visit.

Hannah was deported and left us. The other detainees went home after a couple of months and I was alone again in the gaol except for going to court most days for the trial. I was still in the great dormitory where we had all been together. It seemed enormously empty, especially at night and during the weekend. The matron told me that, despite my earlier refusal to see him, the prison chaplain would like to visit me on Sunday afternoons. I shrank from it at first but finally agreed, partly out of relief at the idea of having someone to talk to, even if only for half an hour.

The chaplain came. He knew of my attitude to the organised church, of my abandonment of my early faith. He talked to me, but not about religion, said a short prayer and gave me a prayer book. That was all. I accepted the prayer book with hesitance as I did not want to hurt him by refusing. During the week that followed I began to look at it. I also had a very small, carefully hidden transistor radio which I had smuggled into gaol one day, a gift from Bram Fischer for us. I used to bring batteries from court, hidden in the knot of hair on top of my head. I could listen to the radio through earphones, always on the alert for the clanking of keys outside the door. The reception wasn't very good but it was a precious link with the outside world. I found myself listening to church services on Sundays, a little at sea at first, then recognising more and more the familiar phrases, hidden until then in my childhood memories. The psalms and prayers I read in my prayer book were familiar too, it was almost like coming home.

Soon I began to talk to the chaplain. At first I was almost too ashamed to pray myself to the God I had neglected for two-thirds of my life. Yet the priest convinced me that I would not be rejected, so I began to pray again, very simply, often returning to my childhood prayers.

When it became clear that the Emergency was dragging to its end and we should soon be released from gaol, returning to our former trial lives, I was full of doubt about what might happen to this renewal of my faith. Would it be strong enough to survive?

It was as I had expected and feared. My faith and my prayers did not survive my return to ordinary life. After a very few weeks the flickering light of my faith was blown out by pressures of all kinds, office and political. Then I would feel ashamed and pray again for a week or two, making resolutions and forgetting them again. I once went to a church service, but I did not feel part of it. I was only on the outside, looking in. Yet I had love and respect for some of the very few Christians I knew, and especially for the priests of the Community of the Resurrection who were supporting us so well in our work for the banished people.

Then came house arrest. From the beginning I received magnificent moral support, both nationally and internationally, for the Minister of Justice had succeeded in making me famous. I was surrounded by warm, concerned friends. All this had helped me to suppress to some extent the feeling of loneliness. I used to say, defiantly, "I may be alone, but I do not know what it means to be lonely!" That was only partly true. I was becoming aware of a deeper level of need, spiritual need, which I suppose was being brought a little nearer to the surface by the enforced solitude of house arrest, just as it had been in gaol.

I became deeply depressed over the major heart operation which Amina had had to undergo. I used to visit her almost daily during my office lunch hour after reporting to the police, for she lived nearby. I feared that she might not survive the operation and somehow this forced me to acknowledge my isolation as nothing else had done. Yet it was at this point that I also became conscious of some indefinable concern and care over my personal agony, of a feeling that I was not really alone, that I never would be, that there was help and love for me if I would only reach out for it. I began to pray again, as I had not done for the three years since I came out of gaol and this time I found myself able to persevere with fewer lapses.

I had come a little closer to my faith, but I was still outside the church. I began to listen regularly to the religious services on the radio and as I listened, some of the voices became familiar, almost personal. Once I heard the Dean of Cape Town say, "A lonely Christian can't be a real Christian." I thought about that a lot and realised how inadequate my own life was, how self-centred my reaching out for faith. I had so often condemned the Christian churches for keeping apart from political issues, but I had not bothered to make Christian friends, apart from the priests of the Community of the Resurrection.

I observed them in their Priory. Their concern and love for all men was wonderful. I thought of Trevor Huddleston and his courageous stand against apartheid and the Sophiatown removals, his commitment to the struggle for freedom and justice. Such people seemed to be the true essence of what I believed the Christian church ought to be.

I realised that if I were to come back fully to my faith, then I ought not wilfully to remain outside the church. True, I was under house arrest, but that did not prevent me from being a member of a Christian church — unless it was to be included in that strange definition of "Organisations that attack, defend, criticise or discuss any principle or policy of the government of a state". If that was so, then almost any church that ever there was must fall into that prohibited category. I soon discarded that line of thinking and decided that it was not for me to exclude myself from the church. That could be left to the government if it wished to take action against me.

I thought long and seriously about what steps to take to return to the church. I finally discussed it with Leo Rakale of the Community of the Resurrection, talking to him many times in the peaceful Priory garden. I found that I could talk to Leo more easily than to anyone else. Eventually I could say to him that if the church would have me, then I wanted to come back, instead of standing aloof — even after forty years of drifting and utter neglect. I wanted to go to Mass again. I wanted the Sacrament of Holy Communion.

Leo handled me gently and with great understanding. He knew that I must not be pushed into this important step, nor even persuaded into it. I must come back at my own pace, in my own time. I do not believe that it was just the loneliness of house arrest. I was a prodigal returning to the father, to complete forgiveness and to a loving welcome. In time of need, yes, but the need was the instrument to satisfy a want which had been suppressed for many years.

The friendship of the Community enriched my life. I was cut off from many friends of former days. They were now in gaol, banned or gone from South Africa. But here was a group of men living under vows of poverty and obedience, having all things in common, inspired and strengthened by their faith.

I became aware of the rhythm of their life. Sometimes when I was working in the library there I could hear their voices in the little chapel singing the cadences of their midday office. Theirs was a life dedicated to God and also to the world. They did not shut themselves away; all people were important to them as individuals.

It was in the fourth year of my house arrest that I at last opened myself to what I hoped would be a new life and to new joys. I had to find out whether I could go to Mass in the hours when I was not under house arrest. The Minister of Justice, however, had declared on an earlier occasion, I discovered, that banned people were not prohibited from attending bona fide religious services.

Father Rakale suggested that I should find myself more at home in the multiracial cathedral in the centre of Johannesburg than in the local Anglican church of Norwood, where there would be an all-white congregation. The Rev Gonville ffrench-Beytagh was then the Dean of St Mary's Cathedral. He was famous for his "political" sermons and for his forthrightness and courage on racial matters, both in the pulpit and out of it.

The only Mass I could attend was at seven o'clock on a working morning. I could leave my house at six thirty and then go on to work after Mass and a quick coffee and toast with the Dean's friendly secretary in her nearby flat. Sometimes I would go to the Priory in Rosettenville for their early Mass and a "breakfast for two" with Father Leo Rakale. My Sunday house arrest prevented me from going to the High Mass in the Cathedral where there is always a large, totally racially integrated congregation.

St Mary's congregation consists of blacks and white, coloured, Indians and Chinese, worshipping together, singing together in the choir. Black and white priests celebrate the Mass side by side, Holy Communion may be received from a black or a white hand. It is a sad comment on the Christian church in South Africa that this should be almost unique.

The Dean asked me whether representations should be made for me to have a couple of hours freedom on Sundays to go to Mass, but I refused because I did not want it said, or even thought, that I had returned to the church merely to get a couple of hours out on a Sunday morning. I said I would reconsider it if the house arrest bans were renewed when they expired the following year.

My second house arrest shocked people even more than the first. Since I now belonged to the Anglican church there were church protests at all levels, from the Archbishop of Canterbury, who wrote me a most concerned letter, to the congregation of St Mary's. I had not yet met most of them, but they took part in an all-night vigil of prayer and protest on my behalf.

I agreed that the Dean should lead a deputation to the Minister of Justice to apply for me to be given permission to leave my home on Sundays so that I could attend High Mass at the Cathedral and also attend the midnight Masses at Easter and Christmas. Permission was granted and I was glad, but I realised that it recognised the power of the Minister of Justice.

Two years later I learned from Winnie that when she was interrogated about me, Colonel Coetzee had in fact said that I was not a sincere Christian and that I only went back to the church so that I could dodge part of my house arrest.

My return to the church brought me one very great honour. The Archbishop of Canterbury came on a brief visit to the Anglican church in South Africa. He wanted to meet Helen Joseph, the Anglican under house arrest. It had, of course to be a meeting of two people only. We met for breakfast at the house of the Bishop of Johannesburg. I don't think I have ever been so shy or so tongue-tied, despite his genial kindness. After a few minutes it became easier to talk and answer his interested questions.

The Archbishop asked me what I intended to do with my theological knowledge when I had completed my studies. I don't know whether he thought I might say, "become a woman priest", but I replied, "nothing, it is an end in itself". He clapped his hands together in obvious delight, exclaiming, "that is the only way to approach learning!"

I was so overcome by this accolade that when he said that he was going to give me a blessing I forgot my ecclesiastical manners and did not kneel for it. Fortunately he is an extremely tall man and could place his hands upon my head without difficulty.

Today I know that I should not agree completely with his attitude towards knowledge, for I am convinced that knowledge and service to humanity are inseparable, that learning ought not to be an end in itself.

The cancer operation of 1971 brought at end to house arrest. I came out of hospital to a "freedom" I had not known for nine years and to full freedom of church worship, no longer by favour of the Minister of Justice.

I went to the Cathedral for the High Mass on the first Sunday I was out of hospital. I took part in the Offertory procession bearing the bread and wine to be consecrated for the Holy Communion. I walked up the aisle, thankful to have a stalwart man beside me carrying the bread in case I stumbled on the way. The Dean had not known I was coming because I wanted to surprise him. When he saw me his face broke into a broad smile of loving welcome, despite the solemnity of the ritual. I walked back to my seat, this time by myself, but not alone, for there were smiling faces on either side in the pews to welcome me back to the cathedral, to life and to freedom. The whole congregation seemed to come alive in greeting and in gratitude to God.

It was in that same year that Father Cosmas Desmond publicly defied his house arrest by attending a church service on Sunday, not once, but every Sunday for six weeks. He had taken a courageous stand. His banning orders did not prevent him from attending religious services, but his house arrest did at the weekend. To violate house arrest could invoke a gaol sentence of up to three years' imprisonment with no option of a fine.

At first I found it difficult to decide whether Cos was politically correct. I had accepted that individual defiance had minimal political value. Mass defiance should be the goal. Cos's Christianity and his priesthood brought a new dimension. He was deliberately confronting the state, denying its right to interfere with his duty as an ordained priest, to celebrate Mass, to conduct religious services on Sunday, denying its right to dictate whether he should or should not worship God in church on Sunday, as Christians are constrained to do.

I came to the conclusion that he had been right to refuse to ask permission to break the house arrest. I realised that I had been wrong earlier in allowing that deputation to approach the minister on my behalf, for in the end I had had to make the application myself. Cos had refused to do this and defied arrest and he was right.

Surprisingly, no police action was taken against him and he was even given a relaxation of his ban to allow him to attend any church services in Johannesburg on Sundays. He had indeed won a victory.

I had returned to the church in 1966, the same year that my second book, *Tomorrow's Sun*, was published in England. I received a very inspiring letter from an Anglican nun in England. Sister Angela of the enclosed Anglican order of Poor Clares, explained that her order was completely enclosed within its convent walls, having no physical contact whatsoever with the outside world. Theirs was a life of contemplation and prayer but also of intercession for the troubled world. They had need, therefore, to keep themselves informed of what was going on in the world by reading newspapers and books. They had no radio or television.

Sister Angela had read my book and felt she wanted to know me. The Mother Superior had given her special permission to write to me and that was how it began, a close and deep relationship. It was at first only by letter and then she was allowed to make tapes to send to me. Legally I could not make tapes for her, for that would be reproducing the statements of a banned person. However, occasionally I managed to send one to her.

All this drew me right into the heart of the enclosed community and it became, in a way, part of my own enforced enclosure. I had photographs of the convent chapel and of their lovely garden. I felt I knew every part of the convent from the kitchen and the nuns' cells to the roofs onto which the nuns climbed by ladder to repair them.

I cannot find words to explain how it was that such a deep bond of love and understanding grew between us. We had never met and never thought we should meet, but our lives seemed intertwined. Later there were also occasional brief telephone calls. We accepted our separation, for she was enclosed in a convent and I was without a passport and too stubborn to plead for one, even when I was no longer under house arrest.

In 1973 the miracle happened. Angela was allowed to visit her seriously-ill mother lest she should not live to return to England to see her daughter again. Angela left her English convent and flew to Sydney. It was Angela, not I, who obtained travel brochures to work out that it would cost no more for her to fly via Johannesburg than via Tel Aviv. She obtained the permission of her Order to spend one day at the Johannesburg airport before flying back to England, but she had to remain at the airport. She was not allowed to come to my house because our being together at all had to be part of her journey so that it would not violate her enclosure.

It was Angela, not I, who thought of booking a room at the Airport Holiday Inn rather than spending our precious time in empty airport concourses. I am sure that never before was any Holiday Inn so blest, for Father Leo brought Holy Communion for us and said Mass with a makeshift altar on top of the central heating pipes. The time was short for us but unforgettable as we laughed and talked all day, Angela the enclosed nun and Helen, the political committed person. Somehow I knew that our closeness would continue always, that she would go on inspiring me with her eager faith and that I should always be stumbling along behind her.

The congregation of St Mary's Cathedral is completely integrated in form. The people, the priests, the choir are black and white together. Yet every Sunday, when the Mass is over, only the memory of that fellowship remains. The reality is dispersed and the people go their ways again, to the white suburbs and the black suburbs, to the white homes and the black homes, with the un-Christian disparity between them. I realised that the very fact that the cathedral was in the centre of a large city would militate against a completely integrated congregation, both socially and politically. Those who come on Sundays come from widely separate and different parts of Johannesburg, Africans from Soweto,

Indians from Lenasia, coloureds from their segregated suburbs and the whites from the northern suburbs. I learned to accept that the wonder lay in the very fact that Sunday after Sunday these people of all races come from all areas to join together in worship, to create, even if only for two hours, a unique togetherness. It was that which Winnie had welcomed when she said, "In there I have seen what we are fighting for." Nevertheless, I knew a sense of disappointment that although my own involvement in the church had brought me personal and spiritual peace, the cathedral and its members were not prepared to walk along the road of involvement with the suffering people of South Africa.

In 1977 there had been that all-night vigil to commemorate the Soweto dead of 1976. That had brought people together for one night, yet many of those at the vigil had come from other congregations or no congregations. The cathedral worshippers had given little support. Was it fear that had kept them away when the Minister of Justice had interfered so ruthlessly? Would they have come otherwise?

Although the Cathedral shuts apartheid outside its doors, the struggle for justice and freedom seems also to have been shut out. The non-involvement of St Mary's congregation is equally true of the Anglican church in general. I have written about St Mary's because it is the church to which I came back to hopefully and to which I still belong.

In the Anglican church and in other churches, there are outstanding committed Christians whose care and concern for the black people of South Africa has taken them far along the costly road of sacrifice. I think of Bishop Trevor Huddleston, of Bishop Tutu, of Father Cosmas Desmond, of Dean ffrench-Beytagh, of the Rev Beyers Naude — and of others. I pay tribute to them all. But there are not enough and the masses in the pews are still silent.

Nevertheless I feel a strong bond of fellowship and communion with St Mary's, its priests and its congregation, just as I do with the priests of the Community of the Resurrection and with Sister Angela and her enclosed community. It is true that I have not entered into the usual activities of my church, nor is it likely that I shall ever do so now. Age and physical disabilities make it difficult for me even to attend Mass on Sundays. My loving friends of the Community of the Resurrection often bring the Mass to me instead. The sacraments and worship of my church are precious indeed.

Sometimes my atheist friends ask me what I really believe and I find myself then most inarticulate. Gandhi has said part of it for me:

> God is that indefinable something which we all feel but which we do not know. To me God is truth and love. God is ethics and morality. God is fearlessness. God is the source of light and life and yet He is above all these. He is even the atheism of the atheist. He is personal God to those who need His touch.

The atheism of the atheists I have encountered is an utterly selfless devotion to a cause, the cause of justice. Most of my friends are professed atheists, they are dedicated people and they have made immeasurable sacrifices. Christians claim to follow Christ. Atheists make no such claim, but they set an example many a Christian could follow.

I am among the millions of Christians who need God's personal touch. I lost it and then found it again. It was God's touch that reached me in gaol and during house arrest. That is what made it possible for me to come back to the Christian faith. A faith I accept in its totality, to which I try to witness as best I can in my personal and political life.

Chapter X

Final word

Right up to the morning of 1 July, I did not know what to expect. Even before the bans were due to expire I was invited to open a women's conference at Wits University — if I was free to speak again. I waited that last month, finishing the draft of this book, eager to be able to speak out again, but was I, I kept asking myself, at seventy-seven, too old to be banned again?

The banning orders were not renewed. I could attend political meetings again and address gatherings of students. I could go on where I had left off two years ago. Without warning, bans could be reimposed. This was not important, merely a risk that had to be taken since I still did not intend to ban myself from speaking in public if I was needed.

The first week was very exciting. Telephone calls came from near and far, telegrams, visits, flowers, press and television interviews — overseas television of course, because the prohibition on quoting me in South Africa still remained. I continued to be a listed person, even though the bans fell away.

The welcome from the Wits students at the conference, my first "free" meeting, moved me very deeply. The ovation as I came forward to speak almost overwhelmed me. I knew that the link with the students had not been broken. Here was the proof that I was still needed, that I could still make my contribution to the struggle for freedom and justice and to the young. I was nervous at first. Could I still hold an audience the way I used to? Would my voice be strong enough? Was age catching up with me? Almost at once I knew that it wasn't so, for the response from the students was there. I spoke of the women's resistance in the 1950s and of the great women's protests to Pretoria — the heritage from the past.

Since I have been unbanned, calls to speak on university campuses have been many. I have been several times to the University of Cape Town, to Wits University and to Natal University, also to Rhodes and to the Indian Westville University. I have had the honour of giving the annual Academic Freedom addresses at five English-speaking universities. Initially I felt inadequate about giving these important lectures, all delivered in the past by very prominent people both in South Africa and from overseas. The lectures are always printed for the occasion and widely distributed. Mine could not be. All this made me feel unequal to the task but I was inspired by the confidence of the students, both in me and in the value of a formal lecture which must be confined to the actual audience.

I am no academic, no ideologue. I could not pretend to be what I was not, so I spoke as simply as I always do, putting academic freedom where I think it belongs, into its true context, beyond the ivory tower. I tried to make it meaningful, to place the responsibility for its survival upon the shoulders of the students. I wanted to show that academic freedom is but a part of the greater freedom for which South Africa must strive. The students on the five campuses showed me plainly by their ovations that I had not reached out in vain. And so I continue today. I am privileged to bring to students and to other audiences, black and white, the message of the struggle for justice and human dignity and the principles of the Freedom Charter.

The political face of South Africa is changing, not only through government effort at so-called constitutional reform, but by the widespread emergence of grassroots community organisations and the development of a fast-growing extra-parliamentary constituency. The old all-white Parliament is gone. We have a new constitution. We have three Houses of Parliament, one for the whites, one for the Indians and one for the coloureds, but nothing at all for African representation, for the voteless millions still left after the shuffling off to the homelands. There is talk of considering their relation to the new parliamentary apparatus. Commissions will sit, but this cannot compensate at this stage, if ever, for the plain fact that the African people, three-quarters of the total population, have been excluded from this new Parliament.

There was referendum for the whites on the new constitution. The result was heavily in favour. The coloureds and Indians had no referendum. They were not asked if they wanted this new dispensation: they were simply called upon to vote for it.

The Indian people had a parliamentary vote for the first time and the coloured people voted again after many years. Each race could only vote for its own House of Parliament. There is no common electoral roll.

When the three Houses come together in this tricameral Parliament, the loading of seats can be clearly seen. The coloured and Indian members are heavily outnumbered by the whites. They are in a permanent humiliating minority, and white supremacy is enshrined in this new dispensation. It was small wonder that when the elections were held, the percentage polls were sensationally low. Boycott campaigns made their mark and some 80 per cent of voters simply stayed away. The Nationalist government forged ahead, undeterred.

The opposition to the new constitution, however, brought into cohesive being a formidable and expanding extra-parliamentary constituency, spearheaded by the United Democratic Front, both the acknowledged leader of the real multiracial opposition and the prime target of government and police repression.

The launching of the United Democratic Front became for me the third high peak of the past thirty years — indeed of my whole life. To the historic gathering in Cape Town came 15,000 people, the old and the young, the black and the white, the professional and the worker, the housewives. I was there. I spoke. I was introduced as "the mother of the struggle". I was elected an Honorary

Patron. Listing barred me from any executive position, but I am proud to be a patron, to know that I belong there, to the people, as much as to the university students.

More than this, so that my cup is really running over, I see the women of South Africa coming together again in many organisations, in many centres, moving forward together to the day when a new Federation of South Africa Women, a truly national unity of women throughout South Africa, will come into being. The thirty-year old dream of the Federation will then come true.

Eighty is a great age. I don't know for how long I shall be able, physically or legally, to speak on platforms. Each year must see me less mobile. I am still unbanned. I know that I must make hay while the sun shines, for I do not know for how long it may shine.

I have been banned four times, gaoled four times, on trial for four years and this is my third period of being unbanned. It is a strange feeling. I speak of joy in being free yet it is only a partial freedom. I am still hedged around with the prohibitions attached to being listed. Winnie and other banned friends may not communicate with me. Nothing I say or write may be quoted in South Africa. I may not belong to any political organisation. Others are banned, many more may be banned. What kind of freedom is this? I do not want a freedom for myself which I cannot share fully with others.

Nelson Mandela, Walter Sisulu, "Kathy" Kathrada, Govan Mbeki, we were all together in those early years, in campaigns, in gaol, on trial for high treason. They are still in maximum security prisons, on Robben Island and in Pollsmoor gaol. Their lives pass by while they wait for the freedom which they know will come for them and for their people. In South Africa's gaols there are more than thirty black political prisoners serving life sentences. There are hundreds of others serving long sentences, some for the rest of their lives and without promise of freedom.

Yet that is not what I really believe. For me there is no doubt that freedom will come in their lifetime — at least for most of them, although there are a few whose lifespan is growing threateningly short.

During the 1950s I was deeply committed to the non-violent struggle, as we all were. We believed that it would be possible through non-violent action to achieve freedom and justice in South Africa, to implement the principles of the Freedom Charter and to live by it. That was before Sharpeville, before the grim 1960s, before the suppression by force of our non-violent campaigns. It was before the outlawing of our non-violent organisations and before the decades of detention and torture.

Non-violence cannot successfully oppose a violent repressive system. The demand by the black people for human recognition and rights is a just demand. I abhor and fear violence of all kinds. I share this abhorrence with millions of human beings, but stronger even than this is the conviction that justice must prevail. If white South Africa persists in its refusal to share the land, the wealth and the power, if it continues to use force to maintain itself in its privileged position, then the black people have no alternative but to use force to obtain their just demands. We must expect a bloody conflict with immense human suffering. Responsibility for what is to come must lie at the door of white South Africans.

Over the years I have become ever more conscious of my white guilt. It is not mine alone. I share it with a few million other whites. That does not make it any less mine. I have never been able to forget Lilian Ngoyi's bitter outburst about my pink skin making me better off in gaol. It makes no difference that I have tried to identify with the struggle of the black people. It makes no difference that I have been gaoled, detained, house-arrested. So have many others. I benefit by this accursed system and I cannot shed my whiteness. I feel shame and contrition for my white skin for I have not been able to expiate it. I cannot do it alone. The real expiation can only come about if the white people of South Africa shed their greed and their fears and stand with the black people of this land in every way.

In this book I have tried to open some windows onto the history of the liberation struggle. I could not open them all; mainly these are the windows through which I myself have looked. We are halfway through this decade and I cannot see clearly how it will end, but I hope that there may then be signs of a new, freer South Africa.

I hoped that I might be able to give some Christian witness in the political world and some political witness in the Christian world. A crazy impractical ideal? I do not know, nor do I know if I have achieved even a part of it. It is for others to judge of that.

There is a plant in South Africa which we call the khakibush. Cut it down, burn it down, it will shoot up again. For thirty years it has grown three feet high over that football field in Kliptown where the Congress of the People was held. Now the invasion of the concrete jungle threatens it and our field lies gravelled over. I can no longer see the khakibush but I know that its roots are there. It will break through elsewhere. For me the khakibush is a symbol of survival, a manifestation of unconquerable growth. Like the khakibush, the African National Congress has grown and spread. Its roots are underground in South Africa. They cannot be seen but they send up shoots. It grows and spreads.

Like the khakibush, the Freedom Charter has resisted all efforts to eradicate it. In this crucial decade it is an article of faith for many people in South Africa and overseas. Thousands of copies are spread far and wide. It is displayed publicly and quoted freely. It has come from the hearts of the people to their lips. Its message can never be banned for it is the message of brotherhood and love.

These freedoms we will fight for, side by side, throughout our lives until we have won our liberty . . . side by side!

AMANDLA NGAWETHU!

Postscript

... Two roads diverged in a wood, and I,
I took the one less travelled by,
And that has made all the difference.

Robert Frost, "The Road Not Taken"

To a great extent that has been true of the past thirty years of my life — I have followed the road "less travelled by", the road of involvement in the liberation struggle. But that road has drawn no sigh from me, as it did from the poet. It draws from me only deep gratitude to know that there was room for me, a white, to walk along that road.

Thirty years ago, it was indeed the road less travelled by. But not any more. Today there are untold millions marching along that road despite all the hardships and suffering that they must encounter. Today it is the onward, accelerating march towards a free, democratic South Africa.

Our story is not yet told; there is still far to go. I cannot write an epilogue to end this book, only a postscript to the part of it that I have written. Other parts, and especially the future parts, must be written by others.

On Sunday, 10 February 1985, a great crowd gathered in a large Soweto sports stadium to honour Desmond Tutu, the Bishop of Johannesburg, on his return from Sweden with the Nobel Peace Prize. There he stood, the people's Bishop, to tell that crowd as he held the Peace Prize in the air, "This award is not for Desmond Tutu. It is for all our people. It is for the woman who sells mealies in the street to pay for her children's education. I say, 'Take it, it is yours!' "

Zinzie Mandela too, stood there, before thousands of people to read her father's reply to the State President's offer of release from gaol on condition that he renounce violence as a political weapon.

She looked so young that day, in her jeans and yellow T-shirt with the United Democratic Front slogan splashed across it, "UDF unites, apartheid divides". I thought that to that great crowd she was everybody's daughter, not only the daughter of Nelson and Winnie Mandela.

Her father's message was one of proud defiance, of loyalty to his people, to his organisation, the African National Congress, as he called upon State President Botha to renounce violence, to dismantle apartheid, to unban the

239

ANC, to free the gaoled, the banished and the exiled and to let the people decide who will govern them.

"My father says, 'I cannot and will not give any undertaking at a time when I and you, the people, are not free. Your freedom and mine cannot be separated. I will return!' "

Nelson's message has rung out, loud and clear, beyond that stadium into the far corners of South Africa and to the world abroad. He closed the prison door upon himself after more than twenty-four years of gaol.

Much has happened since that unforgettable day. Each week, almost each day, the death toll rises with the reports of demonstrations, protest marches met by tear gas and rubber bullets from the police, and cruel whipping of men, women and children. There is burning of cars, houses, offices and shops in black and coloured areas, even in Phoenix in Natal, where once lived Mahatma Gandhi, the protagonist of non-violence. It is becoming endemic as the anger of the people rises against their oppression and the ruthless, violent methods used to crush them.

Official figures reveal that in the past fifteen months more than six hundred and fifty black people have been killed in the townships, two thousand five hundred wounded, more than two thousand persons have been detained without trial and more than ten thousand arrested. Most of those who died were shot by the police. The past five months has seen the greater part of this agony.

Now the children, too, are shot, sometimes killed, whipped by the police, as they continue boycotting their classes in protest against oppression, demanding the release of their fellow students. It is not many days since nine hundred children were taken from their school grounds to the gaols, all in one morning. Some were released to their parents late that night. Many were not.

The army has become an army of occupation in black areas. Soldiers need no longer go to the borders of South Africa to kill their brothers. It happens in the black townships.

Deaths and detentions are almost no longer news. Treason trials multiply. For me there is sickening familiarity about the charges. I have heard it all before. I have been there already. "Hostile intent . . . conspiracy to overthrow the government by force . . ." Once again our leaders are caught up in these lengthy trials, these interminable legal battles. Will they be acquitted as we were?

After twenty-five years, another State of Emergency has been declared. It doesn't really affect the white people. We live undisturbed in our white houses, in our white suburbs, we read about what is happening to people in black areas. We see it on television — some of it — but outside South Africa much more is seen through the foreign media. I am sure that the vast majority of white South Africans remain ignorant of the extent of the violence.

Yet I am sure that white South Africa is frightened as never before, frightened for its wealth and its power, frightened for the continuation of its everyday life of privilege, frightened lest the violence cannot be contained by the armed brutality of the police and the army. And, most of all, fearful now of the world-

240

wide hostility towards South Africa and its apartheid regime, expressing itself in increasing disinvestment and sanctions.

The fine clothes of the emperor have vanished and apartheid faces the world in its naked ugliness.

South Africa has pleaded once again for time to change, has pointed to cosmetic changes already made, which mean but little to the mass of black people. Freedom to marry across the colour line, but no freedom to live in the same area; freedom to share white luxury in expensive hotels and restaurants, but no freedom for the basic human rights too long denied.

As the storm clouds gather, both inside and outside, State President Botha tries anew to appease the outside world, to stave off the financial and political crisis coming ever nearer. There is a new offer; the abolition of influx control and pass laws and the restoration of citizenship to black people in homelands or independent states. No details are forthcoming and the black people, still smarting under earlier broken promises, react with deep suspicion.

It is not enough; it is not a high enough price to be paid for the many dead; for the child of four years shot and killed while playing in her own yard; for the leaders, the heroes become martyrs at the hands of the police, or for the tortured detainees or for those murdered by unknown assailants.

Our anger must be directed against this government, against Botha himself, for he, too, must bear the responsibility for the apartheid system, which has made such violence possible. The blame for the violence that has flared up in all its ugly horror and destruction, from whatever source, lies on the shoulders of the nationalist government, and the men responsible must carry that guilt with them to their graves.

I do not wish this to be a sad and bitter postscript. I do not know what the picture of the coming years may be nor even what the coming months may bring, but my hope and confidence in the future of our country remains undiminished. The cost will be heavy, as it is now, but I believe that South Africa will one day become a united, democratic country.

My hope is grounded in my faith in the extra-parliamentary strength of the people, both those who reject the present constitution and those who are rejected by it.

I draw strength from the United Democratic Front, wounded though it is by constant attacks, by the long trials of some of its leaders, by the detention without trial of others. I do not believe that the UDF can be broken. Thirty years ago, on the eve of the women's protest in Pretoria, Lilian Ngoyi affirmed, "If our leaders are arrested, others will take their places!" That stands as true today as then. Others will take the places of the leaders who are removed.

I have visited some of those accused of treason, some still in gaol, others out on bail. I come away always uplifted by their courage and their spirit. This is a new generation of "traitors" but the strength is the same, the indomitable strength that can carry men through even twenty-four years of prison.

The banner of the Freedom Charter flies as high today as ever. The name of Nelson Mandela is on the lips of the vast majority of the people as the recognised leader. The struggle for justice must follow its course until the hunger of the people is satisfied, for a piece of freedom is no longer enough.

"They have been given pieces, but unlike bread, a piece of liberty does not finish hunger. Freedom is like life. It cannot be had in instalments. Freedom is indivisible. We have it all or we are not free".
Dr Martin Luther King

My book is ended. Our struggle is not, but one day it will be. I do not know if I shall still be here then, for my time is running out, but I know that all that I have lived through, together with the people I love, will not have been in vain.

September 1985

The Freedom Charter
as adopted at the Congress of the People on 26 June 1955

PREAMBLE

We, the people of South Africa, declare for all our country and the world to know:

That South Africa belongs to all who live in it, black and white, and that no government can justly claim authority unless it is based on the will of the people;

That our people have been robbed of their birthright to land, liberty and peace by a form of government founded on injustice and inequality;

That our country will never be prosperous or free until all our people live in brotherhood, enjoying equal rights and opportunities;

That only a democratic state, based on the will of the people can secure to all their birthright without distinction of colour, race, sex or belief;

And therefore, we the people of South Africa, black and white, together equals, countrymen and brothers adopt this FREEDOM CHARTER. And we pledge ourselves to strive together, sparing nothing of our strength and courage, until the democratic changes here set out have been won.

THE PEOPLE SHALL GOVERN!

Every man and woman shall have the right to vote for and stand as a candidate for all bodies which make laws.

All the people shall be entitled to take part in the administration of the country.

The rights of the people shall be the same regardless of race, colour or sex.

All bodies of minority rule, advisory boards, councils and authorities shall be replaced by democratic organs of self-government.

ALL NATIONAL GROUPS SHALL HAVE EQUAL RIGHTS!

There shall be equal status in the bodies of state, in the courts and in the schools, for all national groups and races;

All national groups shall be protected by law against insults to their race and national pride;

All people shall have equal rights to use their own language and to develop their own folk culture and customs;

243

The preaching and practice of national, race or colour discrimination and contempt shall be a punishable crime;
All apartheid laws and practices shall be set aside.

THE PEOPLE SHALL SHARE IN THE COUNTRY'S WEALTH!

The national wealth of our country, the heritage of all South Africans, shall be restored to the people;
The mineral wealth beneath the soil, the banks and monopoly industry shall be transferred to the ownership of the people as a whole;
All other industries and trade shall be controlled to assist the well-being of the people;
All people shall have equal rights to trade where they choose, to manufacture and to enter all trades, crafts and professions.

THE LAND SHALL BE SHARED AMONG THOSE WHO WORK IT!

Restriction of land ownership on a racial basis shall be ended, and all the land re-divided amongst those who work it, to banish famine and land hunger;
The state shall help the peasants with implements, seed, tractors and dams to save the soil and assist the tillers;
Freedom of movement shall be guaranteed to all who work on the land;
All shall have the right to occupy land wherever they choose;
People shall not be robbed of their cattle, and forced labour and farm prisons shall be abolished.

ALL SHALL BE EQUAL BEFORE THE LAW!

No one shall be imprisoned, deported or restricted without fair trial;
No one shall be condemned by the order of any Government official;
The courts shall be representative of all the people;
Imprisonment shall be only for serious crimes against the people, and shall aim at re-education, not vengeance;
The police force and army shall be open to all on an equal basis and shall be the helpers and protectors of the people;
All laws which discriminate on the grounds of race, colour or belief shall be repealed.

ALL SHALL ENJOY HUMAN RIGHTS!

The law shall guarantee to all their right to speak, to organise, to meet together, to publish, to preach, to worship and to educate their children;
The privacy of the house from police raids shall be protected by law;
All shall be free to travel without restriction from countryside to town, from province to province, and from South Africa abroad.
Pass laws, permits and all other laws restricting these freedoms shall be abolished.

THERE SHALL BE WORK AND SECURITY!

All who work shall be free to form trade unions, to elect their officers and to make wage agreements with their employers;
The state shall recognise the right and duty of all to work, and to draw full unemployment benefits;
Men and women of all races shall receive equal pay for equal work;
There shall be a forty-hour working week, a national minimum wage, paid annual leave, and sick leave for all workers, and maternity leave on full pay for all working mothers;
Miners, domestic workers, farm workers and civil servants shall have the same rights as all others who work;
Child labour, compound labour, the tot system and contract labour shall be abolished.

THE DOORS OF LEARNING AND CULTURE SHALL BE OPENED!

The government shall discover, develop and encourage national talent for the enhancement of our cultural life;
All the cultural treasures of mankind shall be open to all, by free exchange of books, ideas and contact with other lands;
The aim of education shall be to teach the youth to love their people and their culture, to honour human brotherhood, liberty and peace;
Education shall be free, compulsory, universal and equal for all children;
Higher education and technical training shall be opened to all by means of state allowances and scholarships awarded on the basis of merit;
Adult illiteracy shall be ended by a mass state education plan;
Teachers shall have all the rights of other citizens;
The colour bar in cultural life, in sport and in education shall be abolished.

THERE SHALL BE HOUSES, SECURITY AND COMFORT!

All people shall have the right to live where they choose, to be decently housed, and to bring up their families in comfort and security;
Unused housing space to be made available to the people;
Rent and prices shall be lowered, food plentiful and no one shall go hungry;
A preventive health scheme shall be run by the state;
Free medical care and hospitalisation shall be provided for all, with special care for mothers and young children;
Slums shall be demolished and new suburbs built where all shall have transport, roads, lighting, playing fields, creches and social centres;
The aged, the orphans, the disabled and the sick shall be cared for by the state;
Rest, leisure and recreation shall be the right of all;
Fenced locations and ghettoes shall be abolished, and laws which break up families shall be repealed.

THERE SHALL BE PEACE AND FRIENDSHIP!

South Africa shall be a fully independent state, which respects the rights and sovereignty of all nations;
South Africa shall strive to maintain world peace and the settlement of all international disputes by negotiation not war;
Peace and friendship amongst all our people shall be secured by upholding the equal rights, opportunities and status of all;
The people of the protectorates Basutoland, Bechuanaland and Swaziland shall be free to decide for themselves their own future;
The right of all peoples of Africa to independence and self-government shall be recognised, and shall be the basis of close cooperation.

Let all who love their people and their country now say, as we say here:

**THESE FREEDOMS WE WILL FIGHT FOR, SIDE BY SIDE,
THROUGHOUT OUR LIVES UNTIL WE HAVE WON OUR LIBERTY.**

Index